YOUR CHILD'S SELF-ESTEEM

A member of Phi Beta Kappa and other honoraries, DOROTHY CORKILLE BRIGGS has worked as a teacher of both children and adults; dean of girls; school psychologist; and marriage, family, and child counselor during the last twenty-five years. Since 1958 she has taught parent-education courses and training in communication and resolution of conflicts.

YOUR CHILD'S SELF-ESTEEM

Dorothy Corkille Briggs

A DOLPHIN BOOK
DOUBLEDAY
NEW YORK LONDON TORONTO SYDNEY AUCKLAND

A Dolphin Book
PUBLISHED BY DOUBLEDAY
A division of Bantam Doubleday Dell Publishing Group, Inc.
666 Fifth Avenue, New York, New York 10103

DOLPHIN, DOUBLEDAY, and the portrayal of two
dolphins are trademarks of Doubleday, a division of
Bantam Doubleday Dell Publishing Group, Inc.

Words from the song, "I've Gotta Be Me" by Walter Marks
© 1967 by Damila Music Inc.

Lines from *The Knowledge of Man:* Copyright © 1965
by Martin Buber and Maurice Friedman.
By permission of Harper & Row, Publishers, Inc.

ISBN 0-385-04020-2

DEDICATED TO THE MEMORY OF

my father, Colonel John D. Corkille,

AND

my mother, Helen Young Corkille,

FOR THEIR MANY CONTRIBUTIONS TO MY PERSON.

Man wishes to be confirmed in his being
by man, and wishes to have a presence
in the being of the other . . . secretly and
bashfully he watches for a Yes which
allows him to be and which can come to
him only from one human person to another.

MARTIN BUBER

MY GRATITUDES:

If there is value for you in this reading, it comes not solely from me, but from interactions with all the people and experiences that have touched my life.

I am particularly grateful to

— Edward Bordin, Duane Bowen, Max Levin, and Lois Southard for teaching that inspired me;

— Thomas Gordon, whose outstanding teaching clarified my thinking concerning anger being secondary, the vital distinction between "I" and "You" messages, the handling of power, and the mechanics of home democracy;

— Frank Barron, S. I. Hayakawa, Abraham Maslow, and Carl Rogers for workshops and concepts that intrigued me;

— Tom Johnston and Sam Warren for a decade of support as I worked with parent groups;

— innumerable children and adults for permitting me to share portions of their private worlds, which has brought into sharper focus the concepts discussed in this book. This allowed me to write from deep personal experience rather than from theory only;

— Myrtle Spencer for confirmation, inspiration, and substituting as "mother" when this manuscript was in its embryonic stages;

— Charlotte Himber for very special support at a crucial point in this project;

— Tom Larson, Mary and Norman Lewis, Nancy Lichina,

Judy Miller, Betty Riley, Sylvia W. Rosen, Jean Schrimmer, Barbara Spaulding, and Elsa van Bergen of Doubleday for personal reactions, editorial assistance, and moral support on this project;

— Mary Baker, Karen Brown, Dorothy McAuliffe, and Mary Starley for their typing skills;

—Laurie and Kerrie Sue, for teaching me so much about human nature and for actively taking over on countless occasions to free me for writing.

To each, I give heartfelt appreciation.

DOROTHY CORKILLE BRIGGS
Palos Verdes Peninsula
California

CONTENTS

OUR CULTURE'S OVERSIGHT

For decades psychologists have focused on mental illness and its cure. But the pervasiveness of psychological disorders is so extensive that there simply are not enough professional people to handle the afflicted. One study of 175,000 people in New York City showed that only 18.5 percent were free of the symptoms of mental illness. The number who limp through life in inner turmoil and whose potentials are mired in unhealthy defenses is of epidemic proportions. Neurotic hangups have become a way of life.

This is a staggering indictment of an unfortunate oversight in our culture: we parents are not trained for our job. Vast sums are spent to teach academic and vocational skills, but the art of becoming a nurturing parent is left to chance and a few scattered classes. And yet, paradoxically, we regard children as our most important national resource!

We turn freely to the medical and educational professions to check on our children's physical and intellectual progress. But for guidance on nurturing children to emotional health, we are left largely on our own. Even when symptoms appear, many parents regard consulting a psychologist as an admission of defeat. It is a last ditch resort.

The discrepancy between our valuing children on the one hand and our failure to give parents specific training for their job on the other hand seems to be based on the assumption that if you are a human being you should know how to raise one. But, becoming a parent does *not* automatically confer upon any of us the knowledge and skills to raise youngsters who are confident and steady and able to live as fully-functioning persons who lead meaningful lives. In short, preventing mental illness has not been given its proper emphasis. Yet, prevention remains our best hope for alleviating the high incidence of emotional disorder.

Most of us do our best, but much of the time we simply fly by the seat of our pants. The fact remains, however, that we, as well as our children, have to live with the results of our *unintentional* mistakes. And these mistakes have a way of being passed on to future generations. The impact of our culture's oversight is to some degree felt by all of us.

In our search for guidelines we parents have turned to the many books available on child-rearing. But here we find the important issues facing us treated on the whole as separate, isolated topics. We have not been given a cohesive, basic framework—the child's self-esteem—into which we may place each important facet of living with children.

This book gives just such a framework. Here is a new way of looking at child development: seeing all growth and behavior against the backdrop of the child's search for identity and self-respect. Step by step, you will be shown specifically *how* to build a solid sense of self-worth in your child. Then, your youngster is slated for personal happiness in all areas of his life. Unless you fully understand the nature of the human fabric and work *with* it, you travel blindly and may pay the price.

This book has been written because of my firm conviction, born of twenty-five years' work in psychology and education as well as from my experiences as a mother, that parenthood is too important for the "by-guess-and-by-golly" approach. Awareness of the facts can help you discharge your responsibilities toward those entrusted to your care, give you confidence as a parent, and point the way to your own personal development.

Over the years, parents in my classes have reported exciting changes in themselves and their children as they began to apply some of the ideas in this book. They have made statements such as the following about their experiences:

"This way of seeing children's growth has given me new confidence. I find I am a freer person, not so afraid of the responsibility of parenthood."

"Our whole family has become much closer and there is far less conflict. As my attitudes changed, so much smoothed out at home."

"I'm more relaxed and patient—even my husband has noticed it."

"I've learned to see myself and my children in a new light; I feel so much more understanding. It has brought my husband and me closer together indirectly."

"I've learned to live *with* my children instead of *in spite of* them!"

"As a father, I thought it was ridiculous to have a class about raising kids. I never realized how blind I've been. A whole new world has been opened to me. I only wish I'd known all this *before* I had children."

The evidence is strong. Knowing what you are doing and having a basic framework as a guide can help you live with your child so that he is emotionally healthy. Then, you don't need to worry; he has his feet on solid ground.

The fact that you are reading this book says that you care about your youngsters and your relationship with them. It suggests that you want your intentions for them to be fully-functioning persons to materialize. This caring, coupled with your interest in reaching out for new ideas, heads both you and your children in the direction of positive growth.

YOUR CHILD'S SELF-ESTEEM

ONE · THE BASIS
OF EMOTIONAL HEALTH

Dreams and realities

You doubtless had a lot of notions about how you would handle your youngsters long before you had any. But behind them was dedication: you were determined to do a *good* job. Most of us take parenthood seriously; in a very real sense, we "go for broke." And then reality thuds against our plans. What looked so simple turns out to be far more complex.

No matter that they come in small packages; children touch off large-sized emotions in us. Joy, sureness, and delight intermingle with worry, guilt, and doubt. Fatigue and frustration come along in good measure. You brave dawdling and messes and torrents of "No's," and the next day it's pinching and tattling and who gets the phone. New sets of problems—they change but never end. There's no turning back.

Regardless, you strive to do your best. All along the way you invest heavily in caring, time, energy, and money. You spare no effort—proper food and clothes, attractive toys, the right medical care, and a constant "taxi circuit" to provide every advantage. Maybe you even scrimp for college and extra insurance.

In spite of good intentions and heartfelt efforts, however, some of you find your youngster not turning out as you would like. He is underachieving, emotionally immature, rebellious, or unduly withdrawn. Maybe he goes around with youngsters who are up to no good. "How can *my* child be having problems when I've done so much and tried so hard?" is a question bedeviling many a well-intentioned parent.

Even if your children are not having problems, hearing about the rising rates of juvenile delinquency, dope addiction, dropouts, venereal disease, and illegitimacy hardly lowers your anxiety level. A nagging uneasiness intermittently pokes its way into your consciousness to make you wonder how to keep your youngsters off such tortured paths. At odd moments uncertainty seeps in: "Am I doing a good job?" "Should I spank, reason, or ignore?" "What do I do now?" Those big ideas—those sure convictions—blur and fade.

Reality can make you lose confidence as a parent. But, regardless, you hold on to the dream of what your child could become. How can you make your dream come true?

The crucial ingredient

If you are like most parents, your hopes for your children are based on more than their avoiding nervous breakdowns, alcoholism, or delinquency. You want life's positives for them: inner confidence, a sense of purpose and involvement, meaningful, constructive relationships with others, success at school and in work. Most of all—happiness. *What* you want is clear. Your uncertainties are more often wrapped around *how* to help them to these goals. We parents hunger for a basic rule of thumb as a guide—particularly during moments of stress and confusion.

Today, enough evidence has accumulated to give you just such a formula: if your child has *high self-esteem*, he has it made. Mounting research shows that the fully-functioning child (or adult) is different from the person who flounders through life.

The difference lies in his attitude toward himself, his degree of self-esteem.

What is self-esteem? It is how a person feels about himself. It is his over-all judgment of himself—how much he likes his particular person.

High self-esteem is not a noisy conceit. It is a quiet sense of self-respect, a feeling of self-worth. When you have it deep inside, you're glad you're you. Conceit is but whitewash to cover low self-esteem. With high self-esteem you don't waste time and energy impressing others; you already know you have value.

Your child's judgment of himself influences the kinds of friends he chooses, how he gets along with others, the kind of person he marries, and how productive he will be. It affects his creativity, integrity, stability, and even whether he will be a leader or a follower. His feelings of self-worth form the core of his personality and determine the use he makes of his aptitudes and abilities. His attitude toward himself has a direct bearing on how he lives all parts of his life. In fact, *self-esteem is the mainspring that slates every child for success or failure as a human being.*

The importance of self-esteem in your child's life can hardly be overemphasized. As a parent who cares you must help your youngsters to a firm and wholehearted belief in themselves.

Two basic needs

Strong self-respect is based on two main convictions:

"I am lovable,"
    ("I matter and have value because I exist.")

and

"I am worthwhile."

("I can handle myself and my environment with competence. I know I have something to offer others.")

Each child, though thoroughly unique, has the same psychological needs to feel lovable and worthy. Nor do these needs end with childhood. You and I have them, and they will be with us until the day we die. Meeting these needs is as essential for emotional well-being as oxygen is for physical survival. Each of us, after all, is our own lifelong roommate. The one person you cannot avoid, no matter how hard you try, is *you.* And so it is with your child. He lives most intimately with himself, and it is of the utmost importance for his optimal growth, as well as a meaningful and rewarding life, that he respect himself.

At this point you may say, "But this doesn't concern me because I love my child and think he is worthwhile." But wait. Notice the prescription does not say, "If you love your child." It says, "If the child feels loved." And there is a big difference between *being* loved and *feeling* loved.

Oddly enough, many parents are sure they love their children, but somehow their youngsters fail to get the message. Such parents have not been able to communicate their love. The seven basic ingredients that permit love to be felt by a child will be discussed in detail in Part II; the important thing to understand at this point is:

It is the *child's* feeling about being loved or unloved that affects how he will develop.

As it is with love, so it is with feeling worthwhile. You must know *how* the message that he is competent and has something to offer others gets across. Then it, too, can become an integral part of his self-picture.

If the most crucial ingredient of mental health is high self-esteem, where does it come from? Stanley Coopersmith's study,[1] among others, indicates that this characteristic is not related to family wealth, education, geographical living area, social class, father's occupation, or always having mother at home. *It comes instead from the quality of the relationships that exist between the child and those who play a significant role in his life.*

Every normal infant is born with the potential for psychological health. But whether that potential flourishes depends on the psychological climate lived in. To know whether the climate surrounding your child nurtures or withers, you must understand:

1. how high self-esteem is built;
2. how a child's self-view affects behavior;
3. what price a child pays when self-esteem is low, and
4. what you can do to foster high self-esteem.

These issues are the basis of Part I, The Phenomenon of the Mirrors.

Once you understand the process by which self-esteem comes about, you need to be aware of the specific ingredients that permit a child to conclude, "I am lovable." This material is discussed in Part II, The Climate of Love.

Then, to understand how a child builds a sense of mastery and competence—those feelings that feed the sense of worth-whileness—you need familiarity with the tasks of selfhood, those specific way-stations of growth that affect self-esteem. When you work *with* a child on his psychological assignments, you help him conclude he has worth. The steps of normal growth and their relationship to self-esteem are examined in Part III, The Journey of Self.

In the remaining sections we'll consider:

1. the influence that feelings have on self-esteem, along with positive ways to handle them;

[1] Coopersmith, Stanley. *The Antecedents of Self-Esteem.* San Francisco: W. H. Freeman & Co., 1967.

2. the influence of different approaches to discipline on self-esteem, as well as constructive methods of discipline;
3. the impact of self-esteem on intelligence and creativity, together with ways to foster mental development, and finally
4. the influence that sex education has on self-esteem.

Understanding what makes your child tick gives you a tool to check the climate you provide. It can pinpoint areas that need change. More important, it goes a long way toward saving both you and your child from the results of trial and error parenting.

The weight of recent research suggests that your good intentions as a parent have a greater chance of becoming reality if you live with your children so that they are quietly glad they are who they are. None of us can afford to be ignorant or casual about a youngster's most important characteristic—his degree of self-respect.

Helping children build high self-esteem is the key to successful parenthood.

PART I · THE PHENOMENON OF THE MIRRORS

TWO · MIRRORS CREATE SELF-IMAGES

Conclusions from mirrors

Have you ever thought of yourself as a mirror? You are one —a psychological mirror your child uses to build his identity. And his whole life is affected by the conclusions he draws.

Every infant is born without a sense of self. Each one must *learn* to be human in the sense that you and I use this word. Once in a while a child has been found who has managed to survive in complete isolation from other people. With no language, no conscience, no need for others, no sense of identity, the "wolf-child" is human only in appearance. Such cases teach that the sense of selfhood or personhood is not instinctual. It is a social achievement, learned from living with others.

Self-discovery

Let's take a typical baby and see how he forges his image of himself.

Red and wrinkled, little Pete is born. His proud parents send announcements proclaiming the arrival of a separate, new individual—their son. No one informs Pete that he has arrived.

And at this point, he wouldn't get the message. Having been one with his mother and his environment for nine months, he doesn't know where he ends and the rest of the world begins. He doesn't know he is a person.

A host of new sensations—touching, being touched, hunger pangs, sounds, blurred objects—arouse his curiosity. Primitive though his equipment is, he begins gropingly to explore his strange new world. When he touches his foot, he gets a feeling there and in his fingers. When he touches his teddy, the feeling is only in his fingers. As days pass, he realizes that his foot is part of him and his teddy is not.

At the same time, he finds people different from things. They come and go, make sounds, and help him feel more comfortable. One day he notices the difference between stuffing a cooky into his mother's mouth and putting one into his own. He begins to sense that he and she are different, but at this stage he still sees himself as an extension of her, perhaps a little like the tail on a dog.

As his brain matures, Pete learns to talk. Language is the tool that finally allows him to feel fully separate. It is essential for self-awareness. Let's see how this happens.

Pete discovers through imitation that certain sounds stand for particular objects. And soon he finds that objects can be labeled qualitatively. He learns, "Fire hot," "Baby hurt," or "Dadda big."

Finally, he learns his own name. Now he has a *symbol* for thinking of *himself apart from others*. This breakthrough is a huge step forward. It allows him to associate qualities with himself just as he did earlier with things. He can say, "Pete hot" or "Pete hurt" or "Pete big." Now he can talk about, describe, and judge himself. He can think of himself in comparison with others, "Me bigger than Bobby," and in terms of time, "Pete go by-by soon."

Around fifteen to eighteen months, Pete gets an inkling of his separateness, but it's hazy. Full awareness will not hit until two or two-and-a-half. Prior to this time, however, his name gives him a kind of frame on which to hang various descriptive labels. First through his senses and then through language, every child builds his picture of himself.

Wordless messages

Long before Pete understands words, however, he gathers generalized impressions about himself (and the world) from how he is treated. He is sensitive to whether he is lifted tenderly or jerked about like a sack of potatoes; he knows whether the arms around him are warmly close or give only vague, disinterested support. He knows when his hunger is respected and when it is ignored. The touch, body movements, muscle tensions, tones, and facial expressions of those around him send Pete an ongoing stream of messages. And his radar is amazingly accurate. (Some infants, of course, are far more sensitive than others, but to varying degrees they are all tuned in.)

Babies are particularly alert to their mothers' emotional states. When Pete's mother is hurried or tense, he's fussy and uncooperative on the diaper table and with eating. When she's relaxed and has time to work around his antics, he's peaceful and quiet as a lamb. A conspiracy? No, he is responding to body language. It tells him whether the psychological weather is fair or foul.

Let's give Pete two different mothers and see how his early impressions of himself depend on the *quality* of their body messages.

Mother A focuses on Pete rather than the task to be done when she bathes him. Her muscles are relaxed, her tone is playful and soft; there's a gentle light in her eyes. She sees his little fat wrinkles and dimpled toes. She delights in his reactions to the water she drips on his stomach. When he gurgles, she responds. If he splashes his fist in the water, he sees her laughing reaction as she joins his game. No words are spoken but the two are communicating. Pete *feels* and *sees* her warm responsiveness. He does not know he is separate, but he has early experiences of being valued.

Mother B consistently uses Pete's bottle time as an opportunity for reading. Her arms hold him loosely and indifferently. Her attention is not on *him* but on her book. If Pete coos, she ignores his sound. If he moves about, her arms are unresponsive. If he grabs her blouse, she loosens his fingers without even looking at him. Pete and his mother aren't sharing an experience. In fact, there is no warm, human, direct, person-to-person encounter at all. Pete's mother is his whole world just now, and his first experiences teach that he isn't worth attention. To him, the world is a pretty cool place in which he has little importance. You can see that Pete would develop quite a different set of early impressions about himself with Mother B than he would with Mother A.

Some experiments with infants suggest that *the degree of warm responsiveness* we provide forms the foundations for a future positive view of self. This responsiveness is made up of the kind of attention, smiles, close cuddling, songs, and talk we give infants. (See Chapter Seven.) Parents who play games with their babies—"How big is the baby?" "Ride a cock horse," "This little piggy," "Peek-a-boo," and all the others—can do so in ways that reflect warm respect and delight. These reflections get babies started toward high self-esteem. Parents who never play with their infants or who care for them with unresponsive, cold efficiency fail to give them early impressions of their importance. There is little joy in reaching out to indifference or rejection.

Before getting anxious about the times you were angry, distant, or tense with your child, keep in mind that single or infrequent messages do not cause permanent damage. What counts is the total number of loving or disinterested messages, together with their intensity. If there are more times of enjoyment, the baby gets the message.

Prior to learning the meaning of words, then, each infant busily gathers the thousands and thousands of impressions about himself that come from the body language of others. These impressions don't jell into clear-cut statements about himself as a person until later. But this fact in no way subtracts from their importance; because later messages rest on them, they pack a mighty wallop.

Word messages

Once a child understands words a new avenue for describing his person to himself opens up.

Toddler Pete snatches his friend's toy, delighted at the fine prize he has captured. At his age concern for the needs of others is nil, and his buddy's wails leave him completely untouched. His mother scolds, "Pete! That's not nice! *Bad* boy!"

To the young child, others—especially his parents—are infallible mirrors. When his mother describes him as bad, Pete concludes this must be one of the qualities he possesses and hangs this label on himself for that particular moment. Her words (*and attitudes*) carry tremendous weight. (See Chapter Nine for constructive ways to talk to children.)

Imagine that Pete's mother consistently sends negative reflections his way. Over the years he hears, "I can't do a thing with this child; he's impossible!" "What do *you* want?" (In an impatient, my-Lord-not-again tone.) "Why can't you get better grades like your sister?" "Pete's been invited away for the weekend." (In a tone of great relief.) "I can hardly wait till the end of vacation and Pete's in school." When he was taken to first grade, his mother's parting words to his teacher were, "Poor you, now you've got him most of the day!" Looking at the barrage he lived with, you can see why Pete would develop a dim view of himself. No wonder he thought of himself as a pain in the neck.

There's no question about it; *words have power*. They can shred or build self-respect. But words must match true feelings. High self-esteem does not come from buttering children up; in fact, nothing could be worse. Unless words and attitudes jibe, children detect the discrepancy. Then they learn not to trust what we say. (Chapter Eight further discusses the importance of matching messages.)

As with nonverbal messages, occasional negative blasts aren't permanently damaging. Every parent loses his temper occasionally. (Even so, negative feelings can be sent nondestructively; see Chapter Nine.) The child, however, who is immersed in verbal character defamations concludes, "I guess I'm a pretty lousy person. If your own parents don't like you, who else could?"

Treatment defines the self-image

High self-esteem, then, comes from positive reflections around the child. You may say, "Nonsense, I know lots of people who, as children, had the worst possible relationships with their parents and life in general. Yet today they are 'successes' who seem very sure of themselves and have many outstanding achievements."

True, there are many such people. But the external trappings of "success" do not ensure inner peace. Often individuals who look successful from the outside inwardly pay the price: living behind masks of phony confidence, alienation, neurotic defenses, and restless malcontent. Loners who dislike themselves, they may use constant busyness as an escape. Yet, they feel inadequate no matter how much evidence of outer "success" they stack up.

Genuine self-esteem, which is our concern here, is how you feel about yourself *privately*, not whether you can put up a good front or accumulate wealth and status.

To build pictures of themselves as truly adequate, to feel thoroughly all right inside, children need *living experiences* that *prove* their lovability and worth. Telling a child he is special is *not* enough. Experience is what counts. It speaks louder than words.

**Children value themselves to the degree
that they have been valued.**

Various factors combine to make you a most crucial mirror in your child's life: his prolonged dependency for physical and emotional satisfactions, his sustained contact with you, and the fact that your reflections of him are the *first* he experiences. To the young child, you are magnified until you take on the appearance of a god.

One four-year-old expressed a child's typical view of parental powers when he and his father drove past some homes one evening. Pointing to a house that had its lights on and shades drawn, he asked, "What are those people doing inside that house, Daddy?"

"I don't know, son."

"Well, why don't you?" he demanded.

To little folk, father and mother are all-powerful and all-knowing; they are literally lifelines. . . . It's quite logical for "threes" and "fours" to believe parents can see through drawn shades!

So the small child reasons, "These all-powerful gods treat me as I deserve to be treated. What they say about me *is* what I am." Using their words and body language to build his picture of himself, he struggles to fit their view of him. It is an image he will live up to as we'll see in the next chapter.

As parents, we must keep in mind that our reflections have a powerful effect on the growing edges of the child's sense of selfhood.

Other people are mirrors

You are, of course, not the only mirror in your child's life. Any person spending long periods with him affects his self-image. It matters little whether such a person is a relative, neighbor, baby-sitter, or maid. Teachers make heavy contributions to a child's view of himself since there is constant exposure and they wield marked power over him. Brothers and sisters are still additional mirrors. Although a child is not so dependent on them for physical and emotional needs, they provide social stimulation, competition, and are an intimate part of his daily life. They react continuously to him as a person.

Around six, the child moves from total dependence on the family. How children outside the home react to him becomes increasingly important. In short order he finds other youngsters value certain qualities. And whether he has them affects his feelings about himself. Boys tend to value athletic ability, sheer physical strength, and courage. Girls ordinarily emphasize physical attractiveness, good grooming, sociability, and friendliness. They give higher priority to tenderness and moral virtue than boys.

The child who has the traits valued by his agemates feels more adequate than the one who does not because he gets repeated positive reflections from the gang. The youngster whose interests and values are noticeably out of step with those his age is likely to feel isolated—then he sees himself as having less worth. Increasingly from age six on into adolescence, each child needs social support from others whose values match his.

Mastery and achievement

Once the toddler realizes he is separate, he tries to overcome his helplessness by mastering himself and his environment. His successes and failures are reflected in his attitude toward himself. Let's see how this works.

Every child's body sends him messages about himself. Ted has inherited long legs and strong, well-coordinated muscles. Whatever the sport, the skills come easily. Other children vie to have him on their teams; teachers and his parents beam warm approval. His competence allows him to see himself quite differently from his friend Clarence, whose small, uncoordinated body feeds his conviction that he has little to offer of what the gang values.

A youngster's rate of growth, energy level, physical size, appearance, strength, intelligence, friendliness, skills, and handicaps are all reacted to. He draws conclusions about who he is partly from his *own* observations of himself in comparison with others and partly from *others'* responses to him. And each reaction adds to or subtracts from his feelings of self-worth.

The attitudes of others toward a child's capacities are more important than his possession of particular traits. The *fact* of any handicap is not nearly so vital as the *reactions* toward it of those around him. Attitudes of pity and scorn make a youngster see himself as unfortunate. Then, his image of himself in that area becomes crippled.

School presents a whole new series of hurdles to clear—in the classroom and on the playground—if the child is to see himself as capable. Here's Jill, a fast maturer both physically and mentally. She finds herself ready to take on school tasks, particularly reading, sooner than many of her friends. She learns to see herself in a different light than does Joel, a late bloomer. She develops a private respect for her mental abilities. She has concrete evidence that she is more than just adequate scholastically.

One second-grade girl whose achievement level in school was high wrote, "I like myself because I do my work well." Awareness of her competence increased her enjoyment of being who she was.

In considering the importance of mastery to self-esteem, we should not overlook that successes carry more weight if they are in areas important to the child. Harlan, at twelve, was an accomplished pianist but a failure at sports. His musical talent meant little to him; it wasn't valued by his friends.

Every activity a child is involved in gives him further information about himself. In clubs, sports, church and social groups, at school, and at work, he continually adds reflections to his growing collection of self-descriptions.

The answers to "Who am I?"

Each child's view of himself is built from the stream of reflections that flow together from many sources: his treatment by those around him, his physical mastery of himself and his environment, and his degree of achievement and recognition in areas important to him. These reflections are like snapshots of himself that he pastes in an imaginary photo album. They form the basis of his identity. They become his *self-image* or *self-concept*—his personal answers to "Who am I?"

It is important to keep in mind that a person's image of himself may or may not be accurate. Every human being has both a self and a self-image. The closer your child's view of himself fits him as he truly is in the present, the more realistically he leads his life.

Mr. and Mrs. K. needed an outstanding child. Lila, absorbing their exaggerated praise, sees herself as a talented singer —an illusion fed by her money-hungry voice teacher. She has trouble, however, because audiences are lukewarm to her singing. If she refuses to change the self-image nurtured by her parents and teacher, she may knock herself out trying to become something for which she has no talent. This can only lead to frustration and failure, if not downright ridicule from others. Then, she has less reason to like herself. If she changes her self-picture to fit her true abilities, she cannot set her heart on becoming a concert singer—her parents' goal.

Naturally, the more any person's self-concept matches his real abilities, aptitudes, and potentials, the more likely he is to have success. Then, he has a greater chance of seeing himself as adequate.

Self-esteem emerges

At the very time that a child absorbs others' descriptions of himself, he takes in their *attitudes toward those qualities.* Mr. T., for example, often says to Lilly, "Lord, but you're boisterous!" A second message—a value judgment—travels with his words. His tone and jaw set say, "And that is bad!" Lilly learns to see herself as boisterous and learns to think of this as a negative trait. She can either push down a natural part of herself to earn approval and add to self-respect, or, if she accepts her father's judgment, she feels a bit less acceptable because of this quality.

Words are less important than the judgments that accompany them.

Mr. S. often calls Sammy a "monster." But his tone is loving and proud. It says, "Son, you're quite a guy!" Sammy refers to himself as a monster but he wears the label with pride. Remember: *body language always speaks louder than words.*

From the judgments of others, the child's own judgment of himself emerges. And the more he likes his self-image, the higher his self-esteem.

By five, each child has usually collected enough reflections about himself to form his first over-all estimate of his worth. He may not feel good about himself at all times, but if, by and large, he feels basically lovable and worthwhile, he can be glad he is himself.

Whenever a person says, "I'm inadequate," he is actually telling us *nothing* about his person. He thinks he is commenting on his personal value (his self). Instead he is commenting on the *quality* of his relationships with others—from which he has constructed his self-image.

In terms of how any person lives his life, there is validity in the statement, "It is not so important *who* you are as who you *think* you are."

Brett, a fifth-grader, turned in this theme when he was asked to write what he would be thankful for on Thanksgiving Day:

> I'm glad I'm not a turkey! I'm thankful that I'm me and you're you. I'm glad I'm getting smart in school. I'm glad I'm here and not there. I'm glad I'm a person and not a dog or cat. . . . I'm glad I go to this school. I'm glad I have nice friends to play with. I'm glad I have a brother to talk to at home. I'm just thankful I'm me!

An eloquent testimonial to the positive mirrors around Brett.

Remember: no child can "see" himself directly; he only sees himself from the reflections of others. Their "mirrors" literally mold his self-image. The key to the kind of identity your child builds is directly tied to how he's been judged. What goes on between your youngster and those around him, consequently, is of central importance.

A positive identity hinges on positive life experiences.

THREE · MIRRORS
INFLUENCE BEHAVIOR

Self-concept and behavior

Lee was happily engineering his "train" of boxes along an imaginary track. His chum, Jeff, angrily circled the train on his tricycle, hurling wild threats. "I'm gonna yank you off your train! You better watch out or I'll punch you in the nose! My trike can beat your train!" Lee blithely ignored the barrage.

Suddenly, Jeff rode over to the nursery teacher, whispering confidentially, "When you were four, were you as strong as me?"

Having been a puny child, his teacher answered emphatically, "You're much more powerful than I was at four."

Jeff sat quietly for a moment, as if digesting this idea. Then he slowly rode off, pedaling peacefully round and round his friend's train without a single added threat.

What triggered this marked change in Jeff's behavior?

Four-year-olds get many reflections of their impotence from their environment and those around them. Like all human beings, small though they are, they seek to counteract such reflections.

Jeff's earlier behavior begged his friend, "Notice my strength. Act scared so I can see myself as powerful." Behind the hostility was simply his wish to like himself. Who can tell, perhaps earlier that morning some experience emphasized his helplessness, leaving a hole in his self-respect that needed patching. Once the teacher supplied the necessary patch, he could tuck away a new picture of strength and his energies were free for peaceful play.

This brief episode illustrates that behavior is directed toward self-esteem.

Every child seeks a self picture as capable and strong. And behavior matches the self-image.

Think about yourself for a moment. Don't you behave differently in situations where you feel confident than you do when you feel inadequate? When you're sure of yourself, you make positive statements about yourself. Then, you are friendlier, more outgoing, and interested in becoming peacefully involved with others. When you feel inadequate and bumbling, you shrink from the limelight. The very term, self-confidence, means inner sureness. It says that at the core you trust your capacities, and you act accordingly. So it is with children.

Even the way a child speaks is colored by his feelings about himself. Ask a stutterer, for example, to tell his name, where he lives, or what he is taking in school, and he stammers in agonizing fashion. Ask him to assume an identity other than his own (deliver a soliloquy from *Hamlet* or adopt a foreign accent), and his disability disappears. Speaking from inadequacy, he stumbles; speaking from strength, he is fluent.

"Spotty" self-confidence

Confidence in one area does not necessarily mean confidence in all areas. Barry, for example, has received over the years many positive reflections of his intellectual prowess. In the classroom, on student panels, and in school organizations, his conviction that he has something to offer shows through. Socially, however, Barry feels like a "dud." Accordingly, at parties he is shy, self-effacing, and stays on the sidelines. He stands, walks, and talks differently in social situations than he does in academic ones.

Adults are no different. We all know men, for example, who are confident and participate freely in business groups. Yet at social gatherings they are fish out of water.

The more broad-spread any child's self-esteem, the more fully he operates with confidence in all areas of his life.

Low versus high self-esteem

Most children have mixed feelings about themselves, but as we have seen, self-esteem refers to their *over-all* self-judgments.

What kind of statements might Bobby make about himself if his self-esteem were low? He would say such things as, "I'm not very important. People wouldn't like me if they really knew me. I can't do things as well as others. There's not much point in my trying anything new because I know before I try that I'll fail. I can't make good decisions. I don't talk in groups because I don't say anything worth listening to. I don't like to go to new places. I hate being alone; in fact, I just wish I were someone else."

If Bobby's self-esteem were high, he would be more likely to say, "I believe I have something to offer others and I can learn from them. My folks think I'm worthy of respect. I can do quite a few things well, although I have lots more to learn. But then, learning is fun. If I can't do something right off, I like to take a second crack at it. In the long run, I believe I can do it. I like being alone or with others. I'm really glad I'm me." Bobby's confidence is obviously greater when he makes this second set of statements.

Let's look at two adolescents, equally attractive and intelligent, to see how self-esteem affects their behavior.

Jean believes in herself, whereas Mary does not. In the classroom you would see Jean volunteer information, go out actively to others, and eagerly take part in discussions. What a contrast to Mary's behavior! Hesitant and awkward, she only answers direct questions. She prefers keeping her opinions to herself because she fears others' reactions. At a teen-age party, Jean goes out to others with warmth and participates actively in games; whereas Mary hangs back. She waits to be coaxed and even then she plays only halfheartedly.

Secretly believing she has nothing to offer, Mary can hardly be expected to be self-assured in *any* situation. Her guardedness and self-doubt prevent spontaneous and wholehearted participation. Such behavior lessens her social impact on others, which in turn nourishes her conviction that she has little value. Unlike Mary, Jean's trust in herself frees her to enter situations without reserve. Each girl's self-image is revealed in her actions.

Whenever a youngster sees himself as a loser, he *expects to fail* and behaves so that success is less likely. Once he stops believing in himself, he is headed for failure. The youngster with a history of past successes expects to do well. His personal sureness gives him *courage* to face obstacles and the *energy* to tackle them.

Little Becky had been surrounded by love and acceptance all her life. People responded warmly to her large dancing eyes, her playfulness, and her sense of humor. "Oh, Mommy," she said one day, "I just love people." Why shouldn't she? Her experiences left her feeling valued and important. Watching her around people was like watching a friendly puppy; she literally bounded out to meet them. She expected to be a winner. And *her expectations colored her behavior*—confident, eager, and outgoing. These very traits brought her still further success.

Why children misbehave

All of us want to avoid the static of misbehavior in children as much as possible. Life is just more pleasant for us and for them without it. Discipline is a topic of such vital importance that we'll look at it specifically in Part V. Meantime, if you know that behavior matches the self-image, you can see that *one cause of misbehavior is a negative self-concept.* The child who believes he *is* bad tailors his actions to fit this view. He plays the role assigned to him. (Why this is so is discussed in Chapter Five.)

Usually, the more a child misbehaves, the more people scold, punish, or reject. And then the more firmly entrenched his inner conviction becomes that he is "bad." Chronic misbehavior can be rooted in a damaged view of self, but low self-esteem is not the only cause of misbehavior.

So many youngsters (and adults) whose behavior is detrimental to themselves and society as a whole—dropouts, delinquents, and dope users—privately believe they are hopelessly inadequate and worthless. They grope for personal meaning and fulfillment. But their misdirected efforts lead to self-defeating behavior.

The youngster with high self-esteem is rarely the problem child. He walks, talks, works, learns, plays, and lives differently from the one who dislikes himself. His inner security radiates outwardly in his actions. As adults, such individuals are better able to work constructively on the problems and inequities that exist in our world. Their solid cores free them to be innovators rather than hostile destroyers. The child with self-respect is likely to be a constructive member of society.

Happiness and behavior

Countless parents say, "I only want my child to be happy." But they are uncertain as to how such happiness comes about.

A study aimed at pinpointing the difference between happy and unhappy people concluded that the single most impressive difference between the two groups was that happy people were *successfully involved with others;* the unhappy ones were not. Low self-esteem acts as a roadblock to personal happiness by preventing peaceful involvements. One of the biggest problems facing almost any organization is that of people who are thorns to others. More progress is snagged on interpersonal relationships than we may fully realize.

The key to inner peace and happy living is high self-esteem, for it lies behind successful involvement with others.

FOUR · THE PRICE
OF WARPED MIRRORS

When self-respect is missing

In his efforts to like himself, every child reaches out for approval and works tirelessly to build skills that eliminate helplessness. If those around him overlook his growing powers, he makes no bones about calling his feats to their attention.

"Daddy, see how strong I am!"

"Know what? *I* can tie shoes now!"

"I can run faster than Billy!"

Bragging? Not necessarily. These statements are simply requests for positive reflections—feedback *needed* for high self-worth.

When children are unsuccessful in building self-respect, they take different routes based on three possibilities (or combinations of them). They

erect defenses: work out various cover-ups for feelings
of inadequacy;

submit:	accept their inadequacy as a fact and live self-effacing lives; or
withdraw:	retreat into fantasies that block out the rejections they suffer.

Each of these choices carries a price tag that diminishes the fullness of living.

The particular path any child travels is influenced by temperament, models, experiences, and the results of trial and error. Most children try a variety of defenses before submitting or withdrawing; these are usually chosen only as a last resort. Children don't give up easily.

Self-esteem and defenses

A defense is but a psychological weapon against anxiety, fear, insecurity, or inadequacy. Its purpose is to help the child maintain his integrity. All of us use devices for defense at one time or another.

Sally's constant tattling is her way of putting her brothers down while upping her own stock. Simon's continual bullying is his attempt to be top dog. Meg's incessant chattering serves to draw attention to herself. She hungers to be noticed.

A whole arsenal of defenses exists. Compensation, rationalization, sublimation, displacement, denial, and projection are common to us all. Sometimes these mechanisms help us adjust, but sometimes they cause trouble, particularly when they are relied on too heavily. (Ordinarily, most children eventually learn that bragging, tattling, and attention-getting behavior bring rejection more often than acceptance.) Our aim is not to deal with the varieties of defenses in detail, as this material is covered in other books, but rather to point out their purpose and examine a few common ones.

Most defenses are rooted in the child's secret belief that he is bad, unlovable, and unworthy. *This secret feeling forms the core of neurosis.* Neurosis is, after all, only the scar tissue around a psychological wound. The youngster with deep self-respect has no need for unhealthy defenses. Remember:

**Defenses are put up around weakness,
not around strength and adequacy.**

Inadequacy feelings and unhealthy defenses go hand in hand. Let's see how one particular child handles her need for self-respect. Vigorous, assertive Suzie senses she is a real disappointment to her parents. Although secretly believing their image of her is accurate, temperamentally she cannot submit passively. As a preschooler, she lashes out in defiance and rebellion; she tries to bulldoze her way to acceptance by direct physical aggression. By age six, she resorts to a cover-up course (compensation) to hide her inadequacy. Inside, she feels small and worthless, but outwardly she is loud, bossy, and overbearing. Telling Suzie to stop this behavior would be like trying to cure the measles by powdering the rash. Feelings of worthlessness are not touched by lectures; in fact, they are only increased.

By age eight, Suzie realizes her tactics only push other children away. Unable to win approval at home, she searches for some way to count in the gang's eyes. Then she discovers she has skill at baseball. Throwing her heart and soul into the sport, she watches the Saturday television games with a critical eye. She uses the hours after school to practice her pitching and batting. By the time she's ten, she has become the outstanding player in her class. The others clamor to get her on their side. Now she has carved out a real place for herself in the gang's admiration.

While taking up baseball was only another form of compensation for feeling unimportant originally, this solution helped Suzie by giving her what she craved—the gang's respect. She is headed for trouble later on, however, when being a good baseball player is no longer valued by her group. Then, unless she develops other ways to gain acceptance, she'll be left high and dry.

Another kind of compensation is seen in the youngster who

drives himself relentlessly to achieve ever higher goals. John, for example, secretly convinced of his worthlessness, "collects" all kinds of achievements to prove his value. But, no matter how thick the "achievement layers," they are rarely sufficient to blot out his private view of himself. Outer evidence does not quell the lurking conviction within.

Compensation is only one of many devices that human beings resort to in an effort to build self-respect.

Defenses and vicious cycles

Not every child (or adult) happens on constructive ways to build self-esteem. Many choose defenses that get them started on vicious cycles of self-defeat. Such patterns usually start in the home.

Suppose Suzie hadn't hit upon the solution of baseball. Suppose, instead, that she continued being bossy, pushy, and overbearing. The more highhanded she becomes, the more rejection she receives. Being an outsider with her schoolmates is added to her family's rejection, and her self-esteem drops even lower.

In Suzie's case, the vicious cycle doesn't stop. The worse her relationships with people, the less she is able to concentrate on schoolwork. From her point of view—from any child's point of view—belonging to the gang is more important than reading or learning the multiplication tables. How can she concentrate on abstractions when inside she is bleeding from the wounds of wholesale rejection?

As the "D's" and "F's" accumulate, Suzie has even more reason to see herself as worthless. Each fresh failure lays the groundwork for future defeat. Failure as a person feeds into academic defeat. Then, it doesn't matter if she has a high intelligence quotient; her personal adequacy quotient is shot full of holes.

One unhealthy defense found in children with low self-esteem is overeating, which starts a vicious cycle that is hard to break.

Jane, an eight-year-old, feels like the odd-ball in her family. Feeling unacceptable creates anxiety and tension. One of her earliest infant memories is that eating felt good; it relaxed inner tensions. As a baby, eating was associated with being held close and comforted. And as a toddler, she noticed her mother's glowing approval when she ate a hefty meal.

Now, on the basis of old memories and associations, she turns to food every time she's frustrated, tense, lonely, or rejected. Finding no comfort from the people around her, she gets momentary satisfaction from food. Eating has its own temporary rewards: food tastes good. To Jane, food becomes the symbol for warmth, closeness, affection, approval, and good body feelings. So she turns blindly to the symbol of old comforts and tries to nurture herself.

In lonely self-indulgence she overeats and becomes steadily heavier. This makes her less attractive and less competent in games, and soon she is the butt of playground jokes. The taunts make her turn even more insistently to food, and the vicious cycle tightens. The fatter she becomes, the more she is teased. Each new rejection sends her racing to food. And Jane retreats into self-hate and alienation.

The phony facade

Some children (and adults) with deep feelings of inadequacy use the defense of putting up good fronts. The model youngster is a case in point. Marie's parents appreciated her only when she was neat, punctual, kind, and thoughtful. As long as she played Miss Sweetness-and-Light she had a solid place in their affections.

She hid her normal feelings of anger, jealousy, frustration, and anxiety. On the surface everything looked fine. The trouble was that she knew these unacceptable feelings lay hidden inside. (The disadvantages of repressed negative feelings and their impact on self-esteem are discussed in Chapter Eighteen.) Marie spent most of her time erecting her "good girl" image to please others. She became a dependent, compliant individual who tailored her every act to win approval and hide her "bad self" from view. But despite her success at covering up, she had no confidence in herself. Her energies were devoted to looking perfect rather than to developing her potential. She became a slave to "shoulds" and drove toward outer evidence of "success." In such cases, "The emphasis shifts from being to appearing," as Karen Horney puts it.[1]

We have all met people who appear confident even when they don't feel that way. Sometimes we're fooled, but often there is a brittleness, an exaggeration, or a tension in their behavior that hints of the inadequacy beneath.

Larry is a little too loud, shakes hands a little too vigorously, laughs too heartily, and cannot sit still. He gives the impression of working to *appear* confident rather than *being* so. We never really feel we know such people as Larry. We cannot get behind the mask to the real person.

Anyone who erects a false self is actually in a bind. He gets reactions about the *mask* he wears, but not about his real self. Such a person knows his facade is not genuine, so he chalks the approval up to his good front. He lives with the belief, "People like my phony self, but that's not the real me." Approval means little; it's for something that's not genuine.

The person that he really is never has a chance to develop because it is removed from its source of nourishment: social interaction with others. Such an individual fears to let anyone see him as he is because he learned in childhood—ordinarily from his parents—that his real self was unacceptable. Carrying this assumption into adulthood, he loses the opportunity to check on how people in his adult life will react to him as he is. While the mask may have been appropriate in childhood, it may no longer be so. He thinks the facade protects him from further rejection. But it is a personal trap. And his relationships

[1] Horney, Karen. *Neurosis and Human Growth.* N.Y.: W. W. Norton & Co., 1950, p. 38.

with others remain counterfeit for as long as he plays this game.

Mildred was born into an extroverted family and learned early in life that for family acceptance she, too, must act the life-of-the-party. She donned the necessary front, but the loneliness of living behind a mask began to wear on her. It sapped her energies until as an adult she spent much of her time in bed with an ever-changing assortment of ailments.

At forty, she entered therapy and learned to accept her true nature—that of a quiet, reflective person. Realizing her life had been one long game of play-acting, she recognized that for her own mental and physical health she had to live according to her intrinsic nature, even though that meant not living up to what had been expected of her earlier.

She was astonished when long-time friends told her they liked the real Mildred better than the phony one. Unlike her family, these friends appreciated the quiet, gentle person she actually was.

Often it is only by reexamining old blueprints absorbed from childhood that we can give up the masks we feel we have to wear. We find to our surprise that they no longer have "survival value." In fact, others like us much better without them, for genuineness is captivating.

Many of us believe we must "look good"—appear strong, efficient, competent, perfect—to have approval. And we spend years polishing up good fronts, never realizing they ensnare us in the long run.

The cocksure adolescent, the woman who "wouldn't be caught dead" without her makeup, the woman who becomes highly anxious if a neighbor drops over when her house is messy, or the exceptionally short man who belligerently throws his weight around: each of these people usually harbors secret feelings of inadequacy. Feeling less than adequate *inside*, they find it particularly important to look competent on the *outside*. Conversely, the person who feels strongly adequate within doesn't have to forever present a flawless image to others.

Masks are worn to hide the "worthless me."

They cover up low self-esteem. When we live with youngsters so that they genuinely like themselves, they need no masks.

Submission and withdrawal

The youngster who fails to work out adequate defenses may resort to submission or withdrawal. These choices are made by Barbara and Harold.

Barbara received little acceptance from her parents, and being passive by nature, she made only mild attempts to win approval. Her father's extreme domination and dislike of females pervaded the home. All during childhood, Barbara watched her mother passively accept the role of the doormat. Using her as a model, Barbara grew up believing she didn't deserve respect. Like her, she chose a life of self-effacement—submission.

Harold's early experiences also convinced him he had little value or worth. He tried to earn his parents' love in many ways, but he never made the grade. Their rejection and the bitter battles he saw between them made him afraid of people. He had little courage to make overtures to others, and the few tentative efforts he made met with similar defeat.

For Harold, the real world and the people in it brought little personal satisfaction or psychological warmth. Frustrated by his inability to gain satisfaction in the outer world, he turned inward to the lonely comfort of daydreams. In his imagination he ordered the kind of world and treatment he craved. Withdrawal into fantasy not only spared him further rejection but gave him a private place in which to feel less threatened. He chose to withdraw.

Usually, the worse the child's behavior, the greater his cry for approval. The more withdrawn or obnoxious, the more he needs love and acceptance. The higher his defenses, the more starved and alienated he is. Yet, the child's very defenses make it less likely that he will win the acceptance he craves. So round and round he goes, spinning the cocoon that becomes his personal dungeon.

Our prisons and courts and hospitals deal every day with people who have paid the personal price of extensive warped mirrors and negative reflections in their lives. In fact, the pages of history are filled with examples of the brutal impact such people have had on the course of human events.

The tragedy is that none of this needs to happen. Vicious cycles *can* be avoided or broken after they've begun. (See Chapters Six through Thirteen.) Each parent and teacher stands in the position of providing reflections that prevent children from becoming ensnared in unhappy, twisted lives. Submission, withdrawal, and unhealthy defenses are choices we can help children avoid. Remember:

If you live with youngsters so that you crush self-esteem, you thwart positive growth; in fact, you foster warped, defensive development.

The benign cycle

When you know the importance of positive reflections, you can get a child started on a benign cycle, rather than a destructive one. This cycle operates in the same fashion except that it is based on positive reflections.

Joe, for example, felt deeply loved and valued by his family. When he went out to other children, his play was peaceful and nondefensive. Naturally, he made friends quickly and kept them. Not needing his energies for protective defense, he could relax in school, give full attention to his studies, and work up to capacity. The positive reflections from home, friends, and school involved him in a benign cycle of increasing mastery and acceptance. The widening circle of positive reflections fed his original belief that he mattered and his confident happiness drew others to him.

How you and I live with our children during their first

years at home sets the stage for whether they are caught in vicious or benign cycles. Even under the best circumstances, however, life experiences and people outside the family come along to give youngsters negative reflections. The fewer negative messages a child has from his family, however, the more he can withstand those coming from outside.

We parents are not *totally* responsible for a child's degree of self-esteem, but we play a major role in his *initial* view of himself and are significant in his life for many years.

FIVE · THE TRAP

OF NEGATIVE REFLECTIONS

Self-concepts change

Self-esteem is not forged for all time, although once established, it is not easily disturbed. A child's view of himself ordinarily changes as he grows and has new experiences. Jimmy's self-respect, for example, goes up a notch when mere physical growth allows him to ride a bicycle.

The process of building the self-image goes this way: a new reflection, a new experience, or a new bit of growth leads to a new success or failure, which in turn leads to *a new or revised statement about the self.* In this fashion, each person's self-concept usually evolves throughout his lifetime.

Rigid self-concepts

Sometimes, however, a child's attitude toward himself becomes rigid. Then, trouble brews. How does this happen?

As we've seen, high self-esteem comes with feeling lovable and worthwhile. Of these two feelings, lovability—believing you matter simply because you exist—is more basic. Once a youngster feels unlovable, evidence of his competence or worth may have little meaning.

The child (or adult) who is firmly convinced that he is no good is sensitized, so to speak, to let in only those reflections that confirm his negative image of himself. The belief, "I am unlovable," acts like a pair of sunglasses that selectively filter out contradictory messages. Disliking himself, the child ignores or rejects reflections that are at odds with his self-image.

The reason for this is that

human beings must make sense to themselves.

We have to feel *internally consistent*—"all of one piece." No person can believe that he doesn't matter and at the same time believe he has value to himself and others. The two feelings are contradictory.

Fourteen-year-old Tina, for example, feels basically unlovable because she has rarely received reflections of her value as a person. She has learned to accept her "unlikableness" as an inborn quality, a kind of given fact. She lacks certain skills respected by her gang; she cannot dance or swim. Believing she is inferior influences her approach to the lessons her parents offer. She has little faith in her ability to learn, but even when she does, her fundamental image of herself as a person does not change. She's convinced of her inadequacy no matter how competent she becomes. She reasons, "Oh, sure, I can swim, dance, play tennis, and the guitar, but so what? Others can do these things, too, and do them much better. My skills mean nothing!"

Tina cannot use her increasing competence to enhance her picture of herself. Feeling unlovable, she *must* focus on weaknesses rather than strengths. Achievements then are hollow victories. With her self-image cast in concrete, her low self-esteem perpetuates itself. Caught on the treadmill of continually reindoctrinating herself, she feeds on what's wrong. Unless her conviction about herself changes, her neurosis will tend to worsen with age. For with each passing year she will add to her collection of evidence against herself. If, instead, Tina had experienced an undercurrent of confirmation from her parents, she could recognize her increasing skills because her successes would then jibe with her basic belief in her value.

An added plus to feeling lovable is that confidence in his person permits a youngster to *accept his lack of particular skills without danger to self-esteem.* Because Mark likes himself, he doesn't believe he has to be perfect. He sees his shortcomings, *not* as proof of personal inadequacy, but rather as areas for growth. June's low self-esteem, by contrast, means that she uses her every frailty as a weapon against herself. She expects perfection; nothing she does is ever quite good enough.

Low self-esteem is tied to impossible demands on the self.

We've all met people who seem wedded to their inadequacies. It is amazing to watch their mental gyrations as they ignore all evidence to the contrary. So we have the girl convinced she is dumb even though an intelligence test shows she is bright. There is the pretty woman who believes she is ugly; the man who reads rejection into situations that others interpret differently, and the highly competent man who always stops short of his goals to feed his view of himself as incompetent. Regardless of the facts, such people cannot believe they have anything to offer. Why? Once the self-picture has jelled, the need for internal consistency pushes each of us to protect and preserve our self-image.

If low self-esteemers were to admit positive reflections, the fundamental assumption on which their lives are based would have to change. This would mean reorganizing their basic belief about themselves—that they are unlovable.

Giving up the only identity you've known for years, even

though that self-image is unsatisfactory, is bewildering. Living with the known, unpleasant as it may be, is far safer. The person who clings to a negative identity protects himself from major change. And change is something people with low self-esteem view with a jaundiced eye. Change involves trying the new, venturing into the unknown; it means giving up the security of the familiar.

The person who has lived with rejection and failure is more threatened by change because, understandably, the new may bring more bad news. And, he's had enough of that. By contrast, the person with positive past experiences has a basis for believing that good will come with change.

Occasionally, we meet a child (or adult) whose self-concept seems to be fixed in a positive direction. He acts as if he were "God's gift to humanity." His picture of himself isn't accurate, of course, for the perfect human being doesn't exist. But he filters out evidence of imperfections. (Remember: High self-esteem does not mean conceit.)

This seemingly "positive" self-concept actually masks deep feelings of inadequacy. Lacking a realistic picture of himself, such a person comes into conflict with others and with his environment. Since he refuses to admit weaknesses, he cannot strengthen them.

Specifics about rigidity

Let's look at a few questions you may have about rigid self-concepts.

If a person is convinced that he's unlovable, can his attitude be changed?

Yes, indeed. Remember: self-concepts are *learned*, not inherited. This means that attitudes toward the self can be altered in a positive direction. The main requirement for change, however, is *positive experiences* with people and life. To feel lovable, the child must experience acceptance from those around him (see Part II); to feel competent and worthwhile, he must *experience* success for his efforts.

If your child has a low opinion of himself, it is easy to think, "My Lord, he's ruined!" But he isn't. Every human being has an amazing capacity for flexibility, bounce, and growth. Counselors working with people in distress are frequently astounded by how well their clients function despite what they have been through.

Even though a child has had many negative experiences, he usually responds to a confirming climate and the "sunshine" of positive reflections. Therapists' records are filled with reports of children (and adults) who, with only one hour of this "sunshine" a week, make enormous changes in their self-images. Think of that for a moment. *Only one hour* out of approximately one hundred waking hours per week for a year or two can help a child change his self-image. What a testimonial to the human being's vast capacity to relearn! It also bears out that man needs only a little "sunshine" each week to blossom.

Parents who shift to providing nurturing reflections find amazing positive changes occurring in a relatively short time, even though the shift may not be made until their youngsters are teen-agers. Often, with no change in home environment, a child with low self-regard takes significant steps toward more positive self-statements when he is around teachers, relatives, or friends who provide a nurturing climate.

How does it happen that some children develop rigid views of themselves as inadequate?

One factor may be heredity. If you have more than one child, you have probably noticed that your words and tones carry far more impact with one child than with another. Some youngsters, by virtue of their particular nervous systems, are more sensitive to all their surroundings—food textures, light, color, sound, approval, or disapproval. Each child has a unique genetic inheritance and responds accordingly. Some children have less capacity to roll with life's punches. The less sensitive child is able to take more negative experiences before he feels damage. He simply responds with less intensity.

In addition, whether low self-esteem becomes rigid depends on *how early in life, how frequently and intensely,* and *from how many sources* a child receives negative reflections.

At what age does rigidity set in?

As we've seen, by five, a child has formed an opinion about himself as a person. Whether his attitude becomes rigid then or later depends on many factors: his heredity, his experiences, and how he organizes them. It takes the converging of many factors, however, to cause rigidity. *No single factor or experience is responsible,* dramatic movies and novels notwithstanding.

How long does rigidity take to soften?

The answer depends on the individual. The fewer hereditary factors operating against the person, the shorter time it takes. The younger the child when he starts receiving nurturing reflections, the more positive reflections he experiences, the less time it takes to change his dislike of himself. Then, too, certain defenses bring more pain than others. The more a child's particular defenses pinch, the more he is apt to *want* to alter his basic attitude toward himself.

Can low self-esteem be broken only *by professional help?*

Therapy may be necessary if the negative attitude is firmly entrenched. But, as the case of Mr. W. illustrates, life's experiences alone sometimes provide the therapeutic ingredients for positive growth.

Mr. W. felt generally comfortable about his person. At fifty, he began working for a supervisor who simply couldn't be pleased. Mr. W. was the "fall guy," and slowly he lost faith in himself. He became tense, withdrawn, and guarded. After seven years in this negative climate, he switched jobs. In the new firm his ideas and experience were eagerly welcomed; he was plainly considered a real asset to the company. Back came his self-confidence, and once again he was warm, confident, and relaxed.

Mr. W.'s experiences are a classic example of the power of mirrors on self-esteem. Negative reflections can tear it down;

nurturing ones can bring it back. This case illustrates again that how we see ourselves is influenced by how we are treated and affects how we behave. It points out that something as simple as a positive job change can be as therapeutic as hundreds of counseling hours.

Many a mother who has made her children her one and only interest in life has gone through a similar experience. When her children leave home, she suddenly feels unneeded and unimportant. Her self-concept changes to, "I have little to offer now," and with this new self-statement comes a lowering of self-esteem. If she get actively involved in a meaningful job or hobby, her sense of personal value returns. Feeling that she matters once more, she has a renewed joy in living.

Retirement for a person whose job has played an important part in his life often brings a lowering of self-esteem unless he finds new activities that give him a sense of fulfillment.

There are many circumstances that prevent low self-esteem: an accepting family; a teacher who respects your person; a job that particularly fits your talents; a warm, confirming friend or marriage partner; a meaningful religious philosophy; an introspective and challenging attitude toward your basic assumptions about yourself; meaningful reading; and individual or group therapy. Each of these situations has actually helped people move from the trap of low self-esteem.

Any life situation that makes an individual feel more personally valuable—that confirms his unique person—feeds high self-esteem.

Rigidity, then, blocks growth and limits the development of potentials.

When a child likes himself, he can absorb new evidence about himself as he grows. He knows he has undeveloped possibilities and is not fearful about exposing himself to new experiences. Then, his potentials have a chance to be realized. The child who feels basically unlovable clings to his negative identity and fails to take in evidence of his competence as it comes along. Only as his self-hatred dissolves is he free to grow.

In one sense, high self-esteem is an insurance policy; it is our best guarantee that a child will make the most fruitful use of his capacities and remain open to change. It is of the utmost importance that we look to our mirrors to check the quality of the reflections we send. We can "polish" our mirrors so that children are not trapped by low self-esteem.

SIX · POLISHING PARENTAL MIRRORS

Seeing through filters

Each of us sees our children to some degree through a haze of filters born of our past experiences, personal needs, and cultural values. They all combine to form a network of expectations. And

these expectations become yardsticks by which we measure a child.

Knowing *what* you expect and *why* is the first step toward polishing your parental mirror. Let's look at some common filters and see how they influence your parenting.

Inexperience

Since each child is different, we all wear the filter of inexperience to some extent. But we usually feel it most keenly with our first child. Mrs. B., for example, explodes when she finds her son's room in shambles after his afternoon rest. She tells him in no uncertain terms that he is a bad boy. A few years later, the wild disorder left by her third son doesn't surprise her. In fact, had she found his room neat, she'd have suspected he was sick. Sheer experience with pre-schoolers and her ability to adapt to reality changed her expectations. She measured her third son's behavior against the yardstick of experience and saw it as normal. Her treatment in both instances resulted from her expectations.

Borrowed standards

Many of our expectations are borrowed unthinkingly. A popular notion is that a quiet child is a "good" child. And our acceptance varies with his output of noise.

Expectations our parents had for us are heavily relied on as guides. These borrowed images allow us to act without thinking, questioning, or experimenting with the natural ways of children. They conserve energy, but they may take their toll.

Blueprints adopted from our culture are legion. "Boys shouldn't cry"; "Girls should play with dolls, but boys never should"; "Brothers and sisters should always love one another"; "Children should never be angry with parents"; "Boys should be athletes." We continuously measure children by many such pat standards, unrealistic though they may be.

In middle-class America, we parents place high value on rapid scholastic achievement, respect for property, cleanliness, sociability, and sexual control. Desirable as these goals may be, expecting such behavior at the wrong ages, or under all circumstances, or expecting children to learn the first, second, or third time around makes our approval conditional on the impossible. Then, we involve a child in a rat race that under-mines self-esteem. *How early* and *how fast* we press for these goals affects each child's view of himself.

Hang-over wishes

Some of our expectations for children are designed to meet our own unmet childhood wishes. One mother tearfully shared this story with her daughter's high school counselor. "I saved for months to give Ginny a matching cashmere sweater and skirt set, only to have her exchange it because none of her friends wore them! I'd have given my eye teeth for those things at her age. Where have I gone wrong to have raised such an ungrateful child?"

An unfulfilled dream made this mother expect gratitude. Her hang-over wish kept her from understanding that her daughter's needs differed from hers.

Current hungers

We may treat our children in ways that feed a current hunger in us. Mrs. T., for instance, is starved for approval. She needs it from everyone. If a visiting neighbor is a strict disciplinarian, she becomes a regular dictator with her children. If her visitor is highly permissive, she lets them get away with anything short of murder. Her response to her children —born of her present, unsatisfied hunger—depends on whom she is with.

If we crave status but cannot earn it through our own efforts, we may unconsciously push our child to fill the gap. We may want him to get all "A's," win the lead in the class play, or get elected to office because of the reflected glory. He must harvest distinctions to feed our needs. On the other hand, we may have heaped many honors on ourselves in our own lives. But if we see children as extensions of ourselves, rather than as separate individuals, we may feel the luster of our own star is dulled if they are less than outstanding. Our expectation is that anything coming from us must shine with equal brightness.

Hungers in our marriage relationship make up another set of filters. If we feel unloved or unappreciated by our husbands or wives, we can easily fall into the trap of maneuvering our children to fill these needs. And we dislike them when they fail. The more satisfying your marriage, the freer you are from asking your child to fill in your voids.

Unfinished business

Expectations for children often help us work out unfinished business from our own childhood. Most of us raise youngsters on the basis of our own needs rather than theirs. An uncomfortable thought, but true.

As a boy, Mr. P. had to do constant battle with an older, dominating brother. He never came to terms with his brother, nor did he lose the urge to get even. Without realizing it, he found a splendid opportunity to even the score, however, with his eldest son. When the older boy dominated the younger one, former memories in him were triggered off. He lashed out at his eldest with exaggerated intensity. He was unaware of why he did this and so was the son who bore the brunt of the unresolved conflict. But the father's unfinished business affected his youngster's self-esteem.

The impact of expectations on self-esteem

Your child measures what he can do against your standards. He then draws his own conclusions as to his value by how closely he fits your expectations.

A basic pattern found in the childhood home of the adult alcoholic is expectations too high to meet. Constantly falling short, the person concludes, "I'm worthless." Feeling no worthwhile resources within, he turns to alcohol as an outside crutch to build a sense of adequacy. Strong dependency and low self-esteem start him on a path that is self-defeating in the long run.

Underachievers most frequently come from homes where there is constant pressure to do more and better. The ever-prodding parent indirectly says to his child, "I have little faith in you." And, "You're not measuring up."

Whenever expectations are too high or too rigid to fit a particular child at a *particular* age under *particular* circumstances, we are disappointed too often. And our disappointments act like termites: they eat at the foundations of self-respect, toppling self-esteem.

Children rarely question our expectations; instead, they question their personal adequacy.

Does this mean that to avoid damaging self-esteem, you must throw out expectations lock, stock, and barrel? *Absolutely not!* Just as expectations that are too high make a youngster feel he is a constant failure, so the *lack* of expectations comes through as, "Why expect anything of you? You probably couldn't do it anyway." Such lack of faith wipes out a child's feeling of value.

Your child feels the force of your expectations; they directly affect his view of himself. Robert Rosenthal, a Harvard psychologist, found that children whose teachers had confidence in their ability to learn spurted ahead with IQ gains of fifteen to twenty-seven points. Nonverbal valuing became positive reflections for each child, enabling him to say, "I can do." The teacher's faith became the child's faith. *The fine line lies in realistic expectations coupled with a warm belief in each child.*

Conditional approval—"Fit my blueprints or go unloved"—tears at self-respect. Mike, by his physical makeup, is a quiet, studious boy, but he is alert to his father's preference for an outgoing athlete. To win approval Mike must give up his natural inclinations and struggle to fit his father's image of what a lovable son is like.

A child's belief in himself is the core that allows him to flourish. When he buckles under to fit preconceived expectations that disregard his essential nature, his self-respect is maimed. Being true to himself means maintaining the integrity of his uniqueness; it is the tap root for his stability. Submitting to expectations that run contrary to his nature always causes impairment. Rigid, unrealistic expectations fairly shriek, *"Be as I need you to be. Don't be you!"*

**Children's confidence has to be in what
they truly are, not in someone else's
images.**

The tragedy of the lost self

An eloquent and tragic example of a youngster faced with
the dilemma of fitting his parents' unrealistic expectations or
going unloved is seen in this summary from a counseling inter-
view.

A fifteen-year-old boy, living with parents whose standards
were rigid, authoritarian, and in no way appropriate to his
nature, said, "I'm completely resigned. There's nothing I can
do about my parents. I can't get them to change, so I'm
going to have to change. Anything I feel or want to be . . .
well, it just means trouble. I really have only one choice; I
have to go their way.

"Of course, other kids are completely ruled by their folks,
so I won't be the only one. But y'know something? I think
something in them kinda dies. You know, I died a long time
ago . . . I guess I died when I was born. The way I really
am couldn't please my family or anybody. How do you get rid
of what you are?"

This young boy sadly resigned himself to the path he must
follow. Never questioning his parents' expectations, he reasoned
it was he who was off-base. His is the tragedy of the lost
self.

Yet he was poignantly aware that a psychological death
occurs when youngsters make this decision. He was willing to
commit this "suicide" for the safety of outward acceptance and
a veneer of peace. But in his immature naïveté he was movingly
aware of a profound psychological truth; many children do not
psychologically survive the tyranny of the parental image!

When expectations cut across a child's grain, they force
him into the dilemma of whether to be or not to be himself. If he chooses to fit our images, he rejects himself; and
for as long as he denies his true self, he is a hollow person

—a carbon copy of the expectations of others. Then he is robbed of becoming the one person he was created to become—*himself!*

The double dilemma

Many a child is pushed into a double dilemma when his parents have different images for the kind of child they could love.

Mr. R.'s picture of an acceptable son is one who is highly outgoing and aggressive. Mrs. R.'s preference is for a son who clings and needs mothering. Their boy stands to lose no matter which image he tries to fit. Meanwhile, the kind of person he innately is may be lost in the shuffle.

Recipe for dependency

Imagine that your blueprints are such that your child can fit them, but only with strenuous effort. You churn out the designs for his feelings, attitudes, values, and goals. You know best, and you teach your child *not* to listen to his inner promptings. He becomes a highly dependent puppet, moving as you pull the strings. His reward? Your approval. (Remember, approval is an oxygen line, particularly for the young child.) The youngster then places his psychological center of gravity outside himself. Others have his answers and his own *self-*confidence never has a chance to flourish. Rigid parental images and tightly held expectations put huge hurdles in the way of movement toward genuine selfhood. They are the cause of the "lost self."

Highly dependent children don't suddenly blossom into emotionally mature, confident adults. Our country suffers when a large proportion of our citizens are highly dependent. Democracies need confident adults who have the courage of their own convictions. Children with high self-esteem become adults with such courage. With their energies free for tackling problems outside themselves, they can contribute meaningfully to our nation. And our country cannot afford to lose them.

Realistic expectations

If standards that are either too high or too low damage self-respect, how can you know if yours are realistic?

Expectations are more likely to be in line if they are based on the facts of child development, keen observation, and consideration of your child's past and present pressures.

You cannot know what is reasonable to expect unless you are familiar with what children *in general* are like. Young Ted's parents constantly expected a miniature adult instead of a child. They were angry when he couldn't handle long excursions for his benefit or waiting for service in a restaurant. They were distressed when his shoes and pants looked shoddy and moth-eaten in a week's time. They couldn't understand his inability to settle down for sleep on visits to his cousins. Common, insignificant situations—compounded by many more —gave Ted daily doses of negative reflections. It was no one's fault; his parents simply weren't familiar with the ways of youngsters.

Not only do you need to know what children are like, but you must know what developmental job is preoccupying them at each stage of growth. (See Part III.) Then, your expectations do not clash with the demands of growth.

Knowing what the average child can and cannot do is, however, not sufficient to make expectations realistic. None of us lives with a child-in-general. (Wouldn't life be simpler if we did!) Each child gives his own special twist to the over-all pattern of growth. And this you *must* attend to. Treating children assembly-line fashion is not respecting individuality. Knowing the basic trend for four-year-olds is helpful, but you must be alert to how Charlie handles this stage. *Close observation is a must.*

Fair expectations always consider past and present pressures. Most of us tend to do this to a large extent.

"Billy's grades fell way down this semester, but he's had a hard time accepting his grandfather's death. They were so close."

"Danny's taken to sucking his thumb, but I'm not surprised since he's adjusting to the new baby."

"Agnes is so grouchy lately, but she's under heavy competition in her accelerated class. She's always been the star pupil, but no more. It must be hard on her."

Each of these parents tailors his attitude to consider the pressures on his youngster. Knowing that *behavior is caused* and periodically looking at a child's world from *his* point of view helps you make allowances in what to expect. When inner or outer pressures are strong, we all appreciate some leeway from those we live with.

Expectation inventory

Since your expectations affect the quality of your "mirroring," you need to examine them. By looking inside, you may unearth one of the various filters that affect your behavior toward your child. Then, you can deal with it, rather than reacting blindly with expectations that meet your needs alone.

During the next few days, observe your behavior toward each child. Try to identify your expectations. Write each one down and look at it in the light of these questions:

Why do I have this expectation?
Where did it come from?
What's in it for me?
Is it based on my needs or my child's?
What purpose does it serve?
Does it realistically fit this particular child at this age and with this temperament and background?

An honest inventory may be painful, but it is the forerunner to change. Your child's self-esteem is at stake.

Working with your inventory

Check each expectation for fairness. How much meaning does it actually have for you and your child?

Perhaps you have been pressing for hearty breakfasts. But your son prefers light ones. When you examine this expectation, you realize he eats well at lunch and dinner and after school. He is rarely ill and his weight is normal. Result? You can toss out a borrowed standard.

Weed out all expectations that you've followed blindly but that have no real meaning for you and your child.

Go through your list again to check for expectations that meet your needs alone. Mr. and Mrs. J., for instance, were both dead-set against their son's flying. They supported any wholesome activity but that. Lloyd's high school teacher told them that of all the boys in his navigation club, none were as interested or talented as their son. After much discussion, they faced the real issue. Their expectation was born of their fear of flying. They decided Lloyd had the right to live his life, unencumbered by their fears. They dropped their objections and went all out to support his genuine talent.

To help children grow strong, you, too, must be able to let go of images that do not fit the uniqueness of your child. Can you drop your dream of an engineer for your animal-loving son? Does Betty have to stay in scouting when she dislikes it? Must Tom study music because *you* think it is a good idea?

Each of us has needs that cannot be dismissed as unimportant, but they must be met through our own efforts. Otherwise, we run the risk of unintentionally asking our children to fill the void.

Ask yourself, "Do I feel loved? Do I have a sense of personal achievement, recognition, and belonging in my relationships with adults?" (This is not to say that children don't provide us with love, a sense of belonging, and achievement. Hopefully, they do. But the point is that they must not be saddled with the burden of being our sole providers.)

Check each expectation to see if it exists to meet your hidden hungers, hang-over wishes, or unfinished business. Be careful, for it is easy to camouflage a need in yourself as a need in your child.

Parenthood means *nurturing;* feeding children the "psychological foods" that help them to self-respect. You do a better job when you yourself are not psychologically starved; that is, when your own needs are met through your own efforts.

You nourish from overflow, not from emptiness.

The more fulfilled you are as a person, the less you will use your children as your personal security blankets.

If you find yourself using your children as your major source of satisfaction, you need to change this arrangement. Mere awareness may be enough to spur you to action. If not, professional help can release you.

People used to think of therapy as only for the mentally ill. Today, however, counseling is increasingly seen as an experience that can free people from low self-esteem, rigid expectations, and help them develop their potentials for fuller, richer lives. Individual and group therapy, parent-education and developing personal potential classes are attracting growing numbers of people who are not mentally ill, but who are aware that they have room for growth.

The sticky wicket

Mrs. L. confided in her neighbor, "If that son of mine doesn't start asserting himself, I'm going to explode!"

Her neighbor, who had known Mrs. L. for some time, said,

"Give him time, he's only four. But who are you to talk? You let people walk all over you."

"That's just the point. I can't stand it in myself, and I hate to see it in him!"

Our attitudes toward others are inextricably bound by our attitudes toward ourselves. As Frederick Perls said, "You do unto others what you do unto yourself." If you are hard on yourself, you are hard on others. If you accept yourself, you can accept others. When you have come to terms with your own hostilities, you are less threatened by hostility from without. So it is that *your ability to confirm your child hinges in large part on your capacity to confirm yourself.*

Moving toward self-acceptance

Because you see others—and particularly your children—in the light of your own self-attitudes, a necessary check on the mirroring you provide involves looking at your own self-esteem. What are your answers to the question, "Who am I?"

Write out your personal feelings about yourself. What kind of person are you? What qualities do you see yourself as having, and how do you feel about them? Do you basically enjoy being yourself or would you rather be someone else?

If you don't like yourself, keep in mind that this attitude is *learned.* Remember: low self-esteem is not a commentary on your value but rather a reflection of the judgments and experiences you have had. *You hold the power of choice* to do something about your low self-esteem.

Just as you cannot afford to ignore the attitudes your child has toward himself, you cannot afford to ignore your attitudes toward yourself. Your own self-image plays a significant part in the quality of the mirroring you do. If you had an insulin or thyroid deficiency, you would doubtless take steps to correct it.

It is even more important to correct a self-image deficiency.

To like yourself, seek people who treat you with respect, for you need experience in being enjoyed. Get involved in activities that give you a feeling of competence and achievement. If your self-concept has become inflexible so that you cannot accept positive evidence about yourself, seek professional help. It can free you from the rigidity of low self-esteem.

Although being around others who enjoy you and having experiences with success will be important to your own personal growth, it is *crucial* that you do not allow others' mirrors to *totally* influence your image of yourself. Every human being will see you to some extent through his own personal filters—his own personal needs. It is vital that you remember that *any one person's view of you* is only *one* of the many reflections coming your way. But that person's view may not always be accurate. In short, the mirrors of others may contain some distortions.

The child uses others to get a picture of himself and tends to believe these reflections. You, as an adult, also cannot see yourself without the mirrors of others. But as an adult, you can and *must keep in mind* that how others see you may in some way be distorted—their mirrors may not be completely accurate.[1]

Hopefully, as more of us become aware of the importance of self-esteem, we will take active steps to strengthen our own self-respect. Our growth pays off, not only for us, but for countless generations to come as our children pass on their self-acceptance to their youngsters and they to theirs. Evolving your own potentials as a human being is a life-long challenge. To be or not to be fully you—that is your life's question.

While you are working to improve your own self-attitudes, your children do not have to go wanting. Expose them to other adults and children who enjoy them as they are. Encourage those activities that bring them success. Positive mirrors they need, but if necessary their self-confirmation can come from sources other than you.

[1] I am indebted to Verne Kallejian for suggesting this inclusion.

PART II · THE CLIMATE OF LOVE

The "stuff" of life

All of us know children need love. The prescription sounds simple and clear: love your youngsters and they'll feel lovable. How often this advice is doled out to us. Yet, countless children whose parents care deeply feel *unloved*. How can this be?

Confusion is rampant as to the meaning of this word love. Ask half a dozen people for their definitions and you'll probably get six different answers. But the confusion doesn't stop here. Ask people how they think love is communicated, and again you'll find a wide variety of ideas. Some youngsters never hear the words, "I love you," but they feel deeply cherished. Others, immersed in verbal affection, feel unloved. So the advice "love your child" leaves parents in the dark. It gives them nothing concrete to work with.

Before you can check on the climate you provide, you have to know what nurturing love is and how it gets across.

Nurturing love is tender caring—valuing a child just because he exists. It comes when you see your youngster as special and dear—*even though you may not approve of all that he does.*

If you feel this way toward your child, then, the crucial issue is how can you communicate your feelings? Many of us have decidedly vague notions about how this basic stuff of life is put across. Before examining the specific ingredients that spell love to children, it's important to look at some common misconceptions.

Common misconceptions of love

We often think of parents as demonstrating love when they are affectionate, repeatedly set aside their own interests for their youngsters, watch over them with vigilance, offer material advantages, spend abundant time with them, or treat them as if they were especially superior. Such behavior, however, doesn't necessarily make children feel loved.

While warm affection and close body contact foster physical, mental, and emotional growth, such affection does not, *in and of itself*, guarantee that a child will feel loved. Cold, impersonal treatment, especially during the early years, damages all aspects of development; yet, responsive affection *alone* doesn't convince a child that he's lovable. He needs much more to be *certain* he is loved. Too many children from affectionate families feel uncherished.

The parent who continually sets aside his own needs to meet those of his child may appear to be loving. But such behavior can mask intense selfishness, low self-esteem, fear of conflict, and even unconscious rejection. Being a child's personal satellite eventually builds resentment in parents (see Chapter Twenty-two), and this feeling is bound to be communicated by body language. Living with martyrdom is not living with love.

The watchful parent who guides and directs at every turn conveys the idea that the world is full of dangers that the child cannot handle. Overprotection says, "You are not competent," rather than, "You are lovable." It undermines self-respect.

Parents are constantly advised to spend more time with children. Yet, it is the *quality* of time and not its *quantity* that affects the feeling of being loved. Mr. H. spends hours with his youngsters, working with them on projects and games. On the surface the time spent looks like proof of devotion. But when you observe, you hear a flow of comments like these:

"Stop dawdling over your turn, Jimmy. Get going!"

"You're not holding that saw right. How many times have I told you to hold it this way?"

"Why can't you pitch that ball the way your brother does? When *will* you learn to throw from your shoulder?"

"You've messed up this paint job. Here, let me do it. For Pete's sake, this time *watch* me. If you're going to do something, do it right!"

The hours with his youngsters are filled with criticisms, lack of respect, comparisons, and high demands. The more time his children spend with him, the less adequate and lovable they feel. Sheer time does not necessarily add up to love.

We've all seen parents who provide lavish material advantages. Yet, as one boy coming from such a home put it, "My father saw to it that I had the best of everything. He actually insisted that I have gold fillings in my teeth, even though he could hardly afford them. But I never felt loved."

Did this father swamp his son with advantages because of love or to satisfy his own unmet childhood needs? Did he do this to fit his image of the "good" father, or to hide from both himself and the boy an unconscious rejection of him? Material advantages can serve as substitutes for love. It is easier to give gifts than to give of ourselves.

Mr. S. is convinced that his son is exceptionally superior. He exaggerates the boy's achievements and expects him to do earth-shaking things. Watching him, we may think he's blinded by "love" for his son. But deep inside, the boy knows his father's picture of him is untrue, and he finds it impossible to live up to his expectations. His son begins to feel inadequate and unloved, as he really is.

Casting a child in a role that meets our needs rather than his doesn't build love. Each child has to feel valued *apart from his achievements.*

Unless we're careful, we can mistakenly think of physical affection, martyrdom, overprotection, high expectations, time spent with children, and material gifts as evidence of love. But they can tangle caring so that it doesn't come through.

The positive ingredients

What, then, are the active ingredients that communicate love—the kind of love that allows a child to build a deep sense of self-respect? How can you prove your love in ways a child can feel?

Love comes through with flying colors when you give *genuine encounter* and *psychological safety.* Let's look first at the kind of encounter that nourishes, and in the remainder of this section we'll consider the six ingredients that build psychological safety. To feel loved, your child needs portions of all of the seven parts of nurturing love.

Genuine encounter

Every child needs periodic genuine encounters with his parents.

Genuine encounter is simply focused attention.

It is attention with a special intensity born of direct, personal involvement. Vital contact means being intimately open to the particular, unique qualities of your child.

Very young children demonstrate focused attention constantly. Watch a toddler as he spies a caterpillar. He becomes thoroughly absorbed in its fuzziness, its particular movements, and way of eating. He is personally engaged with the "particularness" of the caterpillar.

The opposite of genuine encounter involves distancing. You

do not focus attention intimately; you hold back. You see but from a distance, avoiding personal engagement. Many parents are with their children physically, but mentally their focus is elsewhere. Togetherness without genuine encounter is not togetherness at all.

They know when they have it

Children are highly sensitive to the degree of focused attention they receive. Mrs. C. had two elderly baby-sitters, who on casual inspection seemed to handle her children in similar ways. Her youngsters, however, definitely preferred one to the other. Observing closely, Mrs. C. found the answer: the preferred sitter was "all-here" with her children. When they came with a captured insect or an old rock, she gave the same focused attention that she gave to adults.

Mrs. N. was surprised when Molly shared her feelings the night of her birthday. After dinner, her mother had taken Molly for a short walk. Later, as she tucked her into bed, Molly said, "Guess what was the best part of today?"

"Getting that bike you've been wanting?"

"No, I love the bike and my party was so fun. But the best part was our walk tonight—holding hands and talking all about our day."

Focused attention—direct involvement—"all-hereness"; it is a quality that gets love across. It nourishes self-respect at the roots because it says, "I care."

They know when it's lacking

To ease Barby's jealousy of the new baby, Mrs. D. arranged time alone with her each afternoon. At first her daughter's attitude improved noticeably, but soon the old sniping was back in full force. Mrs. D. couldn't understand why the special time no longer bore fruit. Then, she discovered the reason. As her boredom with the childish play grew, Mrs. D. began using this period for mental note-taking. Thoughts like, "I must remember to take the pie out of the freezer," and "I forgot to write Sarah," ran through her mind. She moved into her own private world and Barby immediately sensed the distancing.

Turning her attention away from the games and her personal plans, she focused on Barby's turned-up nose, her broad splash of freckles, the lights that came and went in her eyes. She opened herself to Barby's "particularness." Sure enough, as Mrs. D. became directly engaged with her daughter, Barby's jealousy subsided.

Children are programmed for "inner presence." Without it, time together is wasted or even harmful. Yet, how frequently we give *presents* rather than *presence!*

The twist of nonencounter

Lack of encounter is easily twisted into a negative message. Imagine talking to your husband (or wife). He looks at you but you feel his mind far away. He answers, "Uh-huh," "Yeah," " 'Zat so?" Immediately, you sense that he wishes you'd stop talking so he could get on with his paper, his woodworking, or his inner thoughts. No matter how much he *says* he loves you, if you get this response often enough, you begin to feel, "He's not interested in *me*. He doesn't care—maybe, he doesn't love me." *Consistent* distancing comes through as lack of caring by children and adults alike.

The opposite of love is not hate, as many believe, but rather *indifference*. Nothing communicates disinterest more clearly than distancing. A child cannot feel valued by parents who are forever absorbed in their own affairs. Remember:

Distancing makes children feel unloved.

No matter how we slice it, doses of genuine encounter pound home a vital message. Direct, personal involvement says, "It's important to me to be *with you*." On the receiving end, the child concludes, "I *must* matter because my folks take time to be involved with *my person*."

Busyness cancels out "all-hereness"

How much genuine encounter do you *really* give your children?

We parents are such busy people! We have so much on our minds. It's not that we don't love our children; we do. But we have tasks to complete, schedules to meet, engines and weeds, taxes and jobs, laundry and dirt, appointments and lessons—on, on into the night. We rush to finish this task to start the next "must" on our list. Yet, hectic schedules work against human encounters.

Mrs. R. cares deeply about her children, but where is her focus at breakfast? She mumbles, "Uh-huh," to the story Tom tells while she puts a clip in Kathy's hair, sneaks a quick look at the headlines, gulps some coffee, and tries to remember the bacon that's about to burn.

The family sits down to breakfast and once again Tom starts to share an experience. She interrupts with, "Oh, really, Tom? Kathy, please lean over your plate; you're dropping crumbs all over the place. Bobby, is your P.E. excuse in your notebook? Say, Tom, you'll have to change that shirt; there's a big spot on it."

Unintentionally, not realizing the importance of encounter, we buzz, buzz, buzz. Deep involvement in "all-*thereness*" cancels our "all-*hereness*." Few of us live in the present with focused attention. Locked in the past or concentrating on the future, we are not in the present, which is, after all, the only time we actually have. We try to be everywhere at once. Then, in a sense, we are nowhere.

Every pressure you remove gives you time for *the person of your child*. Each of us needs to ask, "Does my behavior give priority to things and schedules or to human beings?"

One young boy defined grandparents as "people with time for kids." What he left unsaid was, "Parents are often too preoccupied for genuine encounters with children."

Where is your focus?

Do you focus so much on doing things *for* your child that you forget to focus on him as a person? Do you rush so fast to bake the cookies, sew clothes, make money for his education that you overlook *him?*

Or do you take time out—in those small moments when he brings a feeling or thought, or during a special time he can count on—to be *fully* open to him? You answer this question every day by your behavior. You can lose sight of the wonder of your child if you attend habitually to activities, the past, or the future, rather than to his "particularness" at this moment.

Practicing your focus

If you're dissatisfied with your encounters, you can change your focus. Perhaps you have spent so many years hurrying and concentrating on things-to-do that it is hard to switch to being-in-the-present with the person of your child. If so, practice focusing on the present in nonpersonal situations at first.

Choose a time when you are alone. Let go of every thought and concentrate on the here-and-now. No planning ahead or reminiscing.

Become completely absorbed in your task, whether it is washing the dishes or the car. Be fully open to the *feel* of the water. Look closely at the bubbles. Do you see any reflections? Imagine that you are seeing water running over a car or the dishes for the very first time. Whether it is rocking in a chair or driving down a road, close your mind to everything and pay attention—*focused* attention—only to what you see, hear, smell, and feel *at that moment.*

Most of us can stay in the moment—the here-and-now—for only brief periods; then our minds wander. But practice. See if you can increase your focused attention time when you are by yourself.

Next, practice being "all-here" with your child. Be totally with him, even if only for a few moments. Let go of everything except your direct encounter. Look at him with *fresh* eyes. Become directly involved with the wonder of him. Until you become open to your child in the process of becoming, unfolding, and evolving, you don't really see him as he is. Who is he? Look again with *seeing* eyes and *hearing* ears and *sensitive* radar. What is he like? Right now? Check yourself frequently for your "focused-attention rating." It may be fine this month, but then pressures come and you may forget.

Being-open-to-your-child is a skill that can become a habit. Genuine encounter pays big dividends; it pays off in your child's feeling loved.

Quantity of encounter

How often do children need encounter? The more, the better, but constant encounter is unnecessary. We don't ordinarily feel unloved when we lack exclusive attention. It is when others *never* have time to be truly with us that we feel unimportant. If children feel your wholehearted presence periodically, they can tolerate times when your attention is elsewhere.

Booster shots of encounter

A child needs focused attention most when he is under stress. Such events as a new baby's coming, a new school venture, a family move, excessive competition, and heavy disappointments are easier for children if they have booster shots of genuine encounters with those who are important to them. The internal stresses that come when youngsters make major developmental changes (see Part III) are eased by additional person-to-person involvements. Watch for the times when your youngsters especially need your wholehearted attention. Genuine encounters with you actively relieve the pressures that punctuate your child's days.

Appointments for encounter

When you sense your child is facing inner or outer stress, set up a definite appointment he can depend on. It may be twenty minutes once a day or an hour once a week. This arrangement is helpful whether your child needs it or not. One mother who saved each Monday afternoon to be alone with her daughter reported that her child called it her "favorite hour."

Many times our focused attention is saved for misbehavior. Then we zero in like a flash. But youngsters need vital encounters during peaceful times as well. And, of course, the more a youngster is convinced that you care, the less likely he is to misbehave.

You may tell a child many times of your love, but it is how you live with him day after day that proves your point.

Hurdles to encounter

The more fulfilled you are, the easier it is to give focused attention. Inner needs can gnaw so strongly that they literally prevent your being with your child. You can't be half focused and be fully *with* another person at the same time.

Mrs. G.'s self-esteem was extremely low. Her craving for perfection (her own ticket to self-acceptance) influenced her view of everything and everyone. She found it hard to spend time with her daughter because in her day there was always something to be made more perfect.

Even when she was alone with Virginia, she could hardly attend to her. When her daughter smiled, Mrs. G. thought, "Boy, we've got to start saving for orthodontia." Noticing Virginia's profile, her mother was reminded afresh how much she had hoped Virginia would inherit her upturned nose rather than her husband's prominent one. When she looked at Virginia's hair, she worried about its limpness. Her hunger for perfection blinded her to her daughter's uniqueness.

Your own self-acceptance frees you to focus on your child, unencumbered by inner needs. Personal inadequacies do not prevent vital encounters, but if they are insistent, it requires more effort to set them aside for brief intervals.

Genuine encounter is a potent factor in getting love across to children. But it is only one essential. Unless it is combined with psychological safety, it won't do the trick. Let's look at each of the six parts of safety in turn.

EIGHT · THE SAFETY OF TRUST

Antibiotics for neuroses

None of us tries to create problems in children. When symptoms appear—whether asthma, ulcers, underachievement, or promiscuity—we're genuinely bewildered.

Most of us are unaware that neuroses flourish when children feel unsafe. That we may fail to provide safety is a shock. In fact, we usually think of safety only in physical terms and are in the dark when psychological safety is mentioned. Yet,

the CORNERSTONE of the love that nurtures is psychological safety.

Combined with genuine encounter, *the six ingredients of safety are antibiotics that dispel neuroses.* Without them, children learn to wear masks and are launched toward alienation, unhealthy defenses, and twisted growth.

A warning note

Before considering safety, a warning note should be sounded.
No parent provides a consistently safe climate for all children all the time because the perfect parent doesn't exist.

All of us have various deficiencies that, hard as they are to face, sometimes bruise those we love. Living in the psychologically close quarters of the family inevitably causes hurts. This is a fact of life. Fortunately, most children are not unduly fragile. Their psychological bruises heal and they bounce back. They are pushed from within to develop self-respect, and given half a chance, they will.

The first concern

Imagine being suddenly catapulted to Mars and surrounded by strange creatures. Your first concern would be, "How safe am I? What's this place like? Can I trust these creatures?"

Every baby who is precipitated onto our planet is in a similar position. Although he doesn't think in these terms, his early experiences tell him whether he can count on us for friendly help in meeting his physical and emotional needs.

The bedrock of safety is trust.

Without it, later growth rests on emotional quicksand that affects all future development.

Most infants, although not all, experience their needs as intense and immediate; they have little tolerance for frustration. The parent who schedules his baby's feeding to meet the child's needs, respects his signals that he's full, introduces new foods gradually, and weans slowly helps the baby feel safe. Gentle respect for the infant's ways and quiet friendliness build trust.

Relaxed mothers add to their infants' security. Some parents are walking bundles of tension and their babies sense it. Tensions between parents, spoken or otherwise, and tensions born of emotional unrest are quickly picked up by children. These must be worked through if youngsters are to feel safe.

Trust is built in many ways. Let your youngster know when and where you are going and when you will return. Avoid sudden, unpleasant surprises. Help youngsters on visits to the dentist, doctor, or the hospital by frankly discussing what they can expect. Prepare them ahead of time for nursery school and kindergarten. Steer clear of promises you can't keep. These are but a few prescriptions for building a climate of safety.

The mixed-message trap

Many of you might never build distrust in these ways but may unknowingly do so by failing to be honest with your child about your feelings. Let's see how this happens.

Bobby comes home from school to find his mother violently mopping the kitchen floor. Bearing down intensely on the mop with her jaw tightly clenched, she glances up and says tersely, "Hi."

Immediately sensing something is wrong, Bobby asks, "What's the trouble, Mom?"

"Nothing, Bobby," she snaps.

He knows his mother well enough not to say anything more, but he goes out thinking, "Gee, I wonder if she found that frog in the can under my bed? Or is she mad about something else I've done?"

Bobby's confusion is understandable, for he has received two messages: one from his mother's words ("Nothing's wrong") and a contradictory one from her body and tone ("Something is very definitely wrong"). *Whenever words are at odds with body language, a child is put in a "mixed-message" trap.* The confusion shoves him into second-guessing what's up.

Every child first learns to rely on nonverbal clues. When they conflict with verbal messages, he naturally gives the nonverbal priority. He counts on them; yet, he still has to deal with the words.

Disadvantages of mixed messages

Mixed messages create a climate of codes and masks that teach distrust.

When you read the first section of this book about the importance of positive reflections in a child's life, you may have wondered why you couldn't just play the role of the positive mirror. The problem is that how you really feel slips through on the nonverbal wavelength. You know this from your own experience. If your wife pretends to be Mrs. Agreeable, you pick up her phoniness right away. If your husband plays Mr. Patient, you find out soon enough. We cannot live with others, particularly children, day after day and fool them about our true feelings.

Examples of the fact that false fronts don't work are seen in over-permissive homes. Mr. and Mrs. G., for instance, play the role of "anything-you-want-dear" parents even when deep inside they are quite opposed to some of the things their children do. They hide their inner feelings with phony words, but their resentments build up inside to seep out in tense expressions, sarcasms, or false smiles.

Some of the unhappiest children come from over-permissive homes (where parents mask true feelings) because they are immersed in a constant stream of mixed messages. Extreme situations, in which parents continually say the opposite from what they mean, contribute to schizophrenia. The schizophrenic has a profound distrust of people, resulting from the masked and distorted communications he has lived with.

An added disadvantage to mixed messages is that children read their personal concerns into the ambiguity. In our earlier example, Bobby, already feeling guilty about the frog hidden under his bed, first guessed that his secret caused his mother's anger. But if his main concern had been doubt over her love, he could have read this anxiety into the dual messages. He could have thought, "I guess Mom isn't glad to see me come home. Maybe she wishes she didn't have me for a son."

No child can trust unless those around him are open about their feelings. Mixed messages wipe out safety and love.

The single, most important ingredient in a nurturing relationship is honesty.

Probably one reason most of us enjoy young children so much is that they are real. When they're mad we know it; when they're happy, they send the message loud and clear. We know where we stand with them.

The common joke, "I'm going to leave the room now, so you can talk about me," is funny because it's true. Too often we feel that people are polite to us on the surface, but we wonder what they say about us behind our backs. We don't have this feeling with real friends; in fact, we tend to treasure those we can trust because we feel safe. And children respond in kind.

Avoiding mixed messages

Sending mixed messages is a habit that must be broken. Many of us fall into it through imitating others. We may choose this path fearing disapproval if we express honest feelings. We may hesitate to expose ourselves or fear dealing with certain emotions. Sometimes we give phony responses because it's easier than trying to get in touch with our real feelings. At other times we cover up because we are afraid that our openness may hurt others. (Avoiding this pitfall is discussed in the next chapter.) Too much is at stake, however, for you not to make an all-out effort to avoid masking.

How can you side-step mixed messages when you really don't want to share your feelings? Let's go back to Bobby's mother. Suppose she was upset over a personal quarrel but didn't want Bobby to know. She could have said, "Son, I'm upset about a grown-up problem that I don't want to discuss." Now that her words and body language match, Bobby isn't confused by contradictions.

On the other hand, suppose she had found the hidden frog but felt that she had been nagging Bobby too much lately. One part of her wants to vent her frustration, while another part feels it would be wiser to say nothing.

She could, of course, say, "I'd rather not discuss what's bugging me." But then she risks storing up irritations to explode over a minor incident later on. The alternative is honesty about both sets of feelings. She could say, "Bobby, I found your frog, and frankly it bugs me that you haven't followed our family rule. But lately, it seems as if I've been pecking away at you so much that part of me hates to mention it. I'm sitting on top of two feelings. One makes me so frustrated I want to scream, and the other makes me wonder if I expect too much."

Sharing conflicting feelings is part of honesty. Seldom do we have just one reaction to a situation; two opposing feelings—or even four or five—are more frequent. Because children are remarkably sensitive to undercurrents in us, sharing only part of our feelings confuses them.

Is honesty total openness?

You may immediately wonder, "To build trust, am I supposed to be *totally* open *all* the time?"

Definitely not. You may choose to keep certain feelings to yourself, but be honest about your reservations. If Bobby's mother had said, "Son, I'm upset about a grown-up problem that I don't want to discuss," she would have chosen to keep the details to herself. But she would have been frank about her reservation.

If she had felt comfortable about giving him some information, she might have said, "Oh, I'm upset about a quarrel I had with a neighbor, but I prefer not to go into detail." Whatever she says, however, she must *not* say, "Nothing is the matter," when something *is* bothering her—if she wants her son's confidence.

It is simply not appropriate to be totally open about all of your feelings with everyone at all times. You have to decide for yourself when, where, to whom, and how much of your inner world it is *appropriate* to share. Regardless of your decision,

be honest about your reservations; don't mask them.

Watered-down messages

A lesser form of masking comes when you send mild messages to cover strong feelings. Anger is the emotion we most frequently water down. (See Chapter Nineteen for appropriate ways to handle anger.)

Many of us believe that strong feelings are a sign of immaturity. And, therefore, if we feel intensely, we soft-pedal the emotion to fit our image of the mature adult. Many men feel their masculinity is open to question if they show any strong emotion save aggression, anger, or sexual interest. Boys are taught to hide disappointment, tenderness, or sorrow, for instance, lest they be considered poor sports and weak sisters.

The psychologically mature person recognizes that he has feelings and he can share them when it is appropriate. High self-esteem is related to the ability to be open to all inner reactions because human beings, whether male or female, *do* have all kinds of feelings of varying intensity. The person with high self-esteem does not have to deny what he feels. Self-acceptance gives him the security to be open, for he isn't a pawn to others' approval. Open ownership of feelings, then, is a hallmark of high self-esteem. (Feelings that are too intense to fit a particular situation or ones that are inappropriate, of course, signal something amiss.)

Children pick up the discrepancy when we use mild messages for strong feelings, but they do not know *why* we water them down. Many a child concludes, "It's not right to feel intensely. If I don't feel casual, I'd better pretend that I do."

Pretense on our part becomes a model for youngsters to imitate; it teaches them to distrust strong feelings. Then, they think less of themselves privately because of what they harbor inside. Under such conditions, self-esteem can never be wholehearted and unreserved.

You may wonder, "If I do decide to share my feelings, do I share *exactly* how strongly I feel, no matter what?"

Appropriateness must always be considered. Honesty does not mean making children emotional whipping posts. It is possible to match words to feelings and still convey an appropriate message.

Mrs. V., for instance, has had a rough day and her son's lack of cooperation gets to her. For a brief moment she feels, "Oh, I wish I'd never had children!" Sharing such a feeling would devastate George. But she can remain open and yet appropriate by saying, "I've absolutely had it today, George! I need to be alone for a while; I can't take anything from anybody right now!" This response is honest; it expresses her need for time away from her son without damaging his self-respect.

If Mrs. V. had said instead, "George, you're always such a comfort to me; this lack of cooperation just isn't like you," it is quite likely that her body language would tip George off that she masked real exasperation.

If Mrs. V.'s wish that she had never had children is consistent, she needs to get at the source of her rejection. Or she needs to attend to the climate around her children and use constructive discipline so that their behavior is less objectionable. Remember:

Temper openness with appropriateness, but avoid mixed messages.

Do you dare to be human?

The implied question here is whether you dare to be fully human with your children. Or do you feel you must glide along with never a ruffled feather?

The seemingly "perfect" parent is often the masked one. Children need vital contact with real people, not masked robots acting off borrowed blueprints. As a human being you can legitimately own up to feelings of all kinds: weakness, discouragement, worry, fatigue, and confusion. You are no less worthy or strong because of them. In fact, *it takes strength to be open.* Your example demonstrates that feelings are legitimate. Parents who own up to their humanity keep youngsters from hiding theirs.

Many parents ask, "Should I apologize to my child when I do something wrong or say something uncalled for? Won't my child respect me less if I admit to mistakes?"

Would you lose respect for someone who admitted he goofed? Would you respect him less for an apology? Hardly. More than likely your respect would grow because of his honesty.

Mrs. T. used to spank her children for misbehavior. Then, she decided that spanking was a method she wanted to avoid. Sticking to her resolution for quite a while, one day she reverted to the paddle. Immediately, she regretted her act, and she dared to be open with her daughter.

"Tilly, it wasn't fair for me to hit you, especially since I won't let you hit me. I'm awfully sorry. I wish I'd handled my feelings some other way."

She was stunned at Tilly's response, "Oh, Mom, that's O.K. I know you're trying not to spank, just like I'm trying not to cheat at hopscotch. But it's sure hard not to, sometimes, isn't it?" Even very small children are amazingly understanding when we are open and honest. No matter how young or old, we all respect genuineness. Then, we can trust.

Rather than disillusioning children, openness draws youngsters to us. It makes us seem less like distant gods and more like real people. A false notion many of us carry around—one that we need to question—is that we must play gods to earn children's respect. We often fear that children's confidence in our dependability as parents will be undermined if they see us upset, worried, indecisive, or in error. But disguised feelings and whitewashed mistakes only make youngsters aware of our deceits, which ultimately destroys their trust. And it makes them believe they'd better play the same game. Both children and parents are better able to strengthen inadequacies when they feel safe to reveal them.

In addition, our masks encourage children to erect their

own fortresses against psychological intimacy. Then, they are cut off from the source of all human nourishment: close, genuine relationships with other human beings.

Extreme behaviors, of course, tear at a child. If violent moods dominate a parent's life, the most positive action for him is to get professional help, as such upheavals signal internal deficiencies. He can be real with his child by indicating that he is working toward not being buffeted by every feeling. This honesty prevents the youngster from believing that he is the source of the emotional storms.

Trust and self-esteem

What does a climate of trust say to a child?

It says, "You can count on me to help you meet your needs. I am not perfect but you can depend on my being honest with you—even about my imperfections. You can afford to be imperfect, too, and together we can try to strengthen our shortcomings. If I give you anything less than appropriate openness, I shortchange you. Masks aren't good enough because they keep us apart. You are safe with me."

Such an attitude breeds love and respect. It gives a child the security to go out to others in a friendly, open manner, because he has learned this is the way to be. Then, others can trust and respect him.

Every child needs the sure conviction that he can believe what his parents say and depend on them for friendly help in meeting his physical and emotional needs.

Being open with children is not enough, however. Whether you damage or build self-esteem depends upon *how* you tell children about your feelings. If they're to feel safe with you, you must communicate to them in nonjudgmental ways. In the following chapter we'll consider safe ways to share feelings.

NINE · THE SAFETY OF NONJUDGMENT

Reactions vs. judgments

"How can I be honest and open with my child? When I let out my strong feelings, he's either crushed or defensive. I'm not so sure it's helpful!"

This mother's observation is legitimate.

Simply being open with children can have *undesirable* results *even* when you're careful about appropriateness. Some parents tell children how they feel and, in the process, tear down self-esteem. Other parents are open and build mutual respect. What makes the difference?

The distinction lies in *how* you share feelings.

"You're rude!" says Mrs. T. to her son as he continually interrupts while she visits with a friend.

"I'm tired of these interruptions!" exclaims Mrs. M. as her son repeatedly breaks in on her conversation.

Mrs. T.'s words put her in the role of the judge, and she hands down her verdict from on high. The negative label, "rude," slams squarely at her son's image of himself.

Mrs. M., unlike her friend, avoids playing judge. She expresses her reactions toward her son's behavior by saying, "I'm tired of all these interruptions." She conveys inner feelings *without* judgment. Consequently, she does not tamper with self-esteem.

Negative judgments make you a negative mirror for children. More important, they play havoc with self-respect and safety. They belittle, shame, and chastise; they make children feel unloved. Sharing appropriate inner *reactions about behavior*, on the other hand, does not whittle down self-respect, undermine safety, nor erode love.

For safety, children need your real reactions to keep their behavior within bounds. But they must be spared your labels of their person. Nonjudgment is the second ingredient of psychological safety, for

blame—negative judgment—is at the core of emotional disorder and low self-esteem.

As we've seen, each child incorporates negative labels into his self-image and sees himself accordingly. Personal evaluation is always a threat. To nurture truly, switch from being a *judge* to being a *reactor*.

Imagine being a child and having the remarks in the two columns below sent your way. What are your reactions? Which group of statements takes you down a notch?

A	B
"You're impossible!"	"I can't stand all this bickering!"
"You're lazy!"	"I'm worried about your grades."
"You're thoughtless!"	"I don't want to pick up after you!"
"You bad boy!"	"It hurts little Mike when he's pinched. I don't like to see him hurt."

The statements in column A cast *blame*. Don't they make you feel less adequate as a human being? On the other hand, the statements in column B let you know how your parent feels without your feeling personally attacked.

Even positive evaluations (praise) work against safety, for all judgments put the child in the position of living with a labeler. It doesn't take a child—or any of us—long to know that if a person can evaluate positively, he can also evaluate negatively.

You avoid the role of benign judge by simply telling youngsters your personal reaction toward their behavior. You can say, "I really appreciate your remembering to pick up your room," or "It makes me feel so comfortable to know you remember our rules when I'm gone." These reactions are more helpful than the typical judgment, "You are a good boy."

How many of you have heard a dentist or doctor say, "Your son was a good patient!" How much better for the child's self-esteem if he reacts to behavior by saying, "Jackie didn't fuss about my working on him, which made it easier for me. Thanks, Jackie, for helping me out."

So many parents send a child off to a party or to school with that old confidence-shriveler, "Now, be a good boy." Implication? "I have doubts about you." "I hope you remember the rules," tells your child where you are at that moment without plastering him with judgment. As we'll see shortly, doubt about his behavior is quite different from doubt about his worth as a boy.

Here is a distinction that needs careful attention.

Countless books and articles urge parents and teachers to lean heavily on praise. And many experiments show that it far outweighs punishment as an effective behavior manipulator. Of course. Children want positive reflections and they will jump through hoops to get them. They want our approval.

There is, however, a *subtle yet important* difference between positive labels ("good" or "nice") *applied to a child's person* and approval ("I appreciate" or "I like") *directed toward acts*. The point is that to believe in himself a child *must not have to question his worth as a person.* That must always be clearly understood. It is *not* clear to a child when he is told that he is a good boy because you like what he did.

Separating behavior from self

There is a high psychological price tag attached to living with judgments: the child *learns to think of his behavior as synonymous with his person.* The idea that a person and his behavior are separate may be clearer if you think of the sun and its rays. Think of the ball of gases that make up the sun as the inner core of the child. The heat rays from the sun may be likened to his behavior.

Because behavior comes from the child just as heat rays come from the sun, it is easy to think, "Bad behavior, bad person; good behavior, good person." Such thinking fails to separate a child from his acts.

Whenever personal worth is dependent upon performance, personal value is subject to cancellation with every misstep.

A child's self-respect is constantly shifting unless he manages to walk the tightrope of continuously high performance. Such "tightrope walking," however, means constant watchfulness which only undermines safety.

No child always behaves in acceptable ways. When your attitudes and words equate his acts with his person, he lives a yo-yo-like existence. Up and down his personal value goes in accordance with his behavior. Then, the child *cannot develop a solid sense of personal worth* because there is always the "*if*-of-his-performance." Even if you don't believe your child *is* what he *does*, your words can make him think so. "I-reactions" remove this danger.

Avoiding the judgment trap

To avoid judgments, tell your youngster what is going on inside you without using labels.

The labeling words—adjectives and nouns that describe a person—are the ones that cause trouble. Words like "dawdler," "messy," "procrastinator," "sloppy," "rude," "mean," "selfish," "naughty," "nice," "good," "bad," "shameful," and so on are judgmental by nature. Such labels have no place in the vocabulary of nurturing adults.

In general, using "You," and following it by a noun or adjective describing the child, sends a judgment. Ordinarily, "I," followed by what is going on inside you, sends a reaction toward behavior.[1] Let's look again at some messages sent first as judgments, and then as reactions:

"You-judgments"	*"I-reactions"*
"You're such a slowpoke!"	"I'm worried you'll be late for school."
"You're messy!"	"I don't want to clean up these cooky crumbs on the floor!"
"How sloppy can you get!"	"This clutter really bothers me!"
"You're a liar!"	"I can't count on your words when they don't match what you do."
"You have good taste."	"I like the dress you chose."
"You dope! Don't you know any better than to play out in the street?"	"I'm so frustrated I can't stand it! I've repeatedly told you about the danger of street playing. I'm scared stiff you'll be hurt!"

[1] I am indebted to Thomas Gordon for this concept.

It cannot be emphasized too strongly that judgments are troublemakers.

The secret for safety is to react but to suspend judgment.

Practicing nonjudgment

Learning to suspend judgment is far from easy, because most of us have spent a lifetime being judged ourselves. Descriptive labels are our constant mental companions. Let someone be talking to us and even as they do, our "judgment computers" go full blast. We silently judge with a "That's good," "That's stupid," "What a dumb attitude!" "That's the right way to think."

We even do this to ourselves. Mrs. S. says to her friend, "Yesterday I did such and so. Wasn't I *ridiculous?*" Her friend says, "Oh, that's nothing. One time I did this. Did you ever hear of anyone so *stupid?*" Pinning labels on ourselves and others is a national pastime. And we rarely question this way of thinking.

You can move from this habit by first becoming aware that you *are* judging. When you hear yourself do it, translate the judgment into a reaction. Mrs. S., for example, can say, "Yesterday I did such and so. Boy, I sure wish I hadn't." (A reaction, not a judgment.) Her friend can say, "I know what you mean. One time I did this. Was I sorry I did!"

To get off the judgmental merry-go-round, jot down some of the sentences you use about yourself and your children—those sentences with "you" followed by descriptive words. Then, rephrase each sentence to be a statement of your inner feelings.

Obviously, awareness will not eliminate years of habit overnight. Constant watchfulness and practice can convert you, however, and the rewards are well worth the effort.

Benefits of "I-reactions"

"Yes," you may say, "but my child is going to be judged by friends, teachers, and employers, so he'd better get used to it at home."

True, every child will be labeled right and left in the outside world. But he is more likely to shrug off judgments from casual others if the important people in his life haven't marinated him in personal evaluations, particularly during his formative years. Your lack of judgment helps him translate other people's labels into reactions. Then, his self-image is spared unnecessary barbs.

"You-judgments" invite defensiveness and encourage children to tune you out. And, of course, if they are believed, they harm self-esteem, as we've seen.

In addition, when you don't play judge, your children are far more apt to share their feelings with you. And, then too, your "I-reactions" give them a constructive example to use with their friends.

Remember:

Judgments are smoke screens that prevent love from coming through.

When your child lives with a reactor, he can say, "I am lovable even though not all of my behavior is acceptable." The healthy child sees his person as separate from his acts. A sense of personal value independent of behavior is essential to high self-esteem. How you talk to children affects whether they make the vital distinction between behavior and self.

TEN · THE SAFETY OF BEING CHERISHED

Acceptance vs. cherishing

Parents are advised to accept a child as he is. Fine. But acceptance is too mild a word when we consider the climate of love. "Accept" can mean tolerating the inevitable—tornadoes in the Midwest, adolescent acne, or Johnny's lame leg.

Children survive on acceptance but they do not blossom on it.

They need something stronger. They need *cherishing*. They must feel valued and precious and *special* just because they exist. Then, deep down they can like who they are.

Cherishing is not something you necessarily give lip service to; rather it is the feeling you have toward your child. It is sensing his uniqueness and finding it dear. In spite of intermittent irritations, you remain open to the wonder of him.

Why cherishing gets lost

Most of us *do* cherish our children; we'd feel a lifetime ache if they were suddenly to die. In moments of crisis there's no question of our valuing them. How is it, then, that cherishing gets lost so that our youngsters fail to feel it?

One reason is that we tend to take for granted those things we have every day. The right to vote, freedom of religion, good health—we cherish them dearly but we frequently take them for granted until they are threatened.

So it is that we often forget the miracle each child represents as we live with him day after day.

Most of us give preferential treatment to the material possessions we treasure. What a strange phenomenon that we fail to carry this same attitude over to children. We prize them highly; we'd give our lives for them. Yet, how often we put them down.

This inconsistency bears careful scrutiny, because to a child

respectful treatment is translated prizing.

Ask yourself this question: "If I were to treat my friends as I treat my children, how many friends would I have left?"

Few of us would think of shaming or analyzing friends in front of others, jerking them up short with sarcasm, humiliating, embarrassing, hitting, or ordering them about like soldiers under our command. Of course not. But think how commonly these scenes occur:

"Ned is so shy! No matter how much I encourage him he can't seem to get 'with it,'" says Mr. B. while he and his son visit with a neighbor.

"You're just showing off!" Mrs. F. scolds her adolescent in front of four friends.

"Why are you so bossy, Gene? I'm surprised these boys will even play with you," hollers Mr. E. to his son as he watches the gang play softball.

"Billy, if you don't keep out of those chips you're going to be even more of a tub than you are now," sneers Mrs. T. to her overweight son in front of guests.

Repeatedly we treat children as second-class creatures devoid of feelings; and yet, we prize them! At times we blatantly disregard their sensitivities.

Mrs. A. and her ten-year-old daughter are having lunch with Mrs. L. The two women become highly involved in conversation for forty-five minutes, unaware that they're shutting out another person (child though she is) who sits silently eating. Neither of these two women would dream of behaving this way if the third person were another adult. Unthinkingly, they assume that treatment unacceptable for an adult *is* all right for a child. But what about the child's need to be treated with respect? He is no less sensitive because of his size. Disrespect always encrusts caring so that it can't be felt.

A frequent comment in parent-education classes is, "This class has made me start seeing my child as a *person*." Most of us aren't disrespectful willfully. We simply forget and fail to put ourselves in children's shoes. Or we treat them as we were treated.

Your respect for your children is reflected in all the ways you pick them up, hold, bathe, dress, feed, and diaper them. It is reflected in how you talk, play, argue, and discipline them. You have only to apply the Golden Rule to communicate respect.

Any time you make a child feel small, shamed, guilty, non-existent, or embarrassed, you put him down, deny respect, destroy safety, and damage self-esteem.

Sometimes cherishing isn't felt by a child because you focus on what's wrong rather than what's right. Johnny brings home a math test; twenty-seven problems are correct; three are not. What does his father see? The three problems missed! If Johnny's father is questioned about his focus, he says, "I want him to know what was wrong so he won't make similar mistakes." But Johnny hears nothing about his twenty-seven successes from his dad.

In many little ways, we forget to focus on the unique gifts of each child. We focus on what he doesn't have. *When we habitually attend to what's missing, cherishing gets lost.* If your child lacks faith in himself, search to find what he *can* do. Give him plenty of recognition for those things and refuse to focus on what he *cannot* do. His sense of success—victory —is the key to his belief in himself. It feeds his conviction that he has something to offer, which spurs him on to new efforts.

Another fact that muddies cherishing is that we tend to see a child in the light of our own traits. We value qualities in him that are as yet undeveloped in us. Conversely, we tend to reject in the child what we reject in ourselves, as we saw in Chapter Six. And then he pays the price for our own lack of self-acceptance.

Awareness of this phenomenon sometimes helps us be more accepting of ourselves and our children. Mrs. N. confided, "My daughter's sensitivity used to bug the stitches out of me. But, of course, I'm terribly sensitive and I hate it. It takes effort, but now when I run into her strong sensitivity, I say to myself, 'O.K., she's reacting the way I do—the way I wish I didn't,' and somehow just recognizing the tie-in makes her sensitivity less bothersome."

As was mentioned in the last chapter, unless you see your child as separate from his behavior, you give only conditional acceptance. "I-reactions" also play a big part in keeping cherishing from getting lost. There are several things, then, that prevent cherishing from coming through to children: disrespectful treatment, taking a child's specialness for granted, focusing on shortcomings rather than assets, disliking in them what you dislike in yourself, "you-judgments," and confusing behavior with the person.

Enlarging your capacity to cherish

Every effort you make toward enlarging your capacity to cherish is reflected in your child's self-esteem.

For a start, ask yourself how much you value *yourself*. (Remember: you do to others what you do to yourself.) Very few of us take time for a serious "self-inventory." Now is the time to do it. Get by yourself and look within.

How aware are you of your own special qualities as a person? Do you appreciate that there is no other person in the whole world quite like you? You have certain capacities and sensitivities that are uniquely yours. You have special strengths that in some way differ from the strengths of others.

Write out the qualities that make you distinctly you. If you have trouble doing this, check with an intimate friend and see if together you can work out a list of your "specialties."

If you are like most people, you've spent years focusing on what you *don't* have. Now, reverse your focus and concentrate on your positive qualities. Interesting things can happen when you stop taking yourself for granted. You can become the optimist who sees the glass half full rather than the pessimist who sees it half empty.

Next, ask yourself, "Do I treat myself with respect? Or do I play the game of running myself down? Do I sometimes take a trip, buy something, or give myself a little indulgence? Do I quietly, yet firmly, ask that others show respect for some of my needs? Or do I play the game of 'I'm-not-important?'

"Do I respect my body's physical and emotional requirements and do I actively try to meet them? Do I carve out blocks of time to spend with others who enjoy me? Do I save time for doing things I like?" (Remember: the more fulfilled you are, the more you nurture others.)

Then, ask yourself, "Do I think I *am* what I *do?*"

One woman, when complimented for a piece of work she'd done, said, "I'm glad you like *me*." She failed to separate her work from her person. An author said, "If you dislike my book, you dislike me." His sense of personal value was not intrinsic to his being but contingent upon his writing skill. If Mary dislikes Sally's point of view, she dislikes Sally. She fails to disentangle the *idea* from the *person.*

Unfortunately, we live in a "perform-or-perish" culture. We are often valued for what we do rather than because we exist.

If you think of your value only in terms of behavior, it is probable that the important people around you as you grew up sent you this message. Ideally, you should have lived with reflections that told you you had value simply because you were alive. But, you do not have to remain trapped by reflections from the past. You can change your way of thinking either by yourself or with help.

To free children from the bonds of "perform-or-perish" thinking, you *first* have to free yourself from it. You teach this important distinction most pointedly by your own attitudes toward yourself. When you prize your own uniqueness (even though you are aware of your shortcomings), when you respect yourself and focus on your positive qualities, you are freer to cherish children.

When parents can't cherish

What if you agree wholeheartedly to all of this, but honestly can't manage to stir up a prizing feeling even for your potential or that of your children? Your hangup is not being able to cherish.

You need positive mirrors in your life. Go after them. If your friends don't value you as a human being, seek new friends. It may be, of course, that others value you but that you cannot let positive reflections in. Or you may hide behind a mask so that others cannot nurture you. In either case, you can get help to break your low self-esteem.

Sustained effort and growth on your part may be needed but you can learn to find value in yourself by being exposed to acceptance. You can depose the tyrant judge you may carry inside; if not, seek help.

Benefits of being cherished

Not having personal worth tied to behavior permits a child to choose more realistic goals, ones he is more likely to reach. His resulting successes increase his self-respect. When a child knows behavioral errors don't cancel lovability, he is more tolerant of others' mistakes. He can value others. He doesn't have to focus on their frailties because the important people in his life haven't focused on his. This attitude in him attracts others and results in his getting along more peacefully.

When mistakes are not tied to personal worth, they are less overwhelming. Then, the child can see errors as areas for growth rather than as personal catastrophes; they can be faced and worked through.

Scott came from a family that cherished him in accordance with his school success. Consequently, any paper with less than a "B" jarred him to his foundations. To watch him taking a test was to watch a picture of pure tension.

For him, performance was a life-and-death struggle; he believed his personal value was graded with each paper. Tension actually created a hurdle to learning; it literally prevented his thinking clearly. He had to perform in known, approved ways. Having his value tied to his performance sounded the death knell to his creativity.

"Just a minute," you may respond. "In Chapter Two I was told that children need experience with success to feel competent and worthwhile. How does this idea fit in here?"

True, all children need to experience their competence to build self-respect. But each child needs to feel that his person is cherished regardless of his competence.

Successful performances build the sense of worthwhileness; being cherished as a person nurtures the feeling of being loved.

Every child needs to feel *both* loved and worthwhile. *But lovability must not be tied to worthwhile performance.* The more lovable any child feels, however, the more likely he is to perform in satisfactory ways, for then he likes himself.

ELEVEN · THE SAFETY OF "OWNING" FEELINGS

Refusing ownership

"I want a candy bar now," wails ten-year-old Teddy at eleven-thirty in the morning.

Mrs. L. shakes her head, "Teddy, you don't want candy now; it'll spoil your lunch. You can have some for dessert."

Nine-year-old Brian smashes his little brother. His mother orders, "That's enough of that, young man! Now, say you're sorry!"

In countless ways, we repeatedly refuse to let children "own" their feelings. We tell them their emotions are wrong, inappropriate, and even that they are nonexistent. Then, we compound the error by dictating which feeling is appropriate for the occasion. Mrs. L. tells Teddy he doesn't want candy *now*. Brian's mother *orders remorse* to replace anger.

Does this imply that Mrs. L. should let Teddy eat candy whenever he wants? Should Brian's mother allow him to sock his brother at his convenience? Certainly not! But,

**psychological safety is eroded when
ownership of feelings is refused.**

Respect for a child's feelings is part of respecting his integrity.
Emotions well up spontaneously and are an integral part of
each person's private self.

Unintentionally, we treat children like emotional computers
into whom we try to program appropriate reactions. We want
them to feel sorry when we're sorry, hungry when we're
hungry, concerned when we're concerned, and so on. We ask
them to match their feelings to ours and get irritated when
they don't.

When you dictate the feelings a child should have, you
literally ask him to *give up ownership of his personal, internal experiences.* But this he cannot do. He has no power
to manufacture emotions; he can only repress or pretend. Hidden emotions remain very much alive (see Chapter Eighteen),
and in the long run, they invariably have the last word.

Feelings refuse to bow to command.

Please note: *letting a child "own" his feelings does not
mean letting him do anything he wants.* There is a vast difference between stopping an act and dictating to emotions.
Behavior frequently needs to be limited. We are only talking
about the *freedom to feel, not the feeedom to act.* (More
of this in Chapter Eighteen.)

In the candy incident, it is Mrs. L., *not Teddy,* who wants
the candy eaten after lunch. Unintentionally, she asks him
to feel as she does. She could avoid this pitfall by saying,
"Candy would taste so good to you right now, Teddy. (This
says, 'You have a right to your feelings, even if they differ
from mine.') But you'll have to wait till after lunch and have
it for dessert. (Here she limits his act.) If you're hungry,
I'll start getting lunch ready."

Brian pounded his brother because he was mad. His mother's
words do not turn off his hostility. They ask him to lie and

result in greater resentment and guilt. She can let him own his feelings while limiting his behavior by saying, "Brian, hitting your brother has to stop and stop right now! (She limits his act.) But you're really angry, so angry you want to smash him. Use this pillow and show me what you'd like to do to him." (Now she says, "Your inner feelings are your own. Although I have to limit your behavior, I'll help you work your feelings through safely.") For psychological safety, the right to feelings *must be protected.*

Separateness and safety

It is the rare parent who truly allows his child the privilege of owning his separate and distinct feelings. Why? Because you and I have lived with others who insisted that we feel as they did. And unless we're careful, we treat children as we've been treated.

In addition, it is extremely difficult to allow children to have feelings that we have been taught are unacceptable. Their emotions trigger off our own repressed, forbidden feelings. So we back off in alarm and teach children to follow suit.

When a child repeatedly feels that acceptance hinges on becoming an emotional carbon copy of his parents and teachers, his uniqueness and safety are threatened. Too many times the blueprint is "feel as I do to earn my love."

Mrs. D. decides the amount of food her children should eat at each meal and insists on clean plates. Her standards determine the extent of their hunger.

Mrs. W. says to her son when he doesn't like a dish she's prepared, "You don't know what's good." In her eyes, he is clearly out of line when his taste disagrees with hers. This attitude pervades all her relationships. She cannot tolerate or understand anything different from her inner experiences.

We often think we respect individuality when we allow an adolescent to choose his own clothes, class subjects, and vocation. Fringe benefits! It is when you refuse to ask a youngster to deny his feelings that you demonstrate wholehearted respect for separateness.

Parents extol the desirability of individuality loudly, but privately they wonder, "Why isn't Jimmy more assertive like Bob?"

"Science has always interested Marlene. I can't understand why Bob doesn't enjoy it more. Just think, they come from the same family!"

"Lou enjoys social groups; what a shame John doesn't!"

"If only Eric were more like my even-tempered Van!"

And so it goes, ad infinitum:

"Here's - to - individuality;   why - is - this - child - so - different - from - that - one?" All in one breath!

"Long-live-uniqueness-and-creativity! Whew! Our-son-feels-just-as-I-do!"

"I can't understand it; our children are as different as day and night." This commonly expressed observation is rarely said in tones of delight; it is usually said with amazement or weariness.

The wonder is not that children react differently, but that they resemble each other at all. Each human being, save the identical twin, is a unique and unrepeatable event. Add to this inherited individuality the fact that no two children can possibly have precisely the same experiences or environment, and it's not surprising that they differ.

Aside from heredity, you might think that three boys with the same parents, eating the same food, and living in the same house would have the same environment. Externally, this may be true, but their psychological environments differ widely. None of us reacts to each child in the same manner. We are all at a different stage in our own growth and under different pressures with each child. Every youngster has separate neighborhood and classroom experiences. And so it goes. Many factors combine to give each child a unique psychological environment. And each factor plays a part in how that child organizes his reactions.

Whose experience is it?

Letting a child own his feelings raises the whole issue of giving children various kinds of lessons—a hassle in so many homes. Ask yourself, "Who *owns* the experience?"

Who can know for another what will turn on his enthusiasm? Beckon a child into a variety of experiences, but accord him the right to his particular reactions. Safety disappears when you decide what children "should" enjoy. And you tread on dangerous ground when you communicate that children must like certain experiences to have approval.

Said Mary Ann, "Whatever I wanted or preferred wasn't important. My reactions never seemed to be the right ones. Something must be the matter with me."

Respect for separateness proves you care.

Providing for differences

How strongly you pressure children for feelings similar to yours is colored by your capacity to see them as separate individuals and to tolerate differences.

Check your response; it tells about your capacity to change and grow. And it affects whether you permit your children to do the same. Don't brush this issue off lightly. Listen to what you say. Notice how you feel. When difference is seen in a jaundiced light, you teach that uniqueness is wrong. Then you send negative reflections.

Camping bored Thelma to tears, but her family loved each outing. Respecting her preferences, her parents made other arrangements for Thelma when they left. They in no way implied she was a party-pooper because she differed. Their respect allowed her to value her separateness rather than seeing it as a fly in the family ointment.

The star goes on your safety chart, then, only when you **provide for difference without withdrawing approval.**

Checking tolerance for difference

To get a feel for your tolerance for difference, check your relationships with those outside the family first.

Mrs. O. had difficulty getting along with others. Her problem stemmed from her need to have others think as she did before she could relate to them. If you have a similar attitude toward those outside the family, it is highly probable that your children are subjected to an even more concentrated diet of intolerance.

The poem, "The Blind Men and the Elephant," deals with this very point. It tells of a group of blind men who came across an elephant for the first time. Each touched a different part of the elephant and then believed he knew what an elephant "looked" like. The one who touched the tail argued that the elephant was like a rope; the one who held the trunk believed it was like a snake; the one who grabbed the leg insisted that it was like a tree trunk; while another, coming up against the flank, was convinced that the elephant was like a wall.

Each man experienced the elephant differently and each was sure *his* way of organizing his experience was the only "true" way. Yet none of them considered that there might be another point of view equally as reasonable.

We, like the blind men, often have an experience and believe that because we react in a particular way, ours is the only correct reaction. Yet, if we truly accept another's separateness, we must not insist that ours is the only reasonable viewpoint.

To some extent we are all blind men bumping into the various "elephants of life." Each of us brings to any situation our own uniqueness and past experiences and feelings.

Each of us sees a little differently. You need to continually remind yourself that

your way of seeing and feeling is not the only way of seeing and feeling.

A child's viewpoint is as valid for him as yours is for you. Your attitude needs to be, "You are your own person, and your feelings are thoroughly yours." Then, safety and love come through.

If you have trouble accepting differences in others, it may be a clue that your own self-esteem is low. The individual who lacks a strong sense of personal worth is threatened by differences, particularly in his family. He needs them to rubber stamp his various viewpoints *so that he can believe in them himself.* He needs outside support to validate his self-picture. When he doesn't get it, he feels anxious, rejecting, or unloved.

Should this be your case, it simply means you need to get to work on your own lack of self-esteem.

Impact on self-esteem

Allowing a child to "own" his personal feelings and reactions has a strong impact on his self-esteem. It permits him to say, "It's all right to be *me*. My inner experiences are legitimate even when they differ from my folks'. Having certain feelings at certain times in no way detracts from my value as a person."

The child with this conviction doesn't hide behind pretense, nor does he try to ram his perceptions down the throats of others. As a result, he gets along better with people.

Interestingly enough, when you put yourself in your child's shoes, trying to see the world from his point of view, you often discover its reasonableness. Then, you provide the safety of understanding. We'll look at this idea more fully in the next chapter.

TWELVE · THE SAFETY OF EMPATHY

Revealing what's inside

Bruce is out of sorts and his mother says, "Go to your room till you can be pleasant." She allows him to own his irritation, but she plainly doesn't want him around under such conditions. In short, she makes it clear that he invites rejection if his grouchy feelings show.

Strong negative emotions create inner stress; yet unthinkingly we often refuse constructive help when children need it most. We say we want children's confidence, but our responses too often turn them away. And if we cannot accept a youngster's feelings, he too, learns to reject them.

The need for empathy

Think about yourself for a moment. When you share a feeling, you don't want to run into disapproval or reasons why you shouldn't feel as you do. *You want to be heard with understanding.* When you expect to be understood, you feel safe to talk.

Imagine for a moment being deeply worried about some forthcoming surgery for your daughter and confiding your concern to a friend. If he replies, "Oh, *don't worry;* I'm sure everything will turn out fine," you hardly feel understood. His reassurance does absolutely nothing for you. In all likelihood, you think, "A fat lot Helpful Harry knows about it. I'll bet he's never had a child in surgery!"

Suppose, instead, he says warmly, "Boy, these are anxious days for you!" Now his words and tone tell you that he understands how it feels to be you at that moment. You don't share fear to be told that it's groundless; you reach out for understanding to lessen the burden of worrying in isolation. To bear pain in solitude is always more difficult than to know that others are "with" you. *Human understanding brings warm comfort and safety; it bridges the gap of alienation.*

What empathy is

There is a special word for the kind of understanding we all crave. It is *empathy.* Some people confuse sympathy with empathy. But sympathy conveys an "oh-you-poor-thing" attitude. Although we may seek pity at times, it is not nearly so helpful as true understanding.

Empathy is being understood from your point of view.

It means that another person enters your world and proves that he understands your feelings by reflecting back your message. He temporarily sets aside his world to be "with" you in all the subtleties of meaning that a particular situation has for you. As Carl Rogers has pointed out, the empathic person is with you not to agree or disagree, but rather to understand without judgment.

Each of us normally communicates to others by two routes: *words* and *body language.* Ordinarily, our *words contain the facts,* while our *muscles and tones reveal our feelings toward those facts.* The total meaning of our messages is packaged together, and our hope is that others will understand our full message. In terms of being understood, however,

attitudes and feelings are more important than facts.

When your child talks to you, you only demonstrate genuine understanding by reflecting back his *total meaning*. If Ted, for example, slumps into the living room and says despondently, "Well, I finally finished that term paper," his words state that the project is complete. But his tone and posture reveal his feelings toward that fact; he's downhearted and discouraged.

If Ted's father responds only to his son's words, he reflects back only content by saying, "Well, you finished the job." Having his words parroted makes Ted feel heard at one level, but *certainly not fully understood in terms of what this experience means to him*. His feelings toward the project are considerably more important than the literal meaning of his words. But his father's response leaves Ted's feelings untouched.

If Ted's father hears his son's total message, however, he is sensitive to both verbal and nonverbal messages. He proves his understanding if he responds, "Even though it's finished, you feel downright discouraged." Now he captures the full flavor of Ted's world and his son feels the warmth of human understanding.

When you are empathic, you do not try to change a child's feelings. You simply try to learn how he experiences his particular part of the elephant, as it were. You don't attempt to see *why* he feels as he does; you try only to capture all the nuances of his particular feelings at that moment. You come to see how he sees, to feel how he feels.

Empathy is the fifth ingredient of psychological safety.

Because man is a social being, he reaches out to overcome aloneness by establishing psychological intimacy. To do this, however, he must know that he will be heard empathically. Human beings are feeling creatures and for genuine self-respect they need their feelings accepted and understood.

Part of becoming socialized, of course, is learning that *not all feelings can be put into acts*, as was mentioned in the last chapter. But learning that it is safe to reveal inner reactions and that the important people in his life will understand helps a child accept what he truly is—a human being with all kinds of emotions.

Have you ever thought that you may know every statistic and fact *about* a child and yet not *know* him—personally know him—until you understand his point of view? You do not know him until you understand how he personally organizes what happens to him. You cannot know him until you enter his private inner world; it is in the arena of feelings that the human being lives and breathes and dies psychologically. Shut the door to feelings and you cut off life and growth and the essence of uniqueness. Shut the door to empathic understanding and you wipe out intimacy, safety, and love.

Let's look at a typical situation to see it handled first in a manner that undermines safety, and then in a way that builds safety:

Karen, a three-year-old, is frightened by a sonic boom and runs crying to her mother.

Typical response:

Her mother says, "Oh, honey, it's just a sonic boom from a plane. You shouldn't be frightened."

This attempt at reassurance says, in essence, "Don't have that feeling of fear. There is no need to fear airplane noises." Obviously, Karen's mother tries to remove her fear by giving a logical explanation. Loud noises however, *are* frightening to small children, regardless of their source. Logic cancels empathy. And Karen doesn't feel understood. Explanations are more helpful *after* feelings are dealt with. At the moment of strong feelings, the first hunger is for understanding. Explanations are better given second billing.

Empathic response:

Karen's mother pulls her daughter close saying, "Golly, that was a big boom. It's scary!"

In this brief moment, Karen's mother comes into her daughter's frightened world and proves that she understands how Karen feels. The empathic response given first tells Karen, "Mother is 'with' me. She knows how I feel." Once the child knows her fear is understood, she is better able to hear the logical reason for the sound.

Empathy is *listening with your heart* and *not with your head*. If the empathic response is said in cold, matter-of-fact tones, the youngster does *not* feel understood.

You've probably shared an experience only to have the other person reply matter-of-factly, "Gee, that's tough." Then, you don't feel understood. If, on the other hand, he says, "Gee, that's tough!" as if he really means it (his tone and facial expression tell you he is "with" you), then you feel understood. Voice tones and muscles tip you off as to whether another person comes into your world with compassion and understanding or whether he merely mouths words. Tones supply clues as to the sincerity of understanding. (More of this in Chapter Eighteen.)

Prerequisites for empathy

True empathy is a marriage of attitudes and skill. The skill involves the ability to move into another's world with understanding. The parent who is relatively peaceful inside finds it easier to enter his child's world than the one who is tied up with intense conflicts.

"I can hardly hear my kids," said Mr. G., "because it's so noisy inside me. Every time they talk, I get hung up on my own inner reactions." This father must come to terms with his emotions before he can be freely empathic to his children. He has to be able to let go of his own feelings to be "with" them in theirs.

Empathy comes easier when you are sensitive to vocal tones and inflections, to body postures, gestures, and facial expressions. Some of us are not alert to such clues; we are not tuned in to nonverbal talk. Yet, psychologist Albert Mehrabian maintains that only seven percent of a message comes through in words while the rest is carried by tone and muscles.

Sensitivity to body language is essential to empathy.

It can be increased by practice and effort.

The degree to which you can be empathic is affected by your attitude toward your role as a parent. Empathy comes more easily when you see your role as a nurturer, with a large degree of faith in your child's capacity for self-direction. Empathy is more difficult when you believe you should direct and guide children, when you feel you always know best.

Too often, rather than trying to understand, we reason or scold or push to get children to organize their reactions as we would if we were in their shoes. *But the point is that we are not our children.* They have their own unique ways of organizing their experiences, and this uniqueness must be respected. An attitude that tolerates differences and respects the integrity of the other makes it easier to be empathic.

Finally, your attitude toward emotions in general is most important. If you are afraid of them, it is difficult, if not impossible, to be wholeheartedly empathic. Empathy involves hearing and accepting feelings as genuine realities and not as "hot potatoes." Being open to your own feelings and refusing to judge them helps you provide empathic safety for your child.

Benefits of empathy

Empathy is powerful proof of caring. When you set your personal viewpoint aside *temporarily* to be "with" your child, you demonstrate a fundamental respect for him as a separate individual whose personal point of view matters to you. Empathy says, "How you see things is important to me. It is worth my time and effort to be with you in your feelings. I really want to understand how it feels to be you because I care."

Your empathy allows your child to experience himself as a competent communicator. He learns that he can get through to the important people around him. And, success in communication is important to self-respect. Empathy is crucial if lines of communication are to be kept open. Children stop talking when they consistently feel misunderstood.

One of the patterns found in the homes of children with high self-esteem is a great deal of free and easy talk. Such youngsters feel safe to express feelings and opinions. Although others may not always agree with them, they find their personal views respected as legitimate for them. Nothing turns off talk more readily than the knowledge that your views will not be respected or understood.

There is no question about it;

empathy gets love across.

It fosters warm closeness—intimacy; it wipes out loneliness.

Just as empathy draws a child closer to you, it moves you closer to him. For when you walk in another's shoes, when you truly get a feel for his viewpoint, suddenly something happens: his behavior makes sense. Then, it is hard to be angry or upset.

Empathy helps set judgment aside.

Mrs. N.'s report is a vivid example of empathy's role in fostering intimacy and freeing parents from angry judgments. "Gladys was forever sniping at her younger sister, who does have many more strengths than she has. I tried to emphasize her assets and to understand, but she never let up. As I was tucking her into bed one night, she started complaining about her sister again, and I tried to listen with all my heart. Soon, she began talking about the kids at school.

"'Mom,' she said, 'at school it's like it is here at home. The other kids are all stronger than I am in most everything [which was true] and somehow they always win. I'm right at the bottom. They're even stronger than me with words. What they say sometimes hurts so much I get lost in the hurt and can't think of anything to say.'

"As she talked, I caught the flavor of her world, and it kinda broke my heart. Everywhere, she was with kids who could get one up on her. All at once, her sniping at Anne made sense. Home was the one place where she had a possible chance to even up the score. No wonder she was relentless. The whole thing was like a little miracle. Once I really understood, I wasn't angry. I only felt compassion and warmth, and I resolved to take steps to give her more breathing room."

Misunderstood, children feel pushed away and intimacy disappears. They conclude, "My parents don't understand. They just don't care—maybe, I'm not worth caring about." By contrast, whenever any of us, child or adult, feels deeply understood we *feel* loved, for

understanding is the language of love.

(See Chapter Eighteen for further details on the price of empathy's absence.)

Safety is never complete unless empathy is present between a parent and child, but full-time understanding is not essential. Periodic understanding, however, allows a child to say, "At least some of the time my parents understand what it's like to be me."

Check yourself on this important issue: whose eyes do you look out of? If you find that habitually you see only your point of view, you are probably shortchanging your youngsters on love. If, at least at times, you can see the world from their viewpoint, your caring is more likely to come through. Remember the blind men and the elephant. Don't tell your child you understand; prove it by empathy. Then, you prove love.

THIRTEEN · THE SAFETY OF UNIQUE GROWING

The mysterious switch

Four-year-old Linda surprised her mother by asking for a pacifier, a bottle of milk, and diapers before going to bed. Undaunted, Mrs. L. went along with the requests. As she reached for the diapers, Linda said, "Oh, I guess no dipes." With that, she put the pacifier down and went to bed with only the bottle.

Linda was checking her "psychological-safety bank account." Her mother's response said, "Your way of growing is all right. If you want to go backward, I'll respect your need." By proving that Linda was free to grow in her own special way, Mrs. L. gave the next ingredient of psychological safety—the freedom to grow uniquely. With this guarantee, Linda didn't need all the symbols of infant comforts; the bottle was enough.

Mrs. L. could have said, "Good heavens, Linda! You're too big for this baby stuff. Now, act your age and off to bed." These words would have said, "Backward growth is wrong. Shape up and grow *right* (the way I think you should)!"

Faith in growth

Many of us fear that temporary regression halts forward growth. We feel youngsters will never "make it" if they aren't forever going forward. Oddly enough, we have faith in a plant's capacity to grow. We put the seed in a nurturing climate and trust the potential that allows it to develop in its own time, in its own way. Growth plateaus or a few brown leaves don't unnerve us. If things seem amiss, we attend to the nurturing conditions around the plant. But we don't push on it or try stretching its leaves.

We sometimes have less faith in our children's sprouting capacities than we do in our plants'. By pushing and urging and forbidding, we try *to force growth*. When progress bogs down, we focus on *them*, rather than on the *climate* around them. We forget that, like the seed,

the push toward growth lies within each child.

Few of us force a baby to walk because we're sure that in time he'll do so on his own. We accept his reverting to crawling after those first shaky steps. Somewhere along the line, however, many of us lose faith and trot out our "You're-Too-Big-for-This-Nonsense" lecture. Each backward step causes disappointment, worry, or pressure. Such an attitude eats into safety and self-respect.

Every child has an inner timetable for growth—a pattern unique to him. And his particular way must be respected.

Growth: the zigzag path

Growth is *not* steady, forward, upward progression. It is instead a switchback trail: three steps forward, two back, one around the bushes, and a few simply standing, before another forward leap. This zigzag pattern is unfortunate in that we would worry less if every day gave fresh evidence of progress.

A fundamental maxim about growth at all stages is growth proceeds by spurts to the new and regressions to the old. It ebbs and flows like the tide.

Growth is movement by expansion and contraction.

Safety vs. growth

As Abraham Maslow[1] has pointed out, each of us has two pressures pulling on us. One is the pull toward the safety of the known; the other is the attraction to the new. Each bit of growth continually requires a child to leave behind the familiar. To grow is to give up the old.

And the child, poor soul, is asked to give up one thing after another in rapid-fire order: the breast, the bottle, the thumb or pacifier, and the diaper; crawling, mashed foods, and having what he wants when he wants it. He has to move from attachment to mother, from the sanctuary of family, from the safety of peers. He has to balance dependence and independence, submission and dominance, keeping and sharing.

As the excitement of each new frontier beckons, so does the fond remembrance of mother's lap. Even adults would occasionally like to retreat to complete dependence and effortless care. Is it any wonder that hesitation and regression are mixed with expansion and growth? Retreat may be a necessary prelude to surging ahead.

Safety first

Of the two pulls—safety and growth—safety has top billing. Without it, children check in their explorer shoes. Jenny is fascinated by the colors and textures of the produce at the market. She looks up to discover her mother nowhere in sight. All interest in exploring dies as Jenny races for the safety of mother.

[1] Maslow, Abraham. *Toward a Psychology of Being.* New York: D. Van Nostrand, 1964. Chapter 4.

In every nursery school, children who are familiar with the surroundings and have established warm rapport with their teachers are freer to leave their mothers' skirts. Children need safety first; then, they sally forth into the unknown.

All growth involves uncertainty. "What will it be like?" "Will it be dangerous?" "Will there be trouble if I do it?" Movement toward the unknown can turn on anxiety. The child who feels safe to retreat needs far less courage to venture because he hasn't burned his bridges behind.

The option of retreat without dishonor makes any child more likely to embrace the unknown.

Helping growth emerge

Does this mean that you sit back passively and do nothing about growth? No, not at all. Introduce attractive, new experiences as the child seems ready. Gently encourage him into new situations. But at the same time, respect *his* preference if he balks or retreats. Forcing growth only makes the child cling more tightly to the old. Failure to respect preferences and regressions demonstrates lack of faith in sprouting capacities and individuality. Respecting a child's pattern of growth and his need for safety is concrete proof of love.

It is easier to trust a child's push toward growth if others had faith in you as you grew up. Some of you may not have been so lucky, but by sheer determination you insist on trusting your child's way of developing. Many, however, are unable to manufacture faith by determination. If so, seek others who have faith in you. (Every husband needs his wife's belief in him, and each wife needs her husband's faith in her. Too many couples are so focused on their outside activities that they fail to take time to nourish each other. To that extent, they shortchange their youngsters.)

Familiarity with the facts of child development allows you

to work with the over-all plan of growth. (See Part III.) It helps you see today's behavior against the long-range tasks each child must complete. It helps you avoid magnifying fluctuations out of proportion.

The impact of freedom to grow uniquely

Respect for your child's individual growth pattern says, "I believe in your special way of growing. You are no less acceptable because you develop as you do." Then the child is convinced that it is all right to be himself.

Love's climate

Although we have dealt with the ingredients of nurturing love separately, they actually intertwine to form a psychological atmosphere of positive reflections. Seven basic ingredients spell LOVE—that four-letter word embracing the vast difference between the warmth of self-respect and the loneliness of self-hate.

An additional ingredient that rounds out the climate of love is how you discipline your children. Because this topic is a broad one, we'll discuss it in detail in Part V. But keep in mind that the type of discipline used adds an important dimension to the safety you provide.

Safe encounters translate love into terms any child can feel, regardless of age, sex, temperament, intelligence, or abilities. And such encounters can never be faked. Immersed in a safe climate, a child has no other choice but to conclude,

"I am a separate, unique individual.
I know I have value and worth because my parents enjoy, understand, and respect my person.
I don't have to be a carbon copy to matter to the important people around me.

I am cherished even when my behavior has to be limited." These are the statements of high self-esteem.

Because *feeling* loved is so crucial to emotional health and self-respect, it behooves each of us to reexamine the climate we provide. It is only as you establish safe personal encounters that your child confirms himself. Then, you give the priceless gift, not just of biological life, but of inner peace and integrity.

PART III · THE JOURNEY OF SELF

FOURTEEN · JOURNEY OF SELF:
OVER-ALL PLAN

The plan of growth

Human development can be seen as a trip of self-discovery; in this sense, every life is a Journey of Self.

The human plan of growth is orderly, with each task being tied to the sense of identity. Once aware of his separateness, the child sets out on a quest for competence with a zest that reveals its importance to him. When you work with your child on the tasks of selfhood, you help him conclude, "I am worthwhile; I have something to offer others."

For convenience, childhood can be divided roughly into three sections: the first six years, the middle years, and adolescence. Within these periods there are specific tasks which, like stairsteps, must be handled successfully if the child is to be ready for the next one ahead. Not completing a particular task stymies psychological growth. Uncompleted tasks mean arrested development. They sabotage a child's belief in his competence.

The nature of these developmental jobs, how they affect

self-esteem, and how you can help with "psychological home-work" is the basis of the next three chapters.

Benefits of familiarity with the plan

If your child is suddenly irritable, snappy, and refuses dinner, you may feel inclined to tell him to get with it. But when you discover his raging temperature and raw sore throat, your expectations change at once. His behavior makes sense, and you work with him to get him well.

Similarly, when you know what is going on inside children at certain stages, your expectations are different. Without aware-ness, you may press for unrealistic goals that work at odds with growth's plan. Then, you interfere with self-respect. The saying, "Ignorance is bliss; 'tis folly to be wise," does *not* apply to parenthood. You need to be wise to the requirements of the Journey of Self.

In addition, knowing about the plan of growth gives guide-lines for evaluating behavior. You may spend anxious hours before discovering that a child's actions are par for the course. Knowledge reduces anxiety and makes children more enjoy-able to live with. The more you enjoy each child, the more he sees himself as capable of giving delight. Then, he adds positive pictures to his inner photo album. And, of course, knowledge reduces the experimentation your unsuspecting youngsters are subjected to.

No book provides tailor-made specifics to fit each child; no amount of book learning substitutes for actually living with a particular youngster. But familiarity with the tasks of selfhood alerts you to typical behavior patterns, as well as giving an understanding of the purpose they serve. All the benefits are on the side of thorough familiarity with the facts if you would help children to emotional health.

As you read this section, keep in mind that a child is never just one age. Behavior always represents a composite of present development, past stages, and foreshadowings of future growth.

So, when we speak of the characteristics of a particular age, we speak in generalities. Every child brings to each new year the unfinished business of the past, his unique way of responding to present demands from within and without, along with hints of new directions to come.

If you are living with teen-agers, you may be inclined to skip the chapters dealing with the younger years. Do resist this temptation. Your child may be thirteen, but if he is hung up on an earlier stage of growth, he carries invisible satchels of unfinished business. These must be worked through before he can get on with the tasks appropriate to his age.

The next three chapters are ones that bear reading and re-reading. *The one place parents make their greatest number of errors is in their expectations.* Remember: when you repeatedly expect more than a child can do, you are disappointed again and again. And your disappointments become the child's disappointment in himself. The result? Low self-esteem. It is only when a youngster is successfully meeting the challenges of his phase of selfhood that he is convinced of his worth and competence.

Task ✳ 1: Separateness

The child's cooperation up into the second year results from
his not knowing any other way to behave. Awareness of
autonomy, however, opens whole new vistas. He has a brand-
new perception of his little universe.

Down go the heels, out goes the chin, and the "No's!"
flow fast and furiously. No matter that it gets him into hot
water, the flag of independence is raised and family peace
goes by the boards. The revolutionary discovery that he has
a mind of his own must be tested and experimented with in
all its dimensions, particularly with mother. Even if she doesn't
give the "two" opportunities to resist, he's undaunted—he manu-
factures them tirelessly.

Only by *practicing* separateness can the child capture the
feeling of autonomy. It is as if the two says, "To find me,
I must defy you. I have to prove my realness."

"But," asks Mrs. T., "if I accept defiance, don't I teach my
child to be disrespectful?"

A child's capacity to respect others later on is measured by his capacity to respect himself now. During the second year of life the child's primary psychological assignment is to forge a sense of self. To do so,

he or she needs recognition that this self exists.

Awkward and bombastic as his efforts may be, autonomy must be respected. Life with a two is life with a tiny despot. But it is life with a little human being taking his first step toward selfhood.

It is no accident that this is called "The Age of Negativism," or "The Terrible Two's." Actually, these negative labels becloud the fact that an extremely important task in the child's life is underway. It would be more helpful to parents if this period were labeled, "The Age of Separateness."

Just because two's need practice in autonomy doesn't mean throwing out all rules and cowering in the corner. The goal is to avoid head-on collisions when certain behavior is necessary, to accept defiant *feelings* without making the child feel guilty (see Chapter Eighteen), and to channel defiant *acts* into acceptable outlets.

Whenever a child feels guilty because of his emerging selfhood, he concludes, "I'm separate, and this gets me into trouble. Safety lies in being a 'yes-man.'" And he may fail to develop a sense of separateness altogether.

How vigorously any one child goes through this stage depends on inherited characteristics and temperament, the number of frustrations he has faced in his early months, and how cooperative he's found the world around him. If as an infant, Bobby learned that he had to scream bloody murder before anyone came, he's more likely to use dynamite to declare separateness at two.

The degree to which the environment meets his needs, the intensity of competition, how parental power is used, the extent of defiance he sees around him and how it is handled, physical health, and the intensity of home tensions all play a part in the child's handling of this stage.

Unless you know the priority that independence has for the two, his behavior can be confusing. Mrs. G. was puzzled when Walter announced firmly, "Don't wanna ice cream!" But he screamed like a stuck pig when she removed the dish he'd just refused. Bewildered, his mother was downright determined not to give the dessert back.

"I've read about this conditioning stuff and I certainly don't want a spoiled brat. Giving the ice cream back would only reward his being contrary," she said.

From Walter's point of view, his actions were entirely rational; he was not being a brat. One part of him was busy on the task of selfhood; another part wanted the ice cream, but only *after* his separateness was recognized.

Developmental "homework" comes first, but you can imagine Walter's frustration when doing his job caused him to lose out. His "no" to the ice cream was his naïve way of saying, "Mommy, I must defy even when you offer me a goody because my 'person homework' comes first." His "no" was a code for "I'm separate."

Awareness of the job they're doing doesn't make two's any easier to live with; but knowing the purpose of their defiance makes it easier to avoid getting in the way of growth. Their rebellion is *not* disrespect.

Autonomy is the foundation stone to future self-esteem.

Practical suggestions

How can you help the child of two experience his separateness while keeping your own nerves intact?

Fit his environment to his needs, eliminating as many frustrations as possible. His inner pressures are enough for him to handle. The childproofed home beats tranquilizers. Give the two time to move from one activity to another as he resists change. Advance notice that in five minutes it will be time to eat helps him take the shift in stride. Simple games make change more inviting. Instead of saying, "Come in for lunch"— an open invitation for defiance—concoct a game. Say, "Let's be airplanes and spread out our arms. We'll fly in to lunch. How loud can your engine roar?" Instead of "It's time for bed," say, "Let's hop like bunnies into the rocking chair for lullaby time. I'm going to wiggle my nose on the way in; are you?"

Picking up toys is easier if you play a game together: "Let's see if we can get all the toys in the box by the time the record is through playing," or "Let's see how fast we can put the toys to bed."

It may be that this kind of playfulness would feel completely unnatural for you. You would feel like a first-class phony and your child would quickly pick it up. One possibility would be to visit as many nursery schools in your area as possible and watch the teachers there. Shifting children from one activity to another via the route of games is almost always standard procedure. Seeing other adults indulge in such games may give you the sanction you need to feel free to follow suit. Even if you cannot join in the game you may be able to suggest the idea to your child while you stand by to observe his participation.

Positive suggestions are preferable to direct orders. "Now it's time to let the soap wash our hands," as you wash together, meets less resistance than, "Go wash your hands." Using a kitchen timer helps a child avoid seeing mother as the heavy. "You set the timer here and when it bings it will be lunch time," gets Molly involved in working out her own deadline— marginal though it is. Asking a child to color his bath water (a few drops of food coloring does the trick) invites coopera- tion and gives a child some degree of control, underscoring his selfhood.

Invent nonsense games that allow "no's" to be practiced. "Can Teddy fly in the sky like a bird?" "Is milk pink?" "Does the chickie say, 'Moo-moo?'" Providing opportunities to practice autonomy lets the child feel, "I am my own person. My separateness is recognized."

When autonomy is respected, the two does not carry this unfinished task into later stages of growth. In adolescence, the youngster will again concentrate on independence, but he won't have to blast the roof off the second time around if it is already well established.

Tyrants rule the pot

At the very time that two's are establishing independence, many a mother decides it is high time her child was toilet trained. He quickly senses the pressure and may decide to gird himself for battle.

This area is one where a child really *does* possess the power to defy. Strong pressure leads to a power struggle. The issue then is *not* toilet training but *who holds the reins*—mother or child? Bathroom rebellion becomes the order of the day. And the child has most of the ammunition!

You go a long way toward preserving your sanity and your child's self-esteem by either forgetting toilet training during this period, or clearly indicating that he rules this department. Then, most two's are more than willing to cooperate, particularly if they can defy in other areas. Delayed potty training is far less devastating than a crushed sense of self.

Because establishing independence is a monumental task, outside pressures become formidable roadblocks to the two. Yet, around this age parents often decide to take away the bedtime bottle, get the thumb out of the mouth, or remove the security blanket and pacifier. These demands are like asking a confirmed smoker to kick the habit at the very time he takes on a stressful new job.

Because the two's internal pressures are at a peak, you're on safer ground to wait until he's three to make major changes. If you're unsuccessful then, wait until he is five, which is normally a period of inner equilibrium. All of us take outer pressures more gracefully when we feel little inner stress, and children are no exception.

Separateness breeds anxiety

Put yourself in the two's place. Imagine suddenly discovering you are not attached to this all-powerful mother who takes care of your every need. *You are separate!* If you and she are not attached, she can leave you. And you're well aware that she does disappear at times.

Such a situation is like always having swum with a life jacket that you believed was part of you, only to discover that it's removable. This awareness immediately creates anxiety, especially if you are not so sure you can swim.

It may seem contradictory to watch a defiant two-year-old rebel against his mother all day and burst into tears when she leaves. But when you know that separateness breeds anxiety, it's no surprise. The toddler craves independence, but he fears desertion.

For the first time two's have trouble with sleep. They push for a night light or for mother to stay with them at bedtime. Releasing their new-found sense of identity to sleep is disturbing to many toddlers. Two's typically carouse at night or go in for 3:00 A.M. strolls. Safety precautions are needed, of course, but punishing such behavior only adds to anxiety. It makes a child wonder if independence is worth the price.

Separateness means possession

Possession is one device the young child uses to hammer out autonomy. Consequently, ownership takes on special meaning to the toddler set. To them, separateness *means* the right to possess.

Just as babbling comes before talking, so owning comes before sharing. *To fully share, a person must FIRST fully possess.* None of us can share what we don't have. And the little child needs time to get the feel of ownership thoroughly worked into his experience before he can let go. Only fifty percent of "three's" can share and then only briefly; yet, unthinkingly, in our conscientious efforts to teach social graces, we push against the toddler's need to own.

Allowing a child to possess fully for four or five years and then to share on his own terms says, "I respect your independence and your right to decide for yourself what you will share and with whom. I will work with your need for autonomy." With this fundamental respect, children are likely to be more than generous in the long run.

How can you work with the need for possession?

Provide duplicate toys whenever possible. Before visitors arrive, discuss the issue of sharing with your child. Say, "Tommy is coming to play. Let's put away the toys you don't want touched."

Even these precautions may not be sufficient. In the actual situation, the young child may decide he cannot share even his "sharable" toys. It is helpful to ask the visiting parent to bring a few of her child's toys. In any event, protect your youngster's need to possess by saying, "Peter isn't ready to share his truck yet. Maybe later he will." Mere recognition of the rights of ownership may give the child the security he needs to share, if only for a few moments.

Task #2: Achievement and recognition

Once the child realizes he is separate, he reasons, "If I'm separate, I'd better be capable." And he strives to *master himself and his environment.*

Watch the eyes of a child from three to six and you see his glowing pride over each new accomplishment. Joyfully, he repeats his feats for anyone and everyone who will watch.

Because the preschooler is still very little, lacks knowledge, coordination, comprehension of society's complexities, and because the list of things he *can* do is always shorter than the list of things he *cannot* do, each child needs experiences that offset feelings of incompetence. Every time you undercut or belittle or give tasks beyond him, you work against the second task of selfhood—the need for mastery and recognition.

Provide experiences that allow success: an environment that does not overwhelm, simple, sturdy clothes, step stools to reach faucets and light switches, low hooks, noncarpeted floor areas, plastic dishes and glasses that prevent the "tragedy of the crash," sturdy books and toys that take rough treatment, inexpensive furniture scaled to his size, sturdy outdoor play equipment, sand or dirt for digging, plenty of water to splash in outside, and space for running, jumping, and climbing. At this stage he is discovering his environment and what his body will do. Remember:

Mastery underlies the feeling of competence.

Task #3: Initiative

Four-year-old Marnie came into the kitchen proudly announcing she had dressed herself. Her mother turned to see her slip on top of her dress.

About to comment, Mrs. G. noticed the delight in Marnie's eyes. She decided it was more important to encourage her daughter's dawning sense of initiative than to be concerned about proprieties. After all, they were only going to be home that day and there was no harm done. Disapproval would have said, "Don't try new ideas." Then, Marnie would have suffered a little setback in her budding attempts at innovation. If rebuffs are repeated, Marnie will stop initiating.

Some childish innovations, of course, cannot be accepted because they endanger health, safety, or are grossly out of place. But whenever possible, accept each sign of initiative.

Task #4: Attachment to the opposite-sexed parent

As if the "three" to "five" doesn't have enough to keep him busy, another psychological task has to be worked on—attachment to the parent of the opposite sex.

By three, the child is usually aware that he is a boy or a girl. Somewhere between three and five, he needs to experience his maleness (or femaleness) in relation to the opposite-sexed parent.

Before Vernon was four, he didn't care who bathed him or read his bedtime story or tucked him in. But suddenly at four, he wanted nothing to do with his father. He became extremely jealous when his mother talked to other men and tried to get between his parents when his father kissed his mother good-by in the morning. He talked about wanting to marry his mother and throwing his father down the disposal. Was Vernon emotionally disturbed? No, he was simply busy growing according to plan.

Emotional attachment at this age provides each child with his first, safe attempt at establishing a romantic relationship. The flurry dies down around six and heterosexual interest normally doesn't reappear for seven to ten years. If handled wisely, this attachment acts as an embryonic experience upon which the child builds in adolescence. This task begins the establishment of sexual roles.

As in everything else, children vary in the vigor with which they become attached. Regardless of intensity, you help your child by not making him feel guilty about it.

Unless parents are aware of this stage, they may worry needlessly or feel rejected. Many a mother has been crushed to be suddenly pushed out of her daughter's life. Or has interpreted the rejection as a failure on her part. Fathers may object to their sons' attachments to their wives, fearing that their boys will become sissies by clinging to the apron strings. Many a child receives the basic lecture on "Courtesy and Respect for Parents" when he is only attending to his "homework" with all the vigor he can muster.

How can you work with the need for attachment?

When Vera announced in front of both parents that she preferred her daddy, Mrs. B. replied, "Yes, Vera, he's your most important person. You know, *most* five-year-old girls like their daddies best."

This response let Vera know her feelings were acceptable. She was not shamed, nor did she lose approval because for a while she needed to set her mother aside.

By contrast, Mrs. N., knowing nothing about this normal stage of development, spent these years in her son's life believing something was wrong between her son and husband. She thought Randy was rude and ungrateful to his father. She lectured repeatedly and told him that the least he could do was to say hello. But her lectures landed on deaf ears. Randy continued to ignore his father and make derogatory remarks until age six when, in accordance with the plan of growth, he began to prefer him.

Because Randy was made to feel guilty about his attraction to his mother, however, his view of himself can be affected, particularly as it relates to his future relationships with women.

Wise handling of this attachment means accepting it for what it is—a normal stage of development. At the same time, it is important to avoid seductive behavior that accentuates these feelings.

"I like to tease my son by holding hands with my husband as we sit together on the couch. It amuses me to see how upset he gets," said one mother. It may be amusing and flattering to use a child's feelings in seemingly innocent ways, but you tread on *extremely dangerous ground* when you are disrespectful of the child's person and his stage of growth. Any act that accentuates jealousy only emphasizes the child's powerlessness and inadequacy.

You help a child through a period that may involve intense jealousy by avoiding prolonged, affectionate gestures with your husband or wife in his presence. Keep his feelings from becoming more intense by not kissing him on the mouth and by avoiding *sustained* tickling or other stimulating behavior. Hugging is fine but it should not be prolonged or of an erotic nature. The parent of the opposite sex should prevent the child's seeing him in the nude or going to the bathroom during this period, especially if the attachment is strong. Small children have generalized sexual feelings, and it is only common courtesy to avoid arousing them needlessly.

If prior to this period, your child has been free to see you undressed or bathing, say, "Daddy wants to dress by himself," or "Mommy wants to go to the bathroom alone."

You don't have to make a big production out of requests for privacy; it can be done matter-of-factly. If a child rebels, accept his feelings empathically as being real and important for him, but insist on your rights.

If your youngster walks in when you're bathing, the world hasn't come to an end. Let him stay a moment and then casually indicate that you want to be alone. Next time, lock the door.

Authorities on child development differ as to the advisability of allowing children in the attachment stage to see parents in the nude. Usually workers in the field of education see no need for limits. Clinical psychologists are more apt to prefer not allowing this freedom. This difference of opinion may arise because clinicians see children from homes in which disturbed family relationships are more frequent. Their relationships to their parents may reflect other unmet needs that become intensified during this period.

For most children exposure to nude parents, when other family factors are healthy, probably causes no great problem. Nevertheless, you operate on the side of safety if you casually limit such exposures.

Drawing the line on intimacies also includes not having the child sleep with the opposite-sexed parent. Many a mother pulls her sleepy son in for some wee hour cuddling, rather than taking him back to his bed to sit beside him for a few moments. As this can over-stimulate, it's best avoided.

Calm acceptance of attachment needs and the avoidance of provocative acts permit a youngster to say, "My feelings are all right. There is nothing wrong with me for having them. My parents will help me keep them within bounds."

The child's need to be attached to an adult of the opposite sex poses a problem in homes where there is only one parent. Very often, such a child attaches himself to a neighbor, friend, or relative who is especially warm and responsive. But if the parent of the opposite sex is not in your home, actively seek such a person for your youngster to be exposed to.

Task #5: Self-centeredness

"My five-and-a-half-year-old is the most selfish, self-centered youngster imaginable. All she thinks about is taking the biggest and the best. She's too old for this nonsense. Frankly, she's more selfish now than ever." If you live with a "five-going-on-six," you may feel the same way.

Rome wasn't built in a day. And the move from total dependence to strong independence is not accomplished in one neat jump. Even though the child realizes he's separate from his mother, she still looms as being at the center of his world well into the fifth year.

Suddenly around five-and-a-half in girls, and six in boys, an important psychological shift occurs. The center of the child's universe moves from parent to child. No wonder the child becomes a demanding egotist overnight.

When this happens, congratulate yourself, knowing that your child is developing according to plan. Self-centeredness comes before other-centeredness.

The child's need to think of himself first does *not* mean that you should constantly give in to him. It *does* mean that *you must not make him feel guilty* about total self-absorption. Your acceptance of this important inner need helps him accept himself as no less worthy because of his stage of growth. Be empathic but protect your rights.

Task #6: Preference for the same sex

Once the assignment of attachment to the opposite sex has been worked through, the child moves again—this time to a preference for those of the same sex. By six, boys begin preferring masculine company and pursuits, while girls prefer their mothers and other girls.

"There's only one trouble with Neal," said six-year-old Peggy sadly.

"What's that?" asked her mother.

"Well, he's lots of fun and he doesn't grab or cheat, but the whole trouble is, he's a *boy!*" Plainly, his sex made him ineligible as a playmate.

A prolonged period of identifying with his own sex gives the child a feel of masculinity or femininity. It helps establish sexual identity. Although his preference for the same sex begins around six, it increases in intensity until the early teens in girls and the middle teens in boys. (Further discussion of this subject at the end of this chapter.)

Conscience emerges

Most of us want our children to know right from wrong and to be honest, thoughtful, and considerate because they are sincerely convinced that this is the way to live with others.

Yet, few of us realize that the conscience only *begins* to take shape around age six. Even then, however, the sense of right and wrong is shaky at best; it needs much outside support from adults. The conscience is made up of the moral standards a child absorbs. What you preach, however, carries far less weight than what you do. The youngster whose parents live with others in kind, thoughtful honesty is more likely to imitate them.

Even when you provide positive examples, however, remember that absorbing a moral code of ethics is a complex, complicated process. It takes years to accomplish.

When a youngster takes something that doesn't belong to him, talk to him privately, while understanding that such behavior is part of growing up. Help him make restitution, but *without* shame or humiliation. A child must not be made to feel less worthy because his conscience is undeveloped before its time.

The first six years

Autonomy, mastery, initiative, attachment, self-centeredness, and preference for the same sex—a whale of an assignment for little tykes. But only as they complete them do they gain self-respect. Only as they complete them are they free for further growth.

At the very same time that they are working on these psychological tasks, children must learn to handle their bodies, the complexities of language, modern contraptions, and society's rules. Yet, most preschoolers do remarkably well—even when they have to scale the hurdle of our not understanding what they are pushed to do by the plan of growth.

It isn't always easy to accept a child's dirtiness, messes, dawdling, and noise. These needs—so important to him—cut across our adult needs. With a little ingenuity, you can usually provide safe outlets for growth while protecting your requirements for a house that is still standing and a little peace and quiet.

With many jobs to do, strong internal pressures, and mountainous discoveries to make, the preschooler needs understanding cooperation to build self-respect. Remember: slow, nonpressurized learning is always preferable to the rapid, high-pressure variety. Socialization is a long, complicated process. It requires repeated teaching in a nurturing atmosphere.

Make-up work

What can you do if your child missed completing some of the tasks of selfhood during the normal period?

Start today to provide those experiences. Treat your child as a separate, independent person with the right to his own feelings, ideas, and attitudes. Appreciate and recognize what he *can* do—no matter how small the triumph.

As if nature knew we would make mistakes we have a second chance each day. Reminiscing with your child can open locked doors.

"Remember, Toddy, when you built a plane out of two old boards and I told you it didn't look like a plane at all? Well, as I look back, it seems as if I jumped on your ideas right and left. I wish I hadn't done this and I'm going to try to change. If it feels like I'm crowding you or not appreciating your efforts, please let me know. Sometimes I do it without even realizing it. Clue me in when I go astray."

Such invitations, of course, have to be backed up by genuine receptiveness on your part. A change of heart has to be matched by changes in your behavior. Ordinarily, when youngsters find you mean what you say, they're johnny-on-the-spot to complete unfinished business.

Role identification

On page 132 the child's awareness that boys and girls have different sexual organs was discussed. The first fact learned is: humans with vulvas are girls, women (females); humans with penises are labelled boys, men (males). Then very early a second learning occurs: males feel and behave in certain prescribed ways; females in others. (Each culture has its own definitions of masculinity and femininity.)

In our society traditionally strong pressure has been put on boys to be tough, not to cry and to avoid certain activities (playing with dolls) while majoring in others (competitive sports). Similarly we pressure girls to stay within the culturally defined female role.

Tying a person's sexuality to set ways of feeling and behaving is now challenged as limiting potentials. Increasing numbers of adults see children as persons first and foremost and only secondarily as males or females. This challenge to role definition is giving children the go-ahead that allows boys to cry, let their nurturing potentials develop, etc. It is freeing girls to express their assertiveness and choose activities once reserved only for males.

Each of us will be daily deciding our private stand on role identification by the particular freedoms or restrictions we place on our children.

SIXTEEN · JOURNEY OF SELF: MIDDLE YEARS

The mirror of the gang

**Keep out! Warning!
Enter without permishun
and you Get it!**

This brash notice bears happy tidings: Junior is bearing down on the "homework" of self; he is refining his separateness.

Six to twelve is psychologically a quiet time even though these are boisterous years in terms of activity. The rapid physical changes of the first six years are completed and the marked changes of puberty are not in full swing. Identity from family reflections has been established and the youngster does not yet have to reevaluate himself to account for adolescent changes.

The middle years of childhood are directed toward extending mastery and autonomy. But the youngster's primary task is to define his person from reflections *outside the family*. Playmates are his new mirrors as he makes the move from self to others.

Beginning around six, this shift in focus intensifies through mid-adolescence; peer reflections have increasing impact. In our culture, the growing child needs group support to gather the necessary strength to eventually stand on his own. Without it, self-respect may be jeopardized.

Acceptance from agemates, and the mastery of physical and social skills nurture the sense of competence.

Belonging and believing he has something to offer are vital at this age.

The shift to the gang does not mean that you are no longer needed. In fact, your confirmation protects your child from the harsh realities of the group. More than ever, he needs home as a sanctuary. You remain a primary figure as a model and transmitter of values and attitudes. Some research has shown that boys from six to twelve make less adequate adjustments to their agemates when their fathers are absent for prolonged periods (eight to nine months). So, although the child needs to move away, you are nevertheless important to him. (More of this later in the chapter.)

The middle-aged youngster actually operates in two worlds: that of adults and that of peers. *Both* worlds play a big part in his development. But how friends see him increasingly colors his view of himself.

Each youngster has to *earn* a place in the gang. Whether he makes it or not has a real bearing on his self-image. The child on the fringes not only receives negative reflections, but he fails to get practice in relating to others. As his "social knowhow" diminishes, he feels less and less adequate. The more inadequate he feels, of course, the less adequately he behaves, and a vicious cycle starts.

Occasionally, a youngster prefers the company of adults. This may be a clue that he is not "making it" with the gang. To him, grown-ups are less harsh. Highly sensitive or markedly precocious youngsters frequently retreat to spend disproportionate time with adults. Yet, not relating to a group of the same sex is a *misfortune in development*. It is a task left unfinished. A child's peers are *his* generation; he needs to find a place for himself in their community.

All the same, thank you

The ticket of admission with "six to twelve's" is *sameness*. Consequently, noticeable differences are decidedly threatening. An overabundance of freckles, thick glasses, exceptional conscientiousness, fast or slow development, different clothes, an accent, or an unusual name exposes a youngster to blistering attacks. Difference means nonacceptance.

One study of unusually gifted children (IQ's between 160 and 180) indicated they tended to become followers rather than leaders at this age. Because of their abilities, they tried to organize gang play on more complicated levels, but the less gifted would have none of it. To win acceptance, the gifted submerged their talents and followed those less endowed!

The worst fate is to be ignored. Better to be called "Fat Stuff" or "Bird Legs" than to be treated as nonexistent. Many a child deliberately develops mannerisms for the sole purpose of gaining recognition that he exists.

Entering the middle years with solid self-respect enables a child to handle the rough treatment children dish out. Mary, for example, was new in her school, but her self-confidence allowed her to take the initial razzing with good humor. Had she been unduly shy, hostile, or overly sensitive, she would not have been included so quickly. Had she felt personally inadequate, the jibes would have found their mark. By rolling with the punches, she was seen as a good sport and soon was one of the bunch. Confirmation from home gives a youngster a head start as he moves toward the gang.

Contributions from the gang

It is sometimes aggravating to see your youngster a pawn to group values. Gang influence, however, provides important benefits. Playmates force a child to face the realities of his world. In short order and in no uncertain terms, they teach what is acceptable and what is not.

"You brag too much," "I don't want to play with a cheater!" "You poor sport! You always pout when you lose," "Why don't you wash your hair once in a while? It stinks!" "Quit griping; he didn't mean to do it!" "Drop dead!" No, children are not noted for tact and gentleness. They are brutally frank, if not downright cruel, in their honesty with one another. They socialize with blunt, sledge-hammer comments.

As if sensing that moving from the family causes insecurity, youngsters pad their world with rigid rituals that are passed on to succeeding groups of children. Tremendous insistence is put on strict adherence to rules. They are positively compulsive about any child's refusal to follow accepted procedure. It may be only a game of hide-and-seek, but if Paul is "it" and doesn't say, "Here I come ready or not" after he's counted to ten, he has eight important people in his life screaming, "Cheater!" "Unfair!" "You didn't do it *right!*" Tempests in teapots. But they underscore the need for solid structure outside as the youngster edges away from the family nest.

Tongue twisters and chants may seem silly and purposeless, but they are part of belonging. "Twinkle, twinkle, little star, whatever you say is what you are," or "I'm rubber; you're glue; whatever you say sticks to you," are little prescriptions for alleviating hurts.

Belonging to the gang, knowing the "in" talk, and sticking to rigid rules are important to growth. Postpone lectures on the merits of individualism at this age; they only interfere with the job the child needs to do.

Refining separateness

Even though the youngster establishes separateness at two, he continues refining it all during the middle years. "Keep out" signs, secret drawers complete with lock and key, and collections jealously hoarded accentuate autonomy.

What benefits come from collecting 376 rusty bottle caps, 208 green marbles, 452 unmatched playing cards, and a string of 1,000 paper clips? They are *symbols*—psychological tools—that nourish self-esteem. They bring the joy of initiating, the excitement of the hunt, the comfort of status, the fascination of management, and the pride of ownership. The youngster gets experience in controlling, possessing, planning, and trading. It is easier to treat junior-sized junk heaps with proper respect when you know the purpose they serve. If, in a fit of spring house cleaning, you dispose of them, you work against autonomy and control. You emphasize helplessness and nurture seething resentment.

Have you ever noticed that "big secrets" told to chums with all kinds of ceremonial flourish are later casually revealed to you? The *content* of the secret is unimportant; the process of shutting out a brother or friend (maybe even you!) is vital. Deciding whom he will let into his confidence accentuates a child's separateness. This bit of power gives control in a world where so much is still beyond his control. So, signs and secrets and locked diaries are not poor manners nor evidence of rejection. They are part of normal growth.

Destructive gang influences

"I'm well aware that children need to belong," said Mrs. F., "but my son has always been trustworthy. Suddenly, he's started going around with youngsters that everyone knows are just plain delinquent. I know I can't choose his friends, and if I forbid his seeing them, he can see them on the sly. But they have a bad reputation, and I don't know what to do."

This situation signals something amiss. The peaceful child is not attracted to those whose mission is destructiveness. He's more interested in constructive play. Regardless of his former "good" behavior, this boy's choice of friends suggests that feelings of another sort lie beneath his facade of cooperation.

The model child frequently chooses undesirable friends because his repressed negative feelings make him believe he doesn't deserve to go around with "nice" youngsters. Or, he latches onto children who behave as he wishes he could—if only he dared. A youngster often chooses a friend as an emotional counterpart: the shy become attached to the outgoing; model children, to anti-social ones. They become more complete, so to speak, by seeking their "other half."

Whatever the reason, the choice of friends meets inner needs. The obvious solution for Mrs. F. is not to attack the symptom—her son's going around with delinquents—but to deal with his feelings and needs. If she cannot do this herself, she should seek professional help so that her son will reach out for constructive friendships.

Same sex, please

Loud contempt for the opposite sex and close association with his own sex help a youngster establish his sexual role, as was mentioned in the last chapter. In spite of this spoken preference, youngsters in the middle years usually have a secret boy friend or girl friend. Brief chases on the playground, teasing, throwing spit wads, or passing anonymous mash notes are usually as far as such romances get.

Boys of this age can be seen walking arm in arm. Girls get crushes on other girls and exchange love notes, declaring undying affection that lasts from one hour to several months. If you are unaware of this stage of growth, you can think your child is heading for homosexuality. But youngsters need attachment to the same sex to be more fully heterosexual later on.

True homosexuality—barring physical or hormonal abnormalities—is related to a failure in identification. The developing boy, for a variety of reasons (no father, absentee or rejecting father, seductive parents, rejection because of his sex), fails to identify with the male role. Similarly, homosexual girls fail to identify with the female role. Whenever this pattern develops, seek professional help at the earliest possible moment.

When you tease or scold for group dependence, you say, in effect, "Spring full-blown into maturity." No child can accomplish this feat. When you chafe because your child seems wedded to another of the same sex, remember his need to get hold of the feel for his sexual role. Each youngster needs time and understanding support to built these experiences into his self-image.

Adult models

Between eight and ten, the major task of selfhood is *the need for an adult model of the same sex.* The issue of adulthood presses at the edge of awareness. It is as if the youngster thinks, "I am moving from childhood; soon I'll be an adult. What are the ways of a grown man (or woman)?" And he reaches out to imitate.

Ordinarily, children choose the parent of the same sex as models. If ever there is a time when you are a hero, it is during this period. Formerly, you were a god—all powerful, all knowing, all seeing. Now you are not a distant deity, but a flesh and blood hero that they want close association with.

This need is so strong that if a model is unavailable at home, the youngster seeks one outside his family. Girls, of course, have easier access to models than boys. In divorced families, children are usually left with the mother. In school, women teachers outnumber men, particularly at the elementary level. Many fathers are away for long hours and tied up on weekends. It is rare that male relatives live nearby to fill the gap. Smaller families mean fewer older brothers for young boys to imitate.

Actually, it is amazing that boys do as well as they do. Fortunately, the urge is strong, so if models are not readily available, they seek a scout leader or hero in fiction or on television. (Unfortunately, weak, passive television fathers predominate.)

If the appropriate-sexed model is unavailable in your home, seek a substitute. For imitation to occur, the child needs close, *sustained* contact. Finding an adequate model is as important during the attachment period of three to five (opposite-sexed) as during the years from eight to ten (same sex). Turn to relatives, neighbors, or teachers and ask for help. Your minister, rabbi, school counselor, or a member of a service organization may put you on the track of a person who would be delighted to be a foster model.[1]

It is no accident that eight to ten's find Batman, Superman, and Tarzan so appealing. They are figures with whom youngsters identify easily because they have the exact traits each child wants for self-respect: physical strength, power, wisdom, mastery and control over the environment, and invincibility. Immersed in their adventures, children vicariously experience their triumphs. In the dramatic play of boys, the fights erupt over who gets to be Dick Tracy or Davy Crockett. Each wants the role that nourishes self-esteem.

By the same token, young girls turn to biographies of famous women and queens; they eat up tales of undaunted heroines, such as Nancy Drew, who never come out on the losing end. These stories provide additional models that help the potential for competent maleness and femaleness to emerge.

Imitating attitudes

Not only are children this age focusing on the roles of men and women, but they are sharply tuned in to their *attitudes toward their roles.*

Brenda, for example, learns that women, like her mother, are wise and gentle. She learns from her that housework and baking are important, but not nearly so much so as helping children or taking time to share the day's events. She learns from her father's reaction to her mother that women have value and an important part in family decisions.

[1] An organization called Parents Without Partners is available in many communities to help the parent with the problem of raising children singlehandedly.

Kathy, on the other hand, learns from her mother that women are demanding and sharp. They withdraw from life. She absorbs her mother's attitude that men are unreliable bumpkins who must unfortunately be put up with. She learns that success as a woman depends on how efficiently she pushes dirt out the door and how promptly she gets dinner on the table. She senses that adults are too busy for mere children. Kathy's image of womanhood is that it is a hard life with little appreciation and few joys.

Brenda and Kathy carry their impressions about the role of womanhood into adulthood. Even though they may *resolve* to live differently, they may find themselves acting out the patterns they have lived with.

When you enjoy your role as a parent, husband, or wife, your youngsters are more likely to enjoy their roles in the future. Does this mean that mothers who find no satisfaction in vacuuming and cooking are negative models? No, it merely means that *attitudes are contagious*. Mrs. L. found housework unrewarding, but she knew it had to be done. She did the necessary without grumbling and hired help for the jobs she genuinely disliked. Work as a scout leader and a part-time secretary gave her emotional satisfaction, a break from household routine, and extra money to afford outside help.

How any child uses his available models is an individual affair. The boy with a harsh father may pattern himself after a warm uncle. But regardless of his choice, each youngster is pushed from within to work on role identification.

Models outside the home

Nature does not allow children to dally at any one stage. The next assignment between ten and thirteen is to find an adult model of the same sex outside the home. These preadolescent "crushes" on a distant, yet safe, figure outside the family lay the groundwork for giving affection to someone of the opposite sex eventually.

When you can accept not being the star in your child's life and protect him from family taunts, you safeguard his self-respect.

Need for skills

The drive for mastery heightens during the middle years. With expanding social horizons, skills help a youngster participate actively in the games valued by his agemates. With energy to burn, he reaches out to increase his competence in all directions.

No matter that knees are scabby, shins battered and bruised, or that bones break (the cast is a status symbol), the youngster plows ahead relentlessly. Each new mastery proves his value to himself.

Helping with "homework"

Knowing the psychological tasks that your middle-aged youngster is involved with can help you work with him.

Offer broad exposures but let him carry the ball. He'll appreciate encouragement and support, and a little nudge on occasion doesn't hurt. But pressure, humiliation, comparison, or withdrawing approval when he isn't performing his head off steps on his self-respect.

Watch that you don't force activities that he genuinely dislikes. Avoid communicating that he is less worthwhile if he lacks particular skills. Remember: a child needs cherishing as a person *separate* from his performance. His peers will press him hard enough for developing skills.

Competence developed *prior* to adolescence helps a youngster withstand teen-age stresses. Sixteen-year-old Martin's confidence in his swimming, skiing, and ball playing give him blocks of security while he puzzles through how to look suave on a date, how to ditch the girl next door without hurting her feelings, and how to act worldly with the boys in the locker room.

At the same time that the tasks of selfhood push each youngster over new hurdles, each one is subjected to increasing academic challenges at school.

The middle years are time for developing physical, social, and academic competence.

You help with "psychological homework" when you

1. encourage your children to join constructive groups of their age;
2. actively support groups they enjoy;
3. offer opportunities for developing skills with no strings attached;
4. make your home available to friends;
5. avoid giving so many home responsibilities that there's little time for activities with chums; and
6. avoid making them feel guilty for cutting the apron strings.

Many groups that provide adult supervision emphasize the acquisition of new physical and social skills. Supporting them is an investment in your child's emotional health.

Include your child's friends in some of your family activities, extending them the same courtesies you show to adults. The youngster with broad exposures to many different types of children develops wider social responses.

It is tempting when children are young to choose their friends for them. Youngsters, however, learn from negative friendships as well as from positive ones. If you overprotect, the child doesn't discover for himself, while still young, the disadvantages that negative friendships bring. Teach your children to differentiate among friends: to accept their strong points and protect themselves against their weaknesses. Your job is to stand by for support and to teach, but to avoid playing "mother hen."

The older the child, the more he needs to live a life of his own.

Respecting your child's privacy is respecting his separateness. Your act may be as simple as knocking on his bedroom door before entering, extending personal courtesies toward his mail or phone calls, or asking his permission to use something belonging to him. Regardless, if your attitudes and behavior communicate, "You deserve respect as a person in your own right," you give positive reflections for him to absorb.

All during the middle years, a home climate of safe encounter ensures that your child's successes in mastery will be absorbed.

Middle-aged children have few manners and little interest in order. Go slowly as you teach in these areas, for growth exacts so much psychologically. Letting your youngsters live fully as children helps them become mature adults.

When you are familiar with the internal and external pressures children face during these years, it is easier to see why they may periodically be out of sorts, take to nail biting, or fall behind temporarily in one area or another. It isn't easy to shift the center of your world from family to broader horizons.

Conscience during the middle years

From six to twelve, the conscience becomes a more stable part of the personality, but it still needs adult support.

Six to nine's often come with tall tales: "I saw five million grasshoppers today!" "Frank caught a frog one foot long!" "I saw a horse the size of an elephant!" Unlike the preschooler, the child this age *can* distinguish between reality and fantasy. Sometimes yarns are concocted to pep up the drab routine of everyday life. Some whoppers are a code for, "Please, notice me." The child who feels solidly worthwhile doesn't have to resort to shock measures.

Paul casually mentioned that he had found a juicy weed

for sucking on. He didn't run into a bored, "So what?" His father said, "That reminds me of the fun I had sucking sugar cane as a kid. Bring me a sample to try out." Paul didn't have to dream up fictions; his dad appreciated the commonplace.

Tall tales may result from vivid imaginations that have few outlets. Mr. E. repsonded to his son's exaggerations by saying, "Son, that one deserves to be written down." Or, "Let's share that story with the family at dinner; pretend can be fun." He accepted Greg's fancies with good humor and found creative outlets for them.

Genuine lies are frequently born of fear of punishment; harsh reprisals only teach skill in lying. Whenever lying is excessive, examine the climate around your child. Check your expectations. Look to your methods of discipline (see Part V). Lies are symptomatic and the causes need to be removed.

Stealing during this period is not infrequent. It may come from a child's need for friendship. Gertrude stole candy to buy acceptance from others. She didn't need punishment (although teaching would certainly be in order) but needed help in gaining friends in positive ways. Stealing may represent a blind grasping for love. In many homes parents show caring by showering children with material gifts. Things become substitutes for love. Then, when a youngster from such a home needs affection, he steals. He doesn't know why he does; he just has the urge. But the stolen object—the symbol for love—is not what he wants. Like an animal on a treadmill, he repeats the symbolic act but the hunger remains unsatisfied.

Some stealing serves as an outlet for hostility. The youngster who cannot release animosity directly may strike at parental values. Whenever direct routes for meeting needs are closed, children travel by devious ones.

If, on rare occasions, your child takes something that doesn't belong to him, you don't need to suddenly decide that he is starved for love or sitting on mountains of repressed hostility.

His act may only mean that temptation was too strong. The time for concern is when stealing is frequent and prolonged.

Easing tensions

"Ah, for the carefree life of childhood!" Whenever you're tempted to think in these terms, you may be remembering with rose-colored glasses. Children live with child-sized tensions that are as proportionately large for them as your pressures are for you.

You help youngsters discharge tensions by providing ample physical space and vigorous physical activity. Art and dramatic play give outlets for creativity and ease the tensions that accompany growth. One study of youngsters who were provided with a weekly hour of *unstructured* art experiences indicated that they made significant improvements in social and academic progress. Play and free expression are a child's work, and he needs ample opportunity to have fun with others his age. And, don't overlook the benefits of empathic listening.

In successful parenthood you literally try to work yourself out of a job. Each step your child takes toward independence is a badge of "well done" on your sleeve. Increasing self-reliance feeds into high self-esteem. It may be easier to have your child move away from you if you remember that he will always return on a mature level if you have built wisely. And the richness of such a relationship is worth a temporary parting.

SEVENTEEN · JOURNEY OF SELF:
ADOLESCENCE

This younger generation

Teen-ager. Adolescent. The "NOW" generation. What reactions do you have? Do you find yourself wishing they could jump from twelve to twenty-one without going through *that* stage? Does it seem like a prolonged dose of Epsom Salts? Does your anxiety level go up?

Parents have traditionally shaken their heads in exasperation over "this younger generation." But much of our head-shaking today comes from fear and genuine bewilderment. "What's gotten into them?" Many parents are running scared.

To understand the "NOW" generation fully, we must be familiar with the selfhood tasks of every adolescent of every generation in our culture. Next, we need to examine the many roadblocks existing in our society that make it more difficult for young people today to establish a sense of identity. If their behavior is to make sense, we cannot look at the "NOW" generation in isolation. We have to see them in the context of fundamental changes taking place in our culture and in the structure of the family unit. Finally, we'll consider what you as a parent can do to help your adolescent in spite of these roadblocks.

The second childhood

For some parents "teen-ager" is akin to a dirty word. Yet, hundreds of thousands of adolescents move toward adulthood with skill and aplomb. They, however, get little publicity. If you take the developmental point of view, much of their so-called typical behavior makes all the sense in the world. Each characteristic of this period results from important psychological changes necessary for final emergence into adulthood in our culture.

With adolescence, bodies change shape, generalized sexual feelings become specific, and there is an attraction to the opposite sex and new social relationships. At the same time, parents seem less heroic, their shortcomings glaringly obvious, and brothers and sisters are particularly annoying. In the light of these major changes, each adolescent must reevaluate himself to fit new reflections. *Earlier self-statements no longer apply.* The rapid developer must alter his self-image more quickly, which only adds to his insecurity.

Before long, the issues of vocation, marriage, and a basic philosophy of life must be faced, while unresolved conflicts from childhood resurface to be dealt with anew. For some youngsters these concerns are in the forefront of consciousness and cause sharp uncertainty; others handle them without major turmoil.

Reevaluation means refocusing on autonomy, initiative, attachment, and personal and social mastery. But this second time around, the teen-ager needs answers as a budding adult rather than as a child.

The major task of adolescence is the re-evaluation of self.

Reworking his identity is of far greater importance to the adolescent than learning the intricacies of calculus or the sonnets of Shakespeare. We all know the brilliant adult—the precocious quiz kid parading his facts—whose life bogs down because he lacks a solid sense of identity. He finds little meaning in life and cannot relate successfully to others. A factual sponge, he knows all about the "world out there" while his inner world remains a puzzle.

Four areas of reevaluation

Each adolescent brings with him into the teens all his past experiences and feelings. These years cannot be fully understood as an isolated period. Against the backdrop of his past, each one has to reevaluate himself in four major areas. For high self-esteem he needs to

1. establish final independence from family and agemates —to become a "confident other";
2. be able to relate to the opposite sex;
3. prepare for an occupation for self-support; and
4. establish a workable and meaningful philosophy of life.

Movement to the herd

The young adolescent craves group acceptance even more than he did during the middle years. Fourteen-year-old Sam knows the answer to the question asked in class, but he says he doesn't. Why? He wants to be one of the boys and being too smart is frowned on by his crowd. With the insecurity that comes from reshuffling his identity, the young teen-ager needs large transfusions of confirmation from friends.

The need to belong is so central that when a teen-ager appears *completely* indifferent to group opinion, he may be covering feelings of isolation and estrangement. On the other hand, *overwhelming* conformity suggests undue insecurity.

Withstanding some group pressures comes easier for the youngster who *knows* he is adequate and belongs unquestionably. He usually becomes a pacesetter. Ordinarily, only the secure dare to be noticeably different.

Some parents go overboard in pressing for popularity. When
Ellen's dates were few, Mrs. G. fretted and stewed. As Ellen
put it, "When the phone is ringing, I get the glad eye; when
there's a lull, I get the frown, the worried look, and the 'could-
it-be-halitosis' treatment." Such pressures only add to insecurity.

Movement from the herd

After two to four years of being glued to gang values, youngsters start branching out. First in one way, then in another, they
begin to shed group dependence. Somewhere between seventeen and twenty, the youngster should be able to stand apart
with confidence. He should be able to say, "I know who I am
and trust my capacity to handle my life responsibly. I don't
need constant support from outside." (The sequence of the
steps toward maturity is diagrammed on the next page.)

Final separation

In establishing final independence, the teen-ager is not so
subtle as during the middle years. For some youngsters, defiance
of parents (tied to the need for separateness) carries a flavor
reminiscent of the two-year-old. Consequently, this stage has
been called the "Second Age of Negativism." It might be more
productive to think of this period as the "Final Declaration of
Independence."

The teen-ager may be unsure about handling new privileges
but he is the last to admit it. Most need to see parents as outmoded relics from the stone age before they can see them as
the human beings they really are. This view makes pulling
away easier. Your adolescents discover you are far from perfect
(or even heroic) and the toppling of pedestals reverberates
throughout the family. Parents who have held themselves up as
paragons of virtue and as final authorities on most subjects
ordinarily come in for more of this idol-crashing than those
who haven't assumed such positions.

Criticisms and snipings serve to break the chains of de-

DEVELOPMENTAL STEPS TOWARD INDEPENDENCE

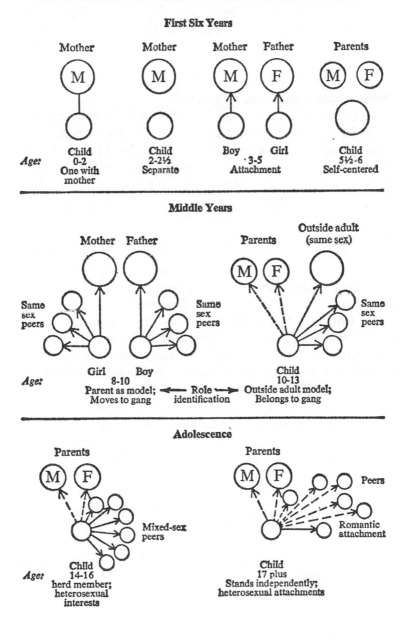

First Six Years

Mother	Mother	Mother Father	Parents
Child 0-2 One with mother	Child 2-2½ Separate	Boy · 3-5 Girl Attachment	Child 5½-6 Self-centered

Age:

Middle Years

Mother Father
Same sex peers

Parents
Outside adult (same sex)
Same sex peers

Age:
Girl 8-10 Boy
Parent as model; Moves to gang ◄── Role ──► identification
Child 10-13
Outside adult model; Belongs to gang

Adolescence

Parents
Mixed-sex peers

Age:
Child 14-16 herd member; heterosexual interests

Parents
Peers
Romantic attachment

Child 17 plus
Stands independently; heterosexual attachments

pendency. Although sixteen-year-old Greta's mother knew her daughter saw her as old-fashioned, she never realized how antiquated she was in her eyes until Greta asked in all seriousness, "Mother, did they wear jewelry like this when you were alive?"

Like the proverbial bull in a china shop, the adolescent may strike at your appearance, values, habits, and the family home. Some of the boy's pecking at his mother and the girl's derision of her father severs the old attachment from the preschool years. The undertones of this embryonic romance lie dormant during the middle years to reemerge with adolescence. Maturing urges combine with cultural mores to tell the teen-ager that he does not want a little-child-attachment to parents any longer. So, he hacks away to free himself for appropriate heterosexual attachments.

How intensely any youngster rebels depends on his emotional hungers and whether autonomy has been encouraged all during childhood. If there are only a few remaining threads to snip, Declarations of Independence are less drastic.

An extremely important factor that contributes to the intensity of rebellion is *how parental power has been handled from birth on.* For years it has been thought that rebellion was normal and necessary to adolescent development. More recently, however, youngsters coming from democratic homes have shown little inclination to engage in out-and-out power struggles. The importance of this evidence is so crucial that the impact of the shift in authority patterns in the home will be discussed in detail in Chapter Twenty-three. At this point, keep in mind that

intense rebellion is not a necessary part of teen-age development.

In any case, adolescent resistance is the cry for autonomy.

Another device that teen-agers use in their push toward final independence is sharing private affairs with those outside the family. This does not signify distrust or lack of love. It is simply easier for them to come to terms with themselves with those to whom they are less emotionally attached. Some youngsters, of course, turn to outsiders because their parents are unempathic, disrespectful, and refuse to give up their power. But even those with empathic, democratic parents often prefer working through some of their feelings with people outside the family.

Relating to the opposite sex

Nature is unkind to adolescents. At the very time they are attracted to the opposite sex and are painfully self-conscious about their peers' opinions, pimples erupt, growth spurts make them resemble ungainly colts, male voices crack, and clothing shrinks overnight.

With puberty, of course, comes interest in the opposite sex. But interest usually *precedes* social "know-how." Along with the awkwardness of physical appearance, there is the pain of not knowing what to say or do.

"I'd like to ask Mary to dance," Guy admits shyly to the chaperone, "but how do you go about it?"

"Asking's no strain," says Martin, "but how do you get rid of her afterwards?"

"How do you keep on talking to boys? I can think of one or two things to say, but then what? There I stand with my mouth hanging open and my hands dangling down. I feel so dumb with boys," moans Gloria.

"Do you keep your eyes open or closed when a boy kisses you?"

How pathetically unsure many teen-agers are as they take those first awkward steps toward heterosexual friendships!

Each teen-ager's attitudes toward his physical and social competence, his body, his role as a male or female, and his new sexual feelings influence how he goes out to the opposite sex. All of his earlier experiences with sexuality play a part in how he relates. (Sexual aspects of self-esteem are discussed in Chapter Twenty-five.)

During early adolescence boys are usually about two years behind girls in development and don't catch up until late adolescence. For this reason, most girls prefer dating boys one or two years older, "because, after all, who wants to baby-sit on a date?" Broad experiences with many different kinds of personalities, of course, give youngsters a more realistic basis for choosing a mate later on.

The more varied the youngster's skills, the more bridges he has for communicating with other teen-agers. Some can make contact only through sex. Said Ralph frankly, "I can't swim or dance or ski or play tennis. I hate card games; I don't have a car, and I have little money for shows. It's hard to know how to talk to girls, so for me dating means making-out."

Going steady faces most adolescents and their parents at some point. In the early years, the term has little meaning. The girl wears the boy's pin or ring, and the "steady" is merely insurance that neither will be left high and dry for some school function. They may go to a school dance together, but hardly see each other until time to come home. The "steadies" of the early teens last for a few days or months and then reassemble along other unsteady "steady" lines. This arrangement is but another outcropping of the need to belong. When thirteen-year-old Anna was asked why she went steady, she said, "Oh, I don't know. It's the 'in' thing." By mid-adolescence, today's teens regard dating a different person every week as unacceptable, "cheap" behavior.

In later adolescence, of course, choosing steady partners becomes an emotional investment. Each youngster usually seeks a partner who typifies his ideals. If relationships with parents have been friendly, boys tend to choose girls like their mothers, and girls choose boys who possess many of their fathers' traits. When strong negative feelings toward parents exist, a youngster is more apt to become serious about a person whose qualities are *directly opposite* from those of his parent.

Paul lived with a dominating brunette mother who drove him relentlessly. He chose as a wife a blond ball of fluff completely dependent on him. Julia's father was a high-principled man who trusted and valued her. She chose a husband who gave her the same treatment.

Serious attachments may reflect emotional needs. Ginny became attached to punitive men. With little self-respect, she looked for those who browbeat her regularly. Teresa hungered for social status, so she refused to date boys who weren't going up the ladder. She needed a man to round out her inadequacies. Mel chose a wife like his mother who allowed him to remain dependent. He didn't want to stand on his own two feet.

The kinds of relationships each adolescent chooses are a reflection of many factors. But, in general, you have less cause to worry when your youngster's self-respect is high and his relations with you are basically friendly.

Adolescent conscience

By late adolescence the conscience ordinarily no longer needs outside support. Until that time, the youngster needs assistance in taking certain moral stands. If Mrs. R. hadn't known this, she might have been completely puzzled by her daughter's behavior.

"Mom, when I get back from the dance with Eddie tonight, come downstairs in five minutes and insist on my going to bed."

"What on earth are you getting at, Edith?" asked Mrs. R.

"Well, I know Eddie. Soon's we get in he'll want to make-out and I'm just not interested. Please do this, and remember, *just* five minutes."

"Sounds like Eddie's a pretty speedy character! I wouldn't dream of waiting a second longer," replied her mother.

With clock in hand, Mrs. R. followed instructions to the second. As she turned to go upstairs after delivering the maternal ultimatum, she heard Edith whisper to Eddie, "She's sure a drag, isn't she?"

Inconsistent? A betrayal of her mother? Not at all. The maneuver makes sense if you're a teen-ager. Edith was in a dilemma. She didn't want intimacies with Eddie, but neither did she want to look like a deadhead. Obvious solution. Make mother the scapegoat and save face.

When youngsters want a way out of situations for which they aren't ready, protect their vulnerability by assuming certain responsibilities until their own capacities to stand firm are stronger. Firmness on moral issues usually comes with late adolescence. This learning takes time.

Vocational plans

At the time when he is least sure of himself, the teen-ager has to make basic decisions about his future. Fairly early in adolescence, he must decide whether to continue his education after high school or go directly to work, and his classes are determined by his choice.

Even under the best conditions, this is a difficult decision, but high self-esteem makes for more realistic choices. The youngster whose aspirations reflect the need to please parents or whose goals are limited by low self-esteem is less able to plan wisely.

Broad educational and job experiences, of course, help each youngster assess his own capacities, but

how youngsters see themselves influence their possibilities for the future.

Bob's self-confidence permits him to prepare for the field of architecture in which his genuine talent for art and math can be used. David has real ability in art and math, but his poor opinion of himself doesn't permit him to recognize it. Consequently, he drops out of school to take a menial and low-paid position. It is all he feels he deserves or can handle.

Many dropouts feel inadequate and worthless. With a history of academic and personal failures, they see no hope. Emotional problems can be so marked that they prevent concentration on academic abstractions. Some youngsters feel schoolwork is basically irrelevant; others drop out as a defiant measure—to flaunt their parents' and society's belief in education.

Vocational choice often reflects emotional needs. Ed's experiences made him fearful of direct contact with people. Defensively, he retreated to become a research librarian. He didn't enjoy the work, but it provided a living while protecting him from sustained contact with others. His dislike for the job pinched less than his fear of involvement with people.

Some youngsters decide on a particular field because it will be lucrative or gives social status. Yet, later, money and position may have less appeal for them. Increasing numbers of young people today are questioning the merits of money and status. With the liberation movement young people are seeking work that sexist notions earlier forbid: men as secretaries, nurses, phone operators; women as politicians, engineers, mechanics. "Jobs that match talents not role expectations" is the theme.

Interestingly enough, a new trend is presently emerging. Top students in law, for example, are refusing jobs with private firms that offer high salaries and status. They are choosing to work in government or in legal programs for the poor. Service to others is more attractive to an increasing number of young people than status and the accumulation of wealth.

Some youngsters head for a profession because telling others they want to be a mechanic or a carpenter would only raise eyebrows. Unfortunately, trade skills do not carry the status of professions, and the youngster whose interests and talents lie in that direction has to accept lowered status. For the youngster with deep self-respect, however, this deterrent is irrelevant.

You help your youngsters with vocational choices by encouraging them to sample widely different subject fields, to work at a variety of summer jobs, and to talk with those already working in the field. Some youngsters need to leave school and work a year or two before they get a feel for their preferences.

Lying fallow may help them discover the direction they want to travel.

Remember: self-esteem plays a large part in any youngster's choice of a vocation, in the goals he shoots for, and in how realistic his choices are. Encourage talents, not roles.

Reevaluating moral concepts

A strong relationship exists between physical maturation and an interest in religious and moral questions. Studies show that the majority of the bull sessions of late adolescence revolve around these two themes.

As each youngster deals with the questions, "Who am I?" and "Where am I going?" his experiences force him to take a certain stance. He is pushed into moral decisions by what goes on around him.

The stronger the youngster's sense of personal worth, the more secure he feels in his group, the easier it is for him to base his decisions on *personal conviction* rather than on the need for group approval. The lower his self-respect, the less he belongs, the stronger the temptation to go along with group pressures to win a place for himself.

Late adolescence is a period of vigorous questioning of religious concepts that have been taught. Living more and more in the world of peers, teen-agers plunge into new thinking. Part of adolescent reevaluation is dealing with such issues as: What is my place in the universal scheme of things? What is the purpose of life? How can I put the apparent conflicts between science and religion into a coherent whole? What do I believe in? What code of ethics can I live by? What is my personal philosophy?

Questioning adult values has traditionally been part of growing up. But because *society's* values are shifting so markedly, the whole issue of values is at the forefront of adolescent dialogues.

In seeking to find himself, the teen-ager needs a meaningful frame of reference from which to operate. He needs to be allowed to question and to think ahead in terms of what certain value commitments will mean to him and others in the long run. A necessary part of his self-discovery is deciding what he stands for. This means that you can expect questioning, doubting, and trying ideas "on for size."

How extensive any youngster's questioning will be depends on his experiences, what and how he has been taught, and whether the teaching makes sense to him in the light of his experiences.

Whether a youngster follows his religious and moral training often depends on his relationship with his parents. Larry's only reason for rejecting his parents' church was that it was valued by them. It was his form of rebellion.

When a teen-ager does embrace a religion, hopefully it will allow him to accept both his clay feet and his holy self. It permits him to accept his own human frailties; yet be true to his own integrity, while freeing him to act responsibly in terms of the integrity of others.

Tom, for example, feels the urge to cheat on a final exam. He does not spank himself for this human desire, but he decides not to because he knows he only cheats himself in the long run and would be acting irresponsibly toward those who have studied for the test. To know that a whole religious body disapproves of cheating gives a bulwark against compromise. He does not feel that he must take a moral position on his own—a difficult thing for a young adolescent to do.

A meaningful and positive religious philosophy gives the teen-ager a sense of direction and purpose; even more important, it supports his need for acceptance and love. It is a source of strength in times of stress and can sharply lessen his feelings of being alone.

When you build friendly, warm, accepting relationships with your children, you increase the chances that they will give your values serious consideration. Few of us even want to look at the values of those whom we dislike and cannot respect. But of course, whatever you teach must be *lived* if it is to convince.

Role rehearsals

Self-doubt in adolescence leads to role rehearsals. Like new clothes, the teen-ager tries first one and then another role and watches for reactions.

Adolescent Ann was a thorn in her brother's side. "One day she's Mata Hari, slinking around like she's Miss Worldly of 2000 A.D. The next day she's Tomboy Tammy, hanging upside down out of trees—next best thing to an ape. Two days later she's taking on like Lady Gotrocks, speaking with an English accent and telling everyone to call her Gwendolynne. And pow, if you misspell it! She wears a French twist, changes her handwriting, and holds her chin up so high she'll need traction to get it down to our level again. Next thing you know, she's talking with a lisp! Whatta pain!"

Many a parent living through this stage with his particular "Ann" reassures his daughter that role-playing isn't the answer. "Honey, you're all right as your own self; you don't have to be a fake somebody else." The only trouble with such well-meant advice is that the Ann's may not be sure who their "own selves" are.

Such role rehearsals actually serve a purpose. When Ann imagines herself a femme fatale, she may work through her disappointment that the local Romeo didn't ask her for a date. In fantasy, she can capture nothing less than a baron or prince. She patches the bruise of rejection and restores self-respect. Her insecurities about social niceties may be handled by forcing herself to out-Emily Mrs. Post. Tree-hanging gymnastics at home may be a welcome outlet for the strain of acting worldly in front of school chums.

Daydreams and adopted roles let Ann practice what are, to her, adult ways of behaving. Miss Worldly, Miss Athlete, and

Miss Highborn protect her while she fathoms out who she really is. Once she's sure of herself, she won't need these roles.

Adolescents need time to consider a whole repertoire of possibilities; they need to project themselves into the future in a variety of ways.

Introspection, or looking inward, is part and parcel of self-discovery. When the teen-ager asks, "Who am I?" he finds not one answer but many. There is the "I" that changes physically; the inner "I" who is socially and sexually uncertain; the intellectual "I" who seeks answers and meaning, and the exterior "I" that must look assured for the benefit of peers. Teen-agers tend to be so immersed in themselves they rarely stop to think that other adolescents are beset by the same doubts; many keep their uncertainties under wraps.

Marked fluctuations

One characteristic that frustrates parents is the marked fluctuation from childishness to maturity. Sometimes the change is so rapid you can't believe your eyes. Back and forth they go—back to the safety of the old, out to the pull of the new.

Some mild mood fluctuations come from major and rapid changes in body chemistry, but much stems from psychological and cultural pressures. Leaving the shelter of childhood can invoke a vague mourning in some youngsters for the security of childhood past. Easy tears, heightened sensitivity, sudden flare-ups, incessant tussling among boys, continuous giggling among girls—these behaviors may come off underlying feelings of insecurity and being out of step. They can be outlets for tension in the struggle to forge a new identity.

When mood swings are too intense or prolonged, it suggests that your youngster is feeling the need for some active help in sorting out his relationship to himself and others. If he seems unduly alienated from constructive friendships, he may need counseling help. A few sessions may untangle some issues that enslave even the confident adolescent. Most teens work best with other adolescents in group counseling, as they still need group support. It is tremendously supportive to discover that other teens feel as they do. Meantime, at home zero in on the seven basic ingredients that spell love and confirmation (see Chapters Seven through Thirteen). And make heavy use of democratic discipline (see Chapter Twenty-three).

The degree of insecurity any teen-ager feels depends on temperament, experiences with success and failure, family relationships, and the group pressures he is exposed to. But the youngster with high self-esteem passes through adolescence with less turmoil.

Idealistic years

"Sometimes I get so impatient with our Peggy," said Mr. F. "She never gets her feet on the ground. Having ideals is one thing, but being so idealistic you ignore reality is another."

How tempting it is, when a teen-ager expounds his dedication to Utopian ideals, to point to reality. Yet, idealism encapsulates or pulls together a teen-ager's insecurities. It gives a feeling of definiteness and structure to believe that all world problems stem from One Evil Influence and all could be solved by One Worthy Principle. Such black and white thinking lessens the confusion within. In his inexperience, the adolescent may be unaware that Grand Ambition has to be pitted against reality and hammered out by sweat and hard work against mountains of indifference and complex cross currents.

Yet, who among us would take away the idealism of youth? Out of the mouths of comparative babes, out of their steadfast refusal to be daunted even in the face of overwhelming obstacles, have come ideas, movements, and innovations that have moved man closer to his ideals. By the same token, the search for the ideal pushes many a youngster to extend and develop budding potentials. Hitching his wagon to a star may provide the impetus to create new, improved ways of living—for himself and others.

When idealism is exaggerated to the point of being excessively unrealistic and persists overly long, the individual may be avoiding psychological issues within.

As an adolescent, Jerry felt strongly about the conditions among the poor. As a young adult he lived in a garret, giving away all his money except what he needed to barely maintain himself. He refused to marry or have children because he said, "That would mean I had less to give to the poor." Jerry's self-imposed martyrdom was his way of punishing himself for the bad person he unconsciously believed himself to be. Through therapy he developed enough self-respect to believe he deserved more that a martyr's existence, even though he still wanted to dedicate his life to bettering conditions for the underprivileged. His earlier exaggerated idealism had been a cover-up for low self-esteem. Once he was personally free, his idealistic wishes were grounded in a healthy recognition of basic realities. Rather than undermining his health, he took care of himself so that in the long run he had more to give.

Inherent or cultural

The myth that adolescent rebellion results solely from hormonal changes has been exploded by studies of primitive cultures. Although their adolescents have similar physiological changes, they do not have many of the teen-age characteristics of youngsters in our society.

With the appearance of sexual maturity, puberty rites in the primitive culture lift the youngster in one neat step from child to adult. A few days or weeks of ceremony bestows full-fledged adulthood with all its privileges and responsibilities. He receives clear-cut reflections from all the community that he is no longer a child.

In our more complex culture, a long delay exists between

the onset of sexual maturity and recognition as adults. The law, rather than sexual development, determines when they can drive a car, be out past curfew without supervision, or marry without parental consent.

Parents provide blurred mirrors for the adolescent as well. We vary tremendously as to when we think youngsters are old enough to date, go steady, or take extended trips with friends. In one situation we dominate them like irresponsible children; in another, we nag because they lack adult attitudes.

The increasing need for education in our technological society further blurs the age at which adulthood arrives. The graduate student may have to remain in a semi-dependent financial position well into his twenties. Traditionally, then, adolescence in our culture has been a period of storm and stress partly because our teen-agers are given the privileges of adulthood in bits and pieces that add to the mosaic of their uncertainty about themselves.

In recent years new hurdles have been added that make building a solid sense of personal worth even more difficult than a few generations ago. Rising divorce rates and increasing mobility cut into a youngster's need to belong to a full family unit and to have an identity in his community.

In times past if an adolescent found few satisfactions in school or in his town, he didn't have to drop out on dope. He dropped out West, where he could readily channel his energies and carve out a nitch for himself. In short, formerly available paths to meet psychological needs are now closed.

Today, an increasing majority of our young people are being raised in large, urban communities and attend high schools where students number in the thousands. It is simply harder to convince yourself that you matter and have an important contribution to make when you are one of a mass.

In our affluent society material goods are easier to come by, and young people are swamped with possessions they haven't worked for. There is less sense of personal achievement in being handed typewriters, stereos, and cars than when you have to work for them.

The fast pace of our times works against genuine human encounters that build a sense of personal worth. And, of course, today's youth lives under the umbrella of larger threats: the bomb, civil unrest, the population explosion, increasing violence in our cities, and economic uncertainties.

Up against these barriers, it is small wonder that many young people, blindly groping for the way to meet their needs, have chosen to withdraw through drugs, drop out of a society that doesn't help them in their struggle, or turned to uncommitted sexual release. These behaviors are but symptoms. *We need to focus on the real villain: the feelings, "I am unlovable; I don't matter or belong; I am not capable of coping."*

If ever there were a time when young people needed a central core of stability, now is that time. The teen-ager who has a faith in himself (born of past successes with life and love) will be less likely to buckle under from outside pressures. The surer he is that he is lovable and worthy, the less security he will need from his environment.

So many of our young people are serious and tense. We this in their dancing; it seems more a release for frantic tension than an expression of the joy of movement. Is it significant that teen-agers today dance apart from their partners? Is it perhaps symbolic of the alienation from others that so characterizes our modern society?

And what is their password? *Love.* In one word they are calling for the curative medicine they need—not only to like themselves, but to feel less tense, less alienated. They need love to scale the hurdles our society has erected. Rapidly becoming a significant majority in our country, young people are asking for a larger degree of control over their own destinies. They are reaching out for respect and recognition. They are telling us they want to belong by having a voice and to contribute meaningfully to the institutions that affect them.

They are asking for personal involvement to counteract the forces that tell them they have no identity. More than ever, we adults are being tested by youth. They want us to be strong, honest, convincing models.

When we look at our teen-agers in the cultural climate they live in, when we know the psychological jobs they have to do, then much of the "NOW" generation's behavior makes a great deal of sense. And as parents, our primary job is to give them a sense of personal security (see Chapters Seven through Thirteen and Chapter Twenty-three) to counteract the uncertainty of the times.

Helping with "homework"

You help your adolescents with the tasks of growth when you
1. respect privacy;
2. make your home attractive. Small considerations such as your neat personal appearance, made beds, and clean kitchen sinks save embarrassment when his friends arrive. Many are keenly sensitive to their peers' reactions toward their parents—even though they themselves need a comb;
3. keep supervision subtle and support constructive group activities;
4. avoid making them feel guilty about the tasks of growth —especially the need to move away from you; avoid sarcasm and teasing about his changing shapes, feelings, or dates;
5. maintain a sense of humor, an antidote to taking this period too seriously;
6. remember that being relegated to the second century B.C. says nothing about you. In a few short years you'll be recognized as back in the twentieth century;
7. keep the long-range view in mind. Millions of doubt-

ing adolescents become steady adults; this stage too
shall pass;

8. casually discuss with your youngsters the adolescent
changes and the pressures they face prior to this period.
Forewarned is forearmed;

9. talk to younger brothers and sisters to enlist their understanding of your teen-agers' pressures and needs;

10. establish basic family policies by democratic procedures
(see Chapter Twenty-three);

11. *listen*—really listen with your heart—to feelings and
points of view. Adolescence is typically a period of intense emotions and empathy actively reduces inner
turmoil;

12. work with the need for competence and recognition;
and

13. attend to the climate around them; they need *safe encounters* in abundance.

Each completed task along the Journey of Self allows the
youngster to sample his competence. Working *with* him cements
the bond of love and directly nurtures his self-esteem.

Your reactions to teen-agers

It is all very well to be told how you should feel toward
adolescents to help them on their Journey of Self. But how
you *should* feel and how you *do* feel may be worlds apart.
You're better able to nurture if you face your inner feelings
squarely.

A question to consider is "What do my teen-agers mean to
me?" Not, "How *should* I feel toward them?" but "How do
I really view this stage?" If you're like most parents, you
probably have mixed emotions.

Ask yourself: "Are my teen-agers insurance against financial
need in the future? Are they investments against loneliness
in the years to come? Are they extensions of me through whom

I can realize my own unmet ambitions? Do I distrust them because I was unreliable as an adolescent or because no one trusted me? Are they emotional and financial burdens when life should be easier and more pleasant?" None of these issues may influence your view of your youngsters, but it is wise to check yourself on each one.

Teen-agers can be threatening. If you fear growing old, seeing your youngsters on the threshold of adulthood can emphasize your own advancing years. Your frustration at not being able to turn back the clock may be expressed in irritations toward them.

Many women enter the menopause as their youngsters hit adolescence. "I'll be quite frank," said Mrs. T. "Much of my anger at Diane comes from being jealous. I shouldn't feel that way, I know, but there she is with all the bloom of youth. I kill myself with exercises, diets, facial creams, and hair dye, but still I look faded. She doesn't do a thing, and she's lovely. My husband treats me like an old shoe, while her dates seem thrilled to go out with her. Talk about teen-agers feeling insecure, how about us poor women going through the change? I try to be supportive of Diane, but much of the time I need support myself!"

Probably the two periods when a woman most needs her husband's active understanding and confirmation are during pregnancy and menopause. The husband making his wife feel that the loss of childbearing capacity in no way dims her womanly appeal literally helps her nurture their children. Feeling important and needed by her husband lessens the threat of their adolescents. Single parents especially need supportive groups and friends and should seek them.

When your youngsters reach the teens, you may experience a sense of urgency in that little time is left to influence them. So, you pour on the pressure. This feeling is more intense if you see your role as a molder rather than as a nurturer.

If you have held the reins of authority tightly, you may feel threatened as your power dwindles with each passing year.

Those of you whose security is tied to money may find adolescent expenses a threat. If your teen-agers become more educated than you, you can feel inferior and resent their "uppity" attitudes. If their vocation puts them in a different socio-economic class, you may feel pushed aside and inadequate. No matter how we look at parenthood, most of us have heavy emotional investments in our youngsters. Few of us avoid a wrench as they move out on their own. But, remember: most youngsters do not want to sever *all* family ties even when we have made many mistakes in raising them. Once they have established independence, they usually want to return as good friends, but on the level of one adult to another. If you have cooperated with the tasks of selfhood and provided safe encounters over the years, they cannot help but cherish your friendship.

The most important step, if you feel threatened by your adolescent, is to *recognize the threat for what it is.* Any problem is easier to solve when you look at feelings honestly. Shoving them aside because you believe you *shouldn't* have them means you are more likely to behave blindly. Accepting your feelings without judgment can free you. You are no less worthy because you feel threatened—only human.

"It's strange," said Mrs. T. in discussing her jealousy of Diane's youthfulness, "but just being able to admit that I am jealous and believing that I'm not such a 'bad' mother because I do feel this—somehow it lessens the feeling. Last night I felt tense as she waited for her date. I told myself, 'O.K., there it is. I wish I were still as lovely as Diane. It's the most natural thing in the world to mourn for what I've lost.' And, then, like magic, I was suddenly glad that my former good looks had passed on to her. I was proud to have borne such a beauty."

Awareness of feelings and sharing them with your husband or wife, understanding friends, or groups of other parents can give you support. Aloneness is lessened when you find that other parents feel the same hodgepodge of emotions—threats and joys—as they live with their youngsters. In many communities adult education classes provide opportunities for such discussions. If your feelings are overwhelming, consult a counselor.

Mothers, particularly, need to prepare *as early as possible* for their children's departure from home. Activities or jobs should be personally fulfilling rather than time-fillers, of course. Some mothers ignore the fact that they have some twenty to forty years of living to do *after* youngsters leave home. The woman who defines herself in terms of motherhood only may define herself as a "shelf-sitter" the last third of her life.

Seeing yourself *primarily* as a *person*, and *secondarily* as a *parent*, allows you to nurture more fully. Your self-definition affects how freely you release your children.

PART IV · NEGATIVE FEELINGS AND
SELF-ESTEEM

EIGHTEEN · HANDLING CHILDREN'S FEELINGS

The great paradox

Most of us handle children's feelings in the *exact* ways that we ourselves dislike. This paradox is one few of us stop to consider.

When you share personal feelings, you don't want judgment, logic, reasons, or advice. You don't want your feelings brushed aside, denied, or taken lightly. Yet, look at these typical responses to children's emotions:

"Mom! Jon just asked me to the Spring Fling! I'm so thrilled, I can hardly stand it!" explodes Katie.

"See, honey, I told you not to worry. All that moping around last week was just wasted energy!" smiles her mother.

(Katie's mother has just told her daughter that her earlier worries were groundless—a fact Katie now knows and doesn't want her nose rubbed in.)

* * * *

"I wish I didn't have a brother; he's nothing but a rat fink!" agonizes Hugh.

"Hugh! That's a *dreadful* thing to say! If anything ever happened to your brother, you'd feel awful for having such thoughts," scolds his mother.

(Hugh's mother has judged and shamed her son rather than moving in to help with the whopping case of jealousy he's sitting on.)

* * * *

"I hate school! It all seems so boring and worthless—the things we learn in class," says Crystal.

"Dear, a good basic education will help you get the kind of job you will want later on," advises her father.

(Mr. T. tells Crystal her feelings of boredom and disinterest are beside the point. He apparently believes that sensible logic erases feelings; yet, nothing could be farther from the truth.)

Each of these adults meant well and each was doubtless unaware that his response was a "feeling stopper." But you have only to put yourself on the receiving end to capture the reactions such remarks would arouse in you. And the pathetic note is that we are unaware that these responses are destructive in the long run.

Regardless of age, sex, race, or condition of life, it is *the search for understanding that makes anyone open up* about feelings in the first place. Yet, when children share emotions with us, we typically dole out prescriptions as to how they should or should not feel.

We rarely give what we ourselves crave when dealing with emotions.

Why feelings are a problem

Why is it that handling feelings constructively poses such a problem?

Most of us have had our feelings handled by the traditional methods rampant in our culture, and we respond to our children in like fashion. Notice when you voice a negative emotion how often you run into reasons, logic, judgment, advice, reassurance, or denial.

Despite the fact that negative feelings are a fact of life, far too many of us have been taught that we *shouldn't* have them. We are convinced we are less worthy or less mature if such feelings well up in us. But, people just cannot live with each other day after day without conflicts and conflicts engender feelings.

Few of us are aware that the fastest way to get rid of negative emotions (and the only way to ensure that they won't erupt in unhealthy symptoms) is to encourage their expression.

Negative feelings expressed and accepted lose their destructive power.

In addition, parents are not given training in the skills necessary to release negative emotions. No wonder so many of us go astray in handling feelings, particularly negative ones.

Feelings cause body changes

Feelings have survival value; they mobilize the body for action. Under the stress of strong emotions, certain glands immediately go to work and major physiological changes take place. The heartbeat increases; blood centered in the digestive system is diverted to large body muscles; sugar from the liver is pumped into the blood stream to provide extra energy; adrenalin is released; the blood coagulation rate increases; breathing becomes more rapid; sweat glands activate; large body muscles tense for action. In short, the body readies itself for fight or flight. Strong emotions make us chemically different people.

At such moments it is totally ineffectual to have someone tell us to calm down. Although we may comply outwardly, our "innards" race on. Our ears hear the request but our glands do not. To work constructively with emotions you must recognize that these physiological changes are triggered off by feelings and they are *not* turned off by order. In fact, being told to stop the feeling only adds to frustration and makes glands work even harder.

Think about a time when you were genuinely upset and instead of telling yourself that you shouldn't feel this way, you did something about your feelings. Maybe you scrubbed the kitchen floor with a vengeance, played a vigorous game of tennis, hacked out weeds, or blasted your golf ball. Maybe you poured out your feelings to an understanding listener, or simply had a "good" cry. The result? Relief.

When feelings are expressed in vigorous physical action, released through clay, art, drama, music, or words, the energy wrapped up in the emotion is discharged. The body, then, returns to its former state of equilibrium.

Feelings expressed discharge emotional energy.

The price of traditional methods

When negative feelings are repressed, the body remains in a state of tension. When sufficient pressures build up, release comes by any of a number of outlets. Bottled-up emotions may be turned against the self (migraines, sleep-walking, hyperactivity, nail biting, head-banging, psychosomatic ailments) or directed outward in hostility toward others and society.

Whether a child's mental ability is *available* for use depends on how emotionally tied up he is. Repression acts like a dam that can narrow the river of intelligence to a mere trickle. There are youngsters whose tested IQ's have jumped 60 to 100 points when emotional blocks have been removed. Children cannot absorb from the printed page when their focus is turned inward.

Energies tied up in repression are not available for constructive purposes. Constant inner turmoil leads to chronic fatigue and lowers resistance to physical disease. Notice how often your ailments follow a period of emotional stress. A further disadvantage is that repression controls indiscriminately. It not only locks in negative emotions but it keeps the lid on warm, positive ones as well. The repressed child is often controlled, distant, and cold.

You might argue, "But look at the model child. He represses his 'bad' feelings but is still 'good.'" Model behavior is not the healthy, positive behavior we're talking about. The model child acts as if he's reading from a page in a book of etiquette. His "good" behavior does not spring spontaneously from an overflow of inner joy and contentment.

Repression's impact on self-esteem

As if these weren't enough disadvantages, repression plays havoc with self-esteem. Our traditional ways of handling negative emotions push youngsters away from us. They tell them that very real parts of themselves are unacceptable. For self-respect, children may try to hide such feelings even from themselves, to block them from consciousness. Then, they become alienated from the fullness of their humanity—out of touch with who they really are.

When a child does not deny forbidden feelings to himself but only keeps them hidden from view, he concludes, "I must be a terrible person to have these 'bad' feelings." And away goes self-respect.

The traditional methods for handling negative feelings have too many disadvantages for you to continue using them. There is a constructive alternative.

Handling feelings constructively

Handling negative feelings constructively is a topic that vitally concerns all of us who live with children. As you start reading here, a number of questions will probably come to your mind—pertinent, legitimate questions that may press so strongly they literally prevent your absorbing some of this first needed material.

To avoid muddying the waters, let's first look at the recipe for handling negative feelings *constructively*. Then, we will consider the many issues you may wonder about when you read this recipe: should feelings ever be limited, your possible fears about accepting them, what benefits come from accepting them, sharing *your* feelings, common pitfalls in using this approach, and finally how to do make-up work if you've been using nonconstructive methods up to this point.

Here's the formula for handling feelings constructively: when emotions come—whether positive or negative—you work on the side of health when you *hear empathically, accept feelings,* and *provide acceptable outlets.*

In Chapter Twelve we looked at empathy's meaning, the importance of voice tone, and the fact that the child's total message is made up of both verbal and nonverbal messages. Before you can accept feelings, you must first be able to *hear* them. (You may find it helpful to reread Chapter Twelve to refresh your understanding of empathy before going ahead.)

Hundreds of articles and authorities urge parents to *listen* to their children, and dutifully parents comply. They attend to their children's words and keep their mouths shut. In *their* view they are following instructions because they are only acquainted with one kind of listening—*passive listening.* Yet, talk to their youngsters and you hear the common complaint, "My parents never listen." Why the discrepancy? Are the young folks distorting the facts?

No. What they want is a *particular kind* of listening—even though they may not be able to verbalize this wish. When they talk, they, like all of us, *seek to be understood from their point of view.* But they do not know whether we have heard—fully understood—unless we *prove* it by a special kind of listening—*active listening.*[1]

---

[1] I am indebted to Carl Rogers for this term.

To handle feelings constructively, you must make a sharp distinction between *passive* and *active* listening. Remember:

Proof of understanding comes only with active listening.

Active listening is

1. sensitive attention to the child's verbal *and nonverbal messages;* and
2. reflecting back the total message empathically.

When a child communicates, he wants concrete evidence that his message has been received. The crucial difference lies in whether you listen passively or actively.

To check the degree of understanding you give, tape record or jot down from memory some actual dialogues with your child in which feelings are expressed. Then go over the record and notice four things:

1. Who does most of the talking?
2. How do you respond to your child's messages? Do you use the traditional "feeling stoppers?" (Judgment, Reasoning, Cheering, Denial)
3. Are you merely quietly attentive, or do you actively reflect back his *total* message empathically?
4. How would you feel if your messages were handled as you treated your child's?

If on your record, you find that you grabbed your verbal shovels and tried to bury your child's feelings in the traditional fashion, take heart. These learned responses can be eliminated. You can change to work constructively with negative feelings so that your child is freed from their clutches. Then he won't have to resort to repression or symptoms.

Listen to others talk. See if you can identify their responses to each other. You will probably be amazed to see how often neither side listens actively to the other. Each person busily sends his own messages while neither proves he has understood the other's point of view.

If on your record, you did little or no talking, you were only passively listening, and your child has no guarantee that you truly understood how he felt. Test this point by asking yourself if you would feel understood if your messages were handled as you handled his. If you used a tape recorder, pay close attention to your tone of voice. It makes the difference between whether you simply label a youngster's message or whether you are with him on his wave length.

None of us feels truly understood by having emotions tagged or catalogued. Intellectual understanding is not what we crave. We want warm understanding from the heart. Cold, objective labeling teaches a youngster to take his feelings elsewhere.

Accepting feelings

Accepting feelings means permitting your child to experience his emotion without being judged. This comes easier when you refuse to judge your own emotions and when you see your youngster as a fully separate person. (See Chapter Eleven.) Acceptance can rarely be feigned; to be helpful, it must be genuine.

An important part of accepting emotions is to shake your mind free of "good-bad" categories. Otherwise, you get hung up on the "Thou Shalt Not's." While such thinking has a place as far as acts are concerned, it is inappropriate for feelings. Emotions exist, and you have to deal with them as the realities they are.

Providing acceptable outlets

Let youngsters around eight and older talk out their feelings. Be an empathic active listener. Younger children cannot always put their feelings into words, particularly when they are in the throes of strong emotions. Then, respond to their body messages and put them into words.

Alison tries to take a piece of candy from the refrigerator. Her mother grabs her toddler's hand and quickly closes the door. Alison goes rigid, turns beet red, doubles her fists, and screams, "E-e-e-ow!" at the top of her lungs. Mrs. R. reflects with intensity, "OO-oo-oo! You don't *want* Mommy to stop you. It makes Alison mad and more, more mad!" (At this moment her mother puts her daughter's body language into words and proves that she *understands* how she feels.)

Alison looks at her mother, gives a terse nod, and scolds, "Bad Mommy, bad, bad," stalking out of the room.

Sometimes a child's emotions need to be acted out, especially if they are intense. Provide outlets that *do no harm to any person or valuable property*. Offer paint, paper and crayons, clay, puppets, or provide substitute targets (stuffed animals, an inexpensive toy, punching bag, or pillow). Of course, there will be times when you are in a situation where there are no acceptable outlets available, as in the grocery store, for example. Then, reflect his feelings verbally, set limits on his behavior, and give him an opportunity to vent when you get home. (More about limiting feelings shortly.)

Gary's mother brought her two-year-old in from play kicking and screaming. Over his cries she reflected empathically, "You're mad; you don't want to come to the store with me. You'd like to hit Mama. Mean old Mommy who makes you do what you don't want to."

Note: Remember active listening is hearing the other person's point of view. It *does not involve agreement or disagreement* with that viewpoint. Here Gary's mother proves she understands that at that particular moment her son does see her as mean because she is taking him from his play. Reflecting his feelings does *not* mean that she agrees with his attitude. She feels justified in taking him to the store. But she lets Gary know that he doesn't have to match his way of seeing to hers—she allows him to own his feelings, which are quite separate from hers at this point.

Gary struggled to land a solid punch. Mrs. L. tossed a couch pillow on the floor between them, and said, "I can't let you hit me but this pillow will be me. Show me, Gary, what you'd like to do."

Gary stomped and pounded on the pillow. Leaning over, he bit it; then, picking it up, he smashed it against the wall. "Feels good to hurt that Mama. Smash and hit and throw. You don't want to come with me, not at all!"

Slowly, Gary's anger subsided; he gave the pillow a last gentle kick and went to his room for his teddy before going to the store.

Gary's mother helped her son express his feelings first by putting them into words and then providing an outlet that allowed him to act out his emotions without doing serious damage. He was allowed to keep his self-respect as a person who was no less worthy because of his violent reactions.

Sometimes children need to release feelings when we don't have time to be with them. Often we can get them busy on releasing until we can return to them.

Billy was pummeling another little boy at recess. His teacher pulled the youngsters apart just as the bell rang. She knew that Billy was a volcano of strong feelings and that he'd probably keep the kindergarten in an uproar if she didn't help him release his feelings constructively. Although she wanted to help him, she had to attend to the other children.

As they entered the classroom, she pulled him aside, saying, "I know you're plenty upset, Billy. Would you like to draw out your feelings?"

"I sure would," growled Billy.

When the other children were quietly engaged in another activity, she went over to him and asked, "Would you like to share your drawing with me?"

Billy handed her a picture of a very large chicken glaring down at a very tiny chick.

"Would you like to tell me about it?" she asked.

"Yeah," he replied emphatically. "This (pointing to the large chicken) is *me*, and this (pointing to the tiny chick) is *you!*"

"Oh, how you'd like to be bigger and stronger than me!" she reflected.

"You bet! You came just when I was winning. I'd sure like to stop you when you're winning. Then you'd see how mad *you'd* be!" (Pause) "Say, what are the other kids doing?" And Billy settled down for the rest of the morning.

Expressing his feelings harmlessly freed Billy to move back into the classroom activities peacefully and forestalled further misbehavior. It also helped him maintain his self-respect.

Not all negative feelings can be released by a single picture, a short sentence, or a nod. Sometimes it takes much longer to drain them, especially when a backlog has accumulated. The length of time for draining pent-up emotions depends on the extensiveness of the backlog and on how safe the youngster feels about expressing them.

As a parent, you are not a therapist; but you can provide a therapeutic climate by helping children express feelings as they develop. (Should pent-up feelings seem excessive or should you feel inadequate to handle them, seek professional help.)

Just because you release emotions today does not mean that more may not need expression tomorrow. Children run into situations daily toward which they develop strong feelings. Getting them expressed as they come along prevents accumulations that literally affect their lives.

Limiting feelings

"I'm going to tell that sitter I don't like her," said Lana to her mother as she was about to go out for the evening.

"You *really* dislike her! I'm glad to know how you feel, but our sitter would not accept this kind of talk," cautioned her mother. "So, please don't say anything to her. Let's talk about it tomorrow and see what we can work out."

* * * *

"Mom, I had an absolute fiasco at school today," said Edith just as her mother stepped to the door to go to the beauty parlor.

"Edith, I really want to hear all about it, but unless I leave now I'll miss my appointment. I'll be back at 4 and put everything aside then to listen."

* * * *

Bobby suddenly wanted to vent his anger while the family ate in a restaurant. "Son," said his father, "you're awfully upset and I want to be with you in these feelings, but we'll have to wait till we get out of here. This isn't the place. We should be through in about fifteen minutes."

* * * *

Are the parents stifling their children's outlets for the expression of negative feelings? No, they are helping them face realistic limits. Even the expression of feelings needs to be limited to particular

people—ones who are capable of empathic understanding,
times—hours that are appropriate, and
places—in the privacy of the family.

As long as a youngster knows he has an outlet, he can use some temporary controls.

There may be times when even you cannot listen empathically. You may have other demands to meet at the moment or you may be too tired, upset, worried, or anxious to give full attention.

Never try to help a child release feelings when your outer or inner pressures mean you cannot *honestly* listen.

Nothing is worse than feigned empathy. It undermines trust —that foundation stone of nurturing relationships.

If your youngster needs to be heard and it is not possible at that time, set the limit. You may say, "I know you need to talk right now, but I'm too upset to listen. Soon as I get my own feelings squared away, I'll try to help you with yours." The promised appointment should be kept as early as possible. Part of helping children deal realistically with feelings is teaching them that release has to come within the limits of appropriate people, times, and places.

Fears regarding feelings

Most of us are so steeped in the belief that negative feelings are best repressed or commanded that we fear their expression, much less their acceptance.

"Look," said Mrs. P., "if I let my kids express their feelings, they'd go on for hours. In fact, they'd just get worse. I can't see any sense in encouraging a lot of griping."

"I agree," said Mr. R., "I used to divert my little girl's attention to something pleasant when she cried. I'd say, 'Barby, you'll feel better in a moment,' or 'Be Daddy's brave girl.' Then, I read about accepting feelings, so the next time she fell I said, 'Gosh, that really hurt.' And she cried louder than ever. Reflecting her feelings only made her more upset than when I used to turn them off."

"You're right!" agreed Mrs. W. "The other day I was terribly hurt by a neighbor's cutting remark after a frustrating morning. A friend phoned later and I nonchalantly mentioned the facts to her. She was so empathic that the first thing I knew, I was blubbering like a baby. Her *understanding only made my feelings worse!*"

These reactions to releasing feelings are extremely common. But let's look more closely.

If for months, Mr. R. had turned off or diverted his daughter's hurt feelings, suddenly allowing her to express them may have brought forth not only the feelings from the present tumble but all the past hurts that had been repressed. No wonder the volume was high!

In Mrs. W.'s case, her morning's frustrations were added to the hurt of her neighbor's remark. Mrs. W. said empathy only made her feelings worse. It would be more accurate to say, "Understanding *made it impossible to keep my feelings under control.*" The feelings already existed; empathy only encouraged their expression.

Understanding never makes feelings worse; it only gives them permission to be revealed.

As a thinking parent, you have to ask yourself, *"What are the alternatives to letting my children express feelings?"* One way or another emotions make their presence felt.

The fear that feelings get worse when they're expressed has some validity unless you take the long-range view. It is comparable to lancing a boil. When the doctor cuts the top layer of skin, the festered material and oozing blood makes the area look worse. But the festered material must come out and underneath lies healthy, pink tissue.

So it is with negative feelings. When first released they may seem worse. As original feelings are accepted, stronger, more intense ones may come forth and this can convince you that you should have left well enough alone. But it is only by getting emotions expressed and accepted that you prevent their doing damage. Only by airing them do you truly get rid of them.

In draining negative emotions, be only an active listener. *Avoid the temptation to probe for the what's and the why's.* See yourself as a "feeling releaser" rather than a "fact finder" or "judger of evidence."

Caution: If, when more intense feelings come, you clobber the child with judgment, the doors to communication are slammed shut. Guard against limited acceptance. You must be prepared to accept the wild as well as the mild.

Most children quickly discover how strongly they dare express themselves. But if you only accept casual feelings, your children are left to handle their intense emotions alone. The result is low self-esteem (they know what's hidden inside), self-alienation (they deny such feelings even to themselves), or disguised release.

Another reservation many of us have about letting children express negative feelings is that they will try to put them into action. Young children may try to do just that. Say to a three-year-old, "You really want to hit your brother," and he'll agree wholeheartedly and proceed to smash his brother's head. Because their controls are limited, it is necessary to set limits on behavior *before* responding to feelings. Then, offer an acceptable outlet quickly.

Teaching children that they can behave irresponsibly does not prepare them to live peacefully in society. Part of maturity is controlling hurtful behavior. Part of teaching children to deal constructively with feelings is insisting that feelings may be acted out *only* in ways that do not hurt themselves, others, or valuable property.

Benefits of releasing feelings

Accepting negative feelings provides emotional relief, avoids repression, and teaches a child that he is no less worthy because of his feelings. He can remain in touch with himself as he truly is and be accepting of the humanness of others.

Releasing feelings helps youngsters see their problems more realistically rather than through the haze of heated emotion. Sixteen-year-old Peggy, for example, storms against her teacher.

Her mother reflects empathically, "You just feel she's impossible!"

"Absolutely. She dishes out all this hard work and never seems to think that we have anything else to do except what she assigns. Doesn't. she know I have five other teachers who also hand out stiff assignments? Stupid woman!"

"Her lack of consideration for your full load *really* gets you," responds her mother.

"Yeah," replies Peggy. "Of course, I guess she isn't the only one who loads us up, but somehow I don't mind it when the others pile it on."

"There's something about Miss Y. that makes it harder to take."

"That's right," says Peggy. She thinks quietly a while and then adds thoughtfully, "You know, I think the reason I don't like her is that she's dishing out math and I hate math. When the other teachers hand out big assignments, it's work I can do without such a struggle, but with math—well, I don't get what we're doing and it's like going up a brick wall—a fight for every inch."

"It's not Miss Y. so much as the math. That's just plain tough!"

"Yeah, you know, Mom, maybe I need some tutoring cuz I'm getting farther and farther behind. It isn't so much that Miss Y. is mean as that I feel mean toward that stupid math!"

Airing her feelings and having them understood helped Peggy define the real problem; then she could work out her own solution, which added to her sense of competence.

The child who is inwardly loaded explodes at the least provocation, sees small hurdles as giant obstacles, and loses his sense of perspective. A child does not get along with others when he is doing constant battle with himself.

All the benefits are on the side of empathic understanding and releasing negative feelings through acceptable outlets. This approach is reflected in physical and emotional health, as well as in intellectual and social competence. It helps a child say, "I have many feelings of all kinds but I'm valued even so. My parents will help me work my feelings through; they won't desert me to flounder alone."

Sending your feelings

To nurture, is a parent only to listen and reflect? Can he never respond from his point of view?

Communication is a two-way street. Both parent and child

may need to send. But the secret lies in the sequence. If listening doesn't settle the issue, the parent needs to talk. But sending your message when a child is upset is like trying to put up wallpaper in a room full of steam. The paper won't stick. Not until you get rid of the steam does the paper adhere. So it is with feelings. Your children can't hear you when they are churning with emotion.

Too frequently when we see a child full of feeling, we rush in with our messages and our words fall on deaf ears. There are times when it is highly appropriate to teach, persuade, use logic, or share reactions (not judgments!), and even to reassure. But the secret lies in the *timing*. The rule is: *Get feelings out first.*

A little device you may find helpful is to remind yourself that you will see this child tomorrow. Try withholding your messages today: simply listen actively. Send tomorrow; they'll be more likely to stick. If that seems too long, then, practice holding back for thirty minutes at least.

As you remember from Chapter Nine, your feelings sent as "I-reactions" rather than "you-judgments" make it more likely that your child will hear you rather than becoming defensive or tuning you out.

Any ideas you share (after the child's feelings are released) are more likely to sink in if they're offered with genuine respect. Mr. P. says, "Son, have you thought about the possibility of . . . ," or "My experience has been . . ." Such an approach is less likely to rouse resistance or antagonize than if he says, "Well, if you wouldn't do such and such, you wouldn't be in this pickle," or "The thing for you to do is . . . ," or "Well, it's obvious that you'd better . . ."

When the problem is one the child owns, all you can do (after having listened thoroughly) is help him think through various alternatives, offer possibilities, or share experiences that you have found helpful in the past. In the last analysis, the youngster is the one who has to carry out the solutions.

The more you help him generate his own ideas, the more you foster independence and self-respect. Swamping youngsters with jewels of wisdom only makes them resist looking at the open doors you may suggest.

(If the upsetting situation involves you, use the democratic approach to handle the conflict.) (See Chapter Twenty-three.)

Common pitfalls

In dealing with feelings you must be alert to certain common dangers. One is the temptation to jump on a youngster for feelings he has revealed earlier.

Margaret's mother listened to her daughter's jealousy toward her sister with real understanding one morning. Two days later, she was furious because Margaret repeatedly forgot to do her chores. She blurted out, "You don't do your chores and you have the nerve to feel jealous of your sister who at least never forgets hers!" When feelings revealed become weapons in the hands of parents, no child will talk.

A common response to the need for listening to feelings is "It takes too much time." Actually, it may take only a few minutes as we saw in the case of Billy, who drew out his reactions for his kindergarten teacher.

Sometimes, however, it does take time. Said Mrs. E., "Last week I listened for a solid hour while Gloria poured out feelings. The next afternoon I listened again and she drew a lot on paper. It wasn't until the third day of talking and drawing that her inner pressures were gone."

If the time spent in empathic listening seems excessive, consider the hours you spend dealing with negative behavior. As Mrs. V. put it, "I feel as if I'm swatting flies all day long. I say, 'Stop that,' and the kids stop doing that particular thing only to start something else just as annoying five minutes later. They stop pinching and start slugging. Some days I ride herd all day long!"

Mrs. V. operated at the "fly-swatting level" because she continually dealt with the negative acts; she never touched the negative feelings.

A basic rule about human behavior is that negative feelings exist before negative acts.

If Sally ran a temperature of 104°, and her mother merely put an icebag on her head, we'd be tempted to say, "Look, lady, don't you know you're only treating the symptom? If you hope to cure the fever, you have to get at its *cause!*" Yet, because so many of us are unaware that *negative emotions* are the "germs" that *lead to negative acts,* we follow the "icebag" approach.

We focus on the act and ignore the feelings causing the act.

Think about yourself. You aren't curt unless you first have an unhappy feeling inside. You don't spank or scold or explode until certain pressures build up within.

Children operate by precisely the same principle. They pinch or hit, weep or worry, hurt or sass after they experience particular feelings. Logically, then, to eliminate undesirable behavior, deal first with feelings. Icebags are not good enough for handling negative behavior. (Discipline is discussed in Part V, but, once you're familiar with this basic principle, you can see that much misbehavior is prevented by getting inner pressures relieved before they are converted into unacceptable behavior.)

A final pitfall is that knowing all about active listening and channeling feelings does no good unless you *use* the skills. *Intentions are no substitute for daily practice.*

Make-up work

What can you do if, as you try to understand your child, you inadvertently revert to a "feeling stopper?" Be honest. Tell him you're learning a new skill or that certain feelings are difficult for you to handle because you were taught they were unacceptable. (This puts the responsibility where it belongs—on your past training—rather than on him.) Enlist his help. You might even make a family game of "Sleuthing for Stoppers." Get everyone involved in detecting those alienators: judgments, denials, ill-timed reasoning, cheering, and advice. You may be surprised how quickly the communication gap narrows. Children are usually eager to help you learn. Everyone stands to benefit as understanding increases.

Even if you miss your child's messages on numerous occasions, your refusal to give up tells him you *care enough to continue trying.*

Youngsters—particularly older ones—may be reluctant to respond to this approach at first. Said Ken, "When my dad started this new way of talking, I wondered what gimmick he had up his sleeve. Figured it was the same old book with a new cover—a little understanding and then, smash, back to the old harangues. I didn't think the old man could change. Now, he seems, sometimes at least, to understand how I feel. And he's quit giving me all this advice I can't use. I'm beginning to think he cares. Funny, I used to think he didn't."

If your youngster has spent twelve or sixteen years being told his feelings are irrelevant and immaterial, he will need time to adjust to your change. You may have to earn his confidence in your sincerity.

Let your youngsters *know* you have a new goal as far as feelings are concerned. It's part of fair play. Then they aren't left wondering, "Why the sudden switch?"

There is a lot to know about negative feelings but handling them constructively avoids so much trouble that it is worth putting your knowledge into practice.

Two particular emotions—anger and jealousy—offer so much difficulty to parents and children that they need to be considered separately. They are alike in that they both cover up other emotions. To deal with them effectively, you need to see them as the codes they are.

NINETEEN · CRACKING THE CODE OF ANGER

Anger comes first

At a sale with her four-year-old in tow, Mrs. N. suddenly finds her son missing. Frantically, she searches the crowds, a cold lump of fear welling up as she remembers the recent kidnaping in her town.

Then, she spies him sitting behind a counter, nonchalantly playing with some papers. Jerking him up, she slams her hand across his bottom, hissing, "You *bad boy!* You know you're supposed to stay right with me! Let *go* of my skirt again and I'll really paddle you good, do you hear?"

Mrs. N. is angry, but this feeling came second. Her first feeling was *fear.*

*   *   *   *

Mr. E. hurries to straighten the garage before visiting relatives arrive. As fast as he puts one thing away, his six-year-old drags out something else. Mr. E.'s frustration mounts at the sabotage. Suddenly he blurts, "Beat it, Bobby! I've had just about enough of you!"

This father's *frustration* turned to anger and with it he blasted his son.

* * * *

At a cocktail party, Mrs. F. sees her husband's attentiveness to a woman considerably younger and more attractive than she is. When he returns to her, she needles, "What's the matter, Romeo? Did Juliet knock you off her balcony?"

Threatened and *jealous*, Mrs. F. cloaked her primary reactions in sarcasm, and verbally slapped her husband.

* * * *

Mr. T. returns home exhausted. As he opens the door, his two sons greet him, loudly requesting allowance increases. "All you kids ever think of is money!" he snorts.

Fatigue was quickly translated into hostility.

* * * *

Ricky cuts up in front of company and his mother's embarrassment grows. Unable to take any more, she snaps, "Go to your room, young man, and stay there till you can act like a gentleman!"

"I will not, you old witch!" he retorts.

Embarrassment became anger, and *humiliation* turned into fury.

Repeatedly, we human beings convert primary feelings into anger. It matters not whether they are worry, guilt, disappointment, rejection, injustice, shock, uncertainty, or confusion. And we dump this second emotion onto those around us.

Rarely, does anger come first.

Anger is a code

Knowing that anger covers a prior emotion helps you deal with it more effectively both in yourself and your children. Seeing it as a code makes it less threatening. If you're unaware of this fact, you are apt to respond directly and only add fuel to the fire.

Bobby's mother says no to his request for another merry-go-round ride. Her reasoning that it is time to go home doesn't dim his wish. Frustrated and helpless to get what he wants, he shouts, "You're mean. I don't like you, you old bag!"

Name-calling is simply a form of hostility. It is less aggressive than hitting but it serves the same purpose. If Bobby's mother hears only his fury, she may become angry herself and give a slap or a lecture. On the other hand, if she senses his frustration (whether or not his wish is reasonable from her point of view), she's less likely to make the situation worse by adding her anger to his.

Breaking the code

"When my daughter called me a name the other night, I reflected her feeling by saying 'Carolyn, you're terribly upset with me,'" said Mrs. H.

"I sure am! How come I have to go to bed at eight and Jimmy gets to stay up till nine? He gets all the privileges around here—just because he's older. I can't help it that I got born too late!"

Invariably, *when we accept anger by active listening, children lead us to the underlying feeling*. The code is cracked and we get to the heart of the matter. Here Carolyn tells her mother that her hostility comes from feeling shortchanged.

"It feels awfully unfair not getting the same privileges, and kinda like there's no way to get ahead of him," reflected her mother.

"Yeah, it sure does," said Carolyn.

"And it makes you mad that Daddy and I allow this kind of thing," added Mrs. H.

"You can say that again. It's all because of you that I got born second anyway. 'Course, I guess if you have more than one kid, someone has to be second, but I don't like being the youngest."

"There are just too many disadvantages to being youngest."

"Right!" said Carolyn more quietly. "Of course, sometimes I like it cuz I don't have to do as many chores as Jimmy does."

"Sometimes you see advantages to being second," responded her mother.

"Yeah, guess I like all the advantages and none of the disadvantages," said Carolyn smiling gently.

By having her feelings put into words and accepted, the steam around them was released, and the cause of the name-calling came to the surface. Not having to defend her position allowed Carolyn to realize that her position in the family *did* have some advantages. In addition, empathy made Carolyn feel no less worthy because of her perfectly normal wish.

Anger is normal

Most of us are taught that anger is "bad" and should not exist. In turn, we teach children that it is unacceptable. And then, they feel less worthy because at times they are angry.

Anger is another fact of life—one of the many emotions human beings are heir to.

The most difficult hostility to accept is that directed toward ourselves. We understand irritations toward friends, brothers and sisters, situations, and perhaps even teachers, but somehow we believe *we* should be exempt.

Yet, parenthood means frustrating children on many occasions. From our point of view our various restrictions make sense. But to the child our limits may not. If we only see "our part of the elephant" then their anger seems unjustified. It's a matter of whose viewpoint you take. You don't have to change your position on a stand you take, but can you *understand* your child's point of view along with your own?

An example of how small children see parents was illustrated by a gifted group of four-year-olds. Their favorite topic for discussion was "How to Get Along with Mothers"! Children have so much reason to feel angry toward us on so many occasions that if they never show it, they are probably hiding the feeling. From a child's point of view, we *are* hard to live with at times—even the best of us.

The child who openly expresses hostility to you actually hands you a double bouquet. You have reared him with enough strength to stand up for himself; he's no wilted violet. And you have made him feel safe to express himself directly.

So, if your child says, "I don't like you," "You're mean," or "I wish I had someone else for a mother (father)," pat yourself on the back and stay with his feeling. He'll take you behind the code and then you can deal with the real issues—the primary emotions.

Causes of anger

All negative feelings can turn to anger, but at each stage of life there are particular situations that cause it more than others.

For the infant, hostility is related to unmet physical and emotional needs. The pain of an empty stomach, the irritation of a soiled diaper, or the need for cuddling make him cry out for help. If his needs are met fairly rapidly, he doesn't cope with overwhelming amounts of frustration. When infant frustrations are kept to a minimum, the number of angry times is obviously reduced. He doesn't spend large portions of his day feeling deprived.

The preschooler's search for power, mastery, and independence cause head-on collisions with those around him and with his environment. Life for him holds thousands of frustrations.

Since young children need large muscle activity, physical restraints represent real frustration. When Bertha was small, her mother's form of punishment was to sit her on a chair for half an hour. With her body crying out for vigorous exercise, Bertha got up loaded with frustration. Her mother considered her extremely willful. "She'll get off that chair and immediately do something she knows very well she's not supposed to." Little did her mother realize that her form of punishment only recharged Bertha's "emotional battery" with large doses of hostility. No wonder, she hopped up determined to get even.

To reduce times of anger, eliminate as many frustrations as possible when your children make major psychological adjustments because of their stage of growth or outside circumstances. Engineer an environment that suits their needs to reduce conflicts. Avoid isolating an angry child, unless he prefers to be alone. Being sent to his room smacks of rejection, which only compounds negative feelings. The goal is to reduce emotional burdens, not increase them.

This does not mean that frustration in and of itself is bad for children. The secret lies in *how much* frustration a child runs into *at what stage* and *how often* it is part of his life. The right amount at the right time increases tolerance for frustration and enhances his competence to deal with it. The infant, for instance, is less capable of handling delays in feeding than the one-year-old; the two's psychological pressures make him less competent to deal with frustration than the three. The child living with excessive frustration at every turn is sensitized to being thwarted. He needs only a tiny scratch to make a loud roar.

At all ages, hostility is spawned by unrealistic standards, destructive discipline, threatening encounters, excessive competition, and continual comparison with others.

You cannot eliminate all anger-provoking situations, but try to reduce their number. There will be enough times when children are angry. Then, your job is to help them express anger directly. You do just this when you give empathic understanding by active listening, accept the emotion, and channel anger into safe outlets.

Handling anger in yourself

The first step toward working effectively with hostility is to accept this feeling in yourself. Shaming yourself or denying your animosities makes it almost impossible to deal with your child's angers. His aggressive impulses trigger off your own forbidden reservoirs.

The second step when anger comes is to see it for what it is: a code signaling the presence of an earlier emotion. The next time you're angry, look for the underlying emotion. Catch hold of the *first* feeling and share *it* rather than the code. Then, you deal with the cause of your anger. It is hard to find solutions for disguised emotions. This habit makes you a positive model for your children. In addition, sharing primary feelings does less damage to self-esteem than do hot verbal assaults. Anger frightens children; sharing primary emotions reduces their times of fear.

When you share those first feelings, send "I-reactions" rather than "you-judgments." (See Chapter Nine.) Invariably, expressions of anger are series of "you-judgments," which destroy self-respect. Check yourself on this point. Write out some of your typical angry tirades and see how frequently they fall into this category. One caution: saying, "I'm mad," is not an "I-reaction" because it does not reveal your *underlying* feeling. Venting only disguises what's really going on inside of you.

In many personal encounter groups the attacker gets Brownie points for being honest. (While such venting may relieve him, it can leave his victim reeling or even more defensive.) When you know that anger is the steam rising off other troubled feelings, then total honesty means communicating your first emotion.

Signs of anger

Young children usually let you know directly when they're angry. The preschooler bites, hits, shoves, screams, spits, or pinches and there's no question he's mad. When he's upset, he may even have a tantrum.

How you see tantrums affects whether you work constructively with them. They are nothing more than intense communications shrieking, "I've lost all control! I'm extremely frustrated!" (Some youngsters, of course, use tantrums as a *form of control*; they've learned that kicking and screaming bring them what they want. If that's the case in your house, there's only one way to remedy the situation: stick to your guns, buy yourself earplugs if necessary, and keep him out of public situations where he may try his most vigorous shindigs in an effort to bend you to his will. Once he learns you will no longer play that game, he'll be most likely to give it up. But be prepared for him to give you his all until he's thoroughly convinced you've changed your tactics.) If you haven't taught your child that you're putty in his hands when he throws his weight around, then the tantrum signals inability to cope.

Paul's parents are unaware that tantrums disguise lost controls. They see "bratty" behavior; consequently, they spank. What are the results of this treatment?

Put yourself in Paul's shoes for a moment. First, he is totally and completely frustrated by some situation he cannot handle. (At four his controls are poorly developed anyway.) At the precise moment when he is overloaded with emotions he can't get on top of, he receives a resounding slap. Now he has a whole new set of feelings to deal with: *hurt* from the slap; *frustration* at not being understood; *resentment* that his folks don't help; *helplessness* to retaliate directly; and *fear* of further punishment. The result: more negative feelings than ever.

"But," counters his father, "when I slap, he stops the tantrum—and right away!" Sure, the *symptom* stops, but why? It stops out of fear. On the surface, the slap looks effective. But what happens to all the feelings that caused the tantrum? And what does Paul do with all the new feelings generated by the slap? He may repress them, but eventually they come out in any of the countless ways that hidden feelings make their presence known. Paul gets a lesson called "Better to Repress than Express."

If there is any doubt in your mind about the wisdom of slapping for tantrums, ask yourself how you would feel if, when you were absolutely beside yourself, the most important person in your life hit you. You know how you'd feel; children have the same reaction. (Some parents allow themselves the privilege of tantrums and hitting, but they wouldn't dream of permitting their children such license.)

When you see the true tantrum for what it is—the communication of extreme frustration—it is obvious that physical aggression from us is the least helpful approach. At such a moment the child needs constructive assistance—active listening and directing his feelings into safe outlets. Remember, when you close the door to the direct expression of anger—via acceptable outlets—you literally insist on repression with all its disadvantages.

Indirect signs of anger

Consistent teasing, tattling, and sarcasm are indirect outlets for pent-up animosity. In most homes they are safer than direct expression. The child has the perfect alibi, "Oh, I didn't mean anything by it."

When children fear to express anger directly, they find substitute targets. Brian's anger toward his mother was released through impudence toward his teacher. Gerald hoarded his hostilities toward his brother, unleashing at boys in the neighborhood. Gretchen let hers out by cruelty to animals. Bill handled his aggression toward his parents by striking at their values. They valued promptness, so he specialized in procrastination; they preached courtesy, he cultivated rudeness; they wanted a weekly letter while he was in college, he couldn't write. Still others find release by joining "hate" groups.

Many youngsters turn their hostility against themselves with asthma, vomiting, continual accidents, and exaggerated fears. The overly "good" and the extremely shy child often mask strong aggression that they have learned is unacceptable. The shy child steers clear of involvement with others so that his secret won't leak out.

The child who is taught that hostility brings disapproval becomes frightened of his own aggressive impulses. Youngsters under six believe that aggressive wishes—that the baby would disappear, for example—will become facts. They may then be overly sweet to deny their wish to themselves and others. The difference between reality and fantasy is hazy to the small child. Even when he doesn't put his aggressive wishes into acts, he believes he is "bad." *You have to actively teach the difference between hostile feelings and hostile acts.*

Depression is another indirect sign of anger. It results from strong, unexpressed anger toward some person or situation, guilt over that anger, and repression. This process occurs subconsciously and the person is only aware of feeling "blue." *Sad so often covers up mad.*

If your youngster uses indirect routes to express hostility, it suggests he feels unsafe to reveal it directly. Then it is up to you to help him find socially acceptable outlets for direct expression.

Working constructively with your child's anger helps him accept *all parts of himself* without negative judgment. And that's the basis of self-respect.

TWENTY · LIFTING THE MASK OF JEALOUSY

The "common cold"

Trying to eliminate all jealousy is like trying to prevent a child's ever catching the common cold. It cannot be done. Jealousy is part and parcel of life.

All of us have felt its pangs and we know it leads to feelings and behavior that cause distress. Our personal experience and our culture's failure to accept negative feelings in general result in our teaching children that jealousy is wrong. They, however, go right on having the feeling despite our best sermons, even though they may feel guilty and less worthy in the process. Far too often we fail to see jealousy as the mask it really is.

What jealousy says

What must another person have to make you jealous of him? More skill, attractiveness, or self-confidence? More recognition, status, or money? Actually, it is immaterial what produces this feeling; the point is that

jealousy comes with feeling disadvantaged.

When you feel securely on top of the heap in areas important to you, jealousy doesn't exist. This emotion masks the conviction that you're unlucky. It is a distress signal crying out, "I feel threatened, cheated, insecure, or left out." It may say, "I'm afraid to share you for fear of not getting you back," or even, "I don't like myself."

Intense and widespread or mild and spotty, it means you feel too far down the ladder for comfort. *Whether the disadvantage is real or imagined makes no difference.* Jealousy is real for the person who feels it.

Why children feel jealous

The very nature of family life has built-in disadvantages for brothers and sisters. Every child wants the exclusive love and attention of each parent; he wants to be *best loved.* This wish makes jealousy in families inevitable.

You have only to imagine living in a society that allows polygamy to appreciate the predicament children are in. In such cultures, rivalries among the wives present quite a problem. All kinds of jockeying goes on for the favored position. Pretend you are a woman living in this society. Wouldn't you want the number-one spot or at least intermittent reassurance that you were still high in your husband's affections? Wouldn't you look for opportunities to needle your rivals and get them in trouble? In all likelihood, you would prefer to get rid of these thorns in your life.

Children are in precisely this position. Bobby watches his mother spend long hours with the demands of the new baby, and his jealousy begins to gnaw. Curly-haired Jane sees her mother putting up her straight-haired sister's hair each night and wishes she had an excuse for the same attention. Sally notices her sister whiz through her homework while she struggles every inch of the way.

Every child lives in the shadow of other children in the family to some degree and feels disadvantaged at some point. Even the only child isn't spared this feeling. He's jealous of children outside the family, perhaps wishing he had brothers and sisters. He may be envious of his parents' attention toward one another.

Jealousy is so normal that when brothers and sisters are always thoughtful and considerate of each other, they may not feel safe to reveal their true feelings. On the other hand, if jealousy is the major theme of a child's life, he's in distress. Either situation—a total lack of jealousy or continual signs of it—means he needs help.

The goal is not to eliminate its presence totally, but to reduce situations that cause it and to work *with* the feeling when it appears.

Advantages of rivalries

It may seem that rivalries among children have no benefits. Yet, brothers and sisters help a youngster face one of life's realities: he cannot have exclusive attention or all the advantages. This is a hard lesson, especially for the young child. He has to learn that love is not like a pie; shared love does not have to mean *less* love.

Brothers and sisters help a child learn to give and take within the family circle. They provide invaluable experiences in sharing and compromise—lessons that the only child has to learn largely outside the family. If rivalries are constructively handled, children learn that the strengths of others do not subtract from their own value as persons.

Normal family rivalries lessen childish egocentricity and develop inner strengths and resources. Uncomfortable as they may be, they provide experience in getting along with others.

Reducing jealousy

As with anger, it is wise to reduce the number of times children feel disadvantaged. First and foremost, by helping a child to high self-esteem, you lessen his conviction that he is unfortunate. Confidence in himself acts as a bulwark against his feeling like low man on the totem pole. The child convinced of his own value is less threatened by the assets of others. He can afford to share his parents' affection because he knows he has a solid place in their hearts.

The child who feels inadequate and unworthy is a sitting duck for jealousy much of the time. With no faith in himself, he feels shortchanged at every turn. He has to grab what he can and look for opportunities to whittle others down. He cannot afford to share time and attention.

Every child gets along best with others—even his own brothers and sisters—when he likes and gets along with himself.

The child with self-respect is less frequently jealous.

He may experience brief flashes, but his positive experiences and belief in himself make them short-lived.

Work with each child to develop his special interests and talents. Treat each one as a separate individual. Holding one accountable for the misbehavior of the other only stirs up intense feelings. Said Sid, "When my brother crumpled the car fender, Dad took the keys away from both of us. I wasn't even with Skip when he wrecked the car. It's like Dad figures if Skip ruined it, I will too. It's that way all the time; he treats us like we're not different people or something."

Safe encounters are antidotes for jealousy. Brian is unhappy about not being chosen baseball captain, but his disappointment is eased when his father plans special times alone with him. Harry feels unlucky that he isn't as tall or strong as his brother, but he senses his parents cherish him regardless of his size and strength.

Rarely do we truly feel the same toward each child all the time, nor do we always treat each one equally. If, however, one child is repeatedly favored, the stage is set for deep feelings of resentment in the less-favored ones.

If you consistently prefer one child, look inside to discover the cause of this favoritism. Does the less-favored one have traits you dislike? (Remember: the trait you least like in a child is often the same trait in yourself that you reject.) Coming to terms with this quality in yourself—and working it through—helps you become more accepting of your child.

As we have seen, a parent may choose one child as an outlet for his own unmet needs and push him unduly. Such treatment leads to intense jealousy toward brothers and sisters who aren't pressured as he is.

When jealousy exists, look at your family situation and check whether you actually give one child more advantages than the others. It is tempting, for example, to make an older daughter an assistant mother. Yet, if you don't compensate for this, she can develop strong resentment toward younger brothers and sisters because of their carefree position in the family. Anna was made responsible for her younger brothers' and sisters' behavior. When they cut up, she got it in the neck. She felt decidedly disadvantaged.

Uneven treatment based on age ("When you're ten you can stay up as late as Bill.") is easier for a child to take than uneven treatment based on sex ("Girls shouldn't roughhouse; it's unladylike."). At least when treatment is unfair because of age, a child knows he has a chance in the future. But when treatment is unfair because of sex, a child is trapped. He may then resent and reject his own sex.

The surest route to breeding jealousy is to compare. Since jealousy comes from feeling "less than" another, *comparisons only fan the fires.*

"I can't see why you don't practice like your sister does. I *never* have to remind her."

"Ken doesn't throw his money around like you do. Because he's saved his allowance he has his own car. But you don't have a thing to show for your money!"

Remarks like these—common fare in thousands of homes— are a deadly poison. They guarantee jealousy, resentment, and inadequacy. They pound home to a youngster that he is less than some other child. To understand, imagine how you'd feel if your boss said, "Why don't you get your reports in on time like John does; he never misses a deadline." Even though you mend your ways, you don't like having someone else held up as a model. If you've had a remark like this thrown at you, you are probably delighted when John comes up short. You may even look for the chance to put him in a bad light with the boss.

Even if you never use such words of comparison with your children, *thinking* in these terms gets communicated non-verbally. Because comparisons are rampant in our culture, you need to remind yourself constantly, "Each child is unique; it is *irrelevant* to compare him to another."

Comparisons only undermine self-esteem, and foster feelings of inadequacy.

Most children make their own comparisons without our doing it; in fact, teaching children *not* to compare themselves with others represents quite a challenge.

To reduce rivalries, let a child know how you feel about his actions directly (with "I-reactions"). Avoid dragging in shining examples of other people's model behavior.

Building self-esteem, avoiding preferential and unfair treatment, refusing to use a child to feed your unmet hungers, and avoiding comparisons prevent unnecessary jealousies.

Family atmosphere influences jealousy

The climate that exists in any home affects how much rivalry exists.

George's family basically enjoyed one another. His parents respected and helped each other. A relaxed atmosphere where people were more important than things made for little family friction. As a group they shared many activities; yet, each felt free to become involved in separate activities; each felt comfortable about bringing in outsiders. George's family worked out their rules cooperatively to respect each person's needs. Naturally, George had a give-and-take attitude, he felt valued, and was seldom jealous of his brothers and sisters.

Pauline, by contrast, came from a highly regimented home where only the father's needs were given preference. She noticed that no matter how hard her mother tried, her father was never pleased. Her home was tainted by suspicion, driving ambition for perfection, material possessions, and status, and the children were actively encouraged to compete with each other. They lived with daily comparisons, little warmth, or humor. The children had to jostle and fight for the small scraps of affection that were dropped. The total family climate was such that no one enjoyed anyone.

It is small wonder that Pauline saw being a girl as a disadvantage or that jealousies ran high in her family. Feeling deeply inadequate, Pauline lived with the suspicion that everyone was more favored than she. She was ready to bicker and fight at the drop of a hat.

How you and I live with our husbands and wives, how responsibility is divided, and how needs are met affect family morale and jealousies. A relaxed, accepting, cooperative family atmosphere reduces the number of times children feel disadvantaged.

Times of flare-up

Certain periods in every child's life make jealousy more prevalent. Keeping this thought in mind, you can be ready to help.

Most of us know that a new baby almost always triggers off jealousy in older children. No matter how much they look forward to the new arrival, they are bound to feel somewhat displaced, especially after the novelty wears off or the baby becomes a personal inconvenience.

An increase in jealousy can be expected with each new developmental task because the child feels less sure of himself. Insecurity within makes him more sensitive to the advantages he thinks others may have, regardless of the facts.

Outer events can also cause insecurity and make jealousy more likely. Starting to school for the first time; adjusting to a new teacher; giving up friends who move away; moving to a new community; running into stiffer academic subjects; adjusting to a separation, death, or divorce in the family—any new pressure can trigger off flare-ups among children.

Jealousy is more heated between children of the same sex who are close in age. Tom and Dick, at four and five, both need close attachment to their mother. Their battles are far more intense than if Tom were four and Dick were fifteen.

When a youngster goes through inner or outer pressures that may threaten his adequacy, move in with empathic support.

Handling jealousy constructively

Even when you reduce situations that foster jealousy, it will still appear at various times. Your job is not to decide whether your youngster *should* have this feeling but rather to work with it as real for him.

Jealousy is particularly well waterproofed against reasoning and logic. As was discussed in Chapter Eighteen, the most constructive path toward reducing negative feelings of any kind is to encourage their expression—in words, drawing, painting, music, clay, dramatic play—while truly hearing and accepting those feelings—from the child's point of view. The jealous child hungers to be *understood empathically*.

Jealousy that seems illogical to us is particularly hard to accept. Yet, most of us know from our own experiences that *feelings are not always logical*. A youngster's belief that he is being left out or cheated may not square with the facts. But that is beside the point. The issue is that *he* feels unlucky at this time. And you must work with what he is experiencing at the moment; otherwise, he may conclude, "My parents don't understand."

Look at this typical jealous statement that bursts on the scene in most families from time to time:

"You do more for Teddy than you do for me!" pouts Gene.

"Oh, Gene, that's ridiculous!" says his father. "Don't I spend every Saturday afternoon with you at Little League? Didn't we buy you a bike for Christmas? And don't you go to Scout camp during the summer? Each session costs $64.00, and we don't spend that kind of money on Teddy yet. You actually get far more privileges than he does. Now cut out this jazz!"

Gene's father has bombarded his son with the fact that he has no logical *reason for his feelings*. How can his father accept an irrational feeling that doesn't fit reality? The point is that feelings may be irrational, but when you accept them as legitimate because they exist, a child defines the real issues and becomes more realistic in his reactions. Trying to argue jealousy out of existence only further convinces the child that he is unlucky.

How can Gene's father handle his son's feelings more constructively?

"You do more for Teddy than you do for me!" pouts Gene.

"Feels like you're coming out on the short end of the stick," responds his father, trying to get into his son's world.

"Yeah, every night you let him sit on your lap and you read

those stupid nursery stories to him," Gene smirks. (Because his first feeling has been accepted, Gene lets his father in on what's really bugging him.)

"You don't like his getting this treatment from me," reflects his father.

"Well, why should I? Just because he's little, he gets all this gushy attention, like he's a privileged character around here or something!"

(How tempting it would be at this point to remind Gene that he'd had the same when he was small, but such a message would cut off further communication. Reminding him of something he received five years ago doesn't touch his *present* feeling. Watch how further empathy brings the real issue to the surface.)

"It's hard to share me with Teddy," says his dad.

"Yeah, it is, Dad," says Gene softly. "I know you spend every Saturday afternoon with me at Little League, but that's only once a week. Teddy has you *every* night."

"You'd like my time a little more often, is that it?"

"Yeah. Maybe if one Saturday afternoon I rode over with Bob and his dad to Little League we could have about twenty minutes after Ted goes to bed each night for a game of checkers. It's not that I want to be read to like a baby, but I'd love a good game or two."

Empathy helped Gene's father get to the source of the trouble; it helped Gene move from the irrational statement that his father did more for him than his brother. Gene was able to consider his father's time limitations and together they could work out a solution that would feed his hunger for more frequent time with his father.

Here a mother helps her daughter express her jealousy in both words and actions:

"I hate Janet," wailed Bonnie one night. "Either she leaves or I do!"

"You just *can't* take any more of your sister," empathized her mother.

"No, I can't. She is so tough, I can never hit her hard enough to make her cry." (Bonnie moves from the code of anger, lifts the mask of jealousy to reveal feelings of frustration and inadequacy.)

"You'd like to be the strong one, so you could get even for a change."

"Would I! But there's no chance. She just always will be stronger than me."

"Feels like you could never even up the score."

"That's it, Mom," said Bonnie more quietly; "there is no way to get back at her, so I just want her gone."

"Feels like the only way out—just get rid of her," mirrored her mother.

"Yeah, only I know you won't do that." (Here Bonnie recognizes her wish is unrealistic. Her wish is normal for someone who feels she will always be the underdog, but without any logic given by her mother, Bonnie knows the facts. Her mother's empathic understanding makes it more likely that she can and will face reality.)

"No," replied her mother, "I can't get rid of her, but you can pretend this doll is Janet and do whatever you want to her." (Her mother recognized the limits on behavior but she offered Bonnie an acceptable channel for the intense feelings that needed expression.)

With that, Bonnie began to slam the doll against the floor, to jump on it, screaming, "You stupid, big, strong thing! Now you're not so strong; now see who the strong one is! You're the little, weak one and I will make you into jelly! Stupid, weak, jelly blob!" Angrily Bonnie pounded the doll, screaming over and over, *"you're the little one! Take that and that and that."*

While her mother continued to be with her daughter by putting her feelings into words, Bonnie vented her fury. Then, looking up, she said, "I'm tired. I'm going to sleep."

Not knowing whether all the feelings of being disadvantaged were drained, Bonnie's mother was prepared to have further sessions about her feelings. The next morning, however, Bonnie was full of good spirits, even offering to butter her sister's toast. The storm was past; the feelings had been worked through so that the affection Bonnie also felt could be expressed. There might be—and probably would be—other times when Bonnie would rebel at her older sister's strength but her mother can help her work through these feelings as they arise.

By providing empathic listening and a safe outlet, Bonnie's mother worked constructively with her daughter's feelings. She offered no solutions, reasons, condolences, or judgments. She merely stayed with her daughter and tried to understand how she experienced her world. Bonnie was not made to feel "bad" because of her jealousy and anger. Her negative feelings dissipated when they were expressed and accepted as real for her.

Many children are less endowed by nature than their brothers and sisters. It is only natural that they should have feelings about such disadvantages. Empathic understanding can help them accept the inevitable.

Many times one child in the family will get a special privilege by virtue of his age or a particular circumstance. Then you can lessen jealousy by giving the others a corresponding privilege; if not, help them accept their lot more readily by understanding how they feel.

Empathy says, "You are no less lovable and valuable because of your feelings. I will understand and try to help you work them through." The refusal to accept jealous feelings makes children feel guilty, less lovable, and unworthy. Lack of acceptance of feelings always works against self-esteem.

Signs of jealousy

A child is often not direct about revealing the feelings behind his jealousy. He doesn't say, "I'm afraid to share you," or "I'm feeling left out." In fact, he may not even be clearly aware of what the trouble is.

More often he talks in codes. He hits us with a resounding "you-judgments" (perhaps because he models his talk after ours!), by saying, "You don't love me," or "You always give Karla her way."

Then, because we don't recognize the code, we respond to the *literal* message of the words. We say, "Why, honey, of course, I love you," or "That's not true! I work overtime to be fair to both Karla and you." But because the underlying feeling hasn't been heard, our facts fail to impress; they don't touch his belief that he's out in left field.

Frequently, the only clue that a child feels unlucky is that he is unduly cross and seems to itch for a fight. Or he may start tearing another youngster down. We human beings operate on the "pulley system." Feeling down, we try to pull those around us down—particularly those who are too high for our comfort. It's as if we figure that by undercutting the other person, we elevate ourselves.

Another sign of jealousy may be a sudden increase in dependency. Martha, aged six, showed her true feelings toward her baby brother only by regressing to bed-wetting, thumb-sucking, and sudden clinging.

A subtle sign of jealousy may be an increase in demands for things. When a child suddenly begins to demand more and more material items, what he may need is not more toys but more time—focused-attention time.

Many children who feel shortchanged suddenly start misbehaving. Peter ups the television volume until it blasts the rafters every time his father helps his younger brother with homework. It is his childlike way of saying, "Gosh, I want attention, too!"

"Including Peter in the homework times—letting him have first chance to show his brother how to do a problem when he could—stopped his monkeyshines. He began to show real pride in his brother's progress," said his father, "and his whole attitude changed." (Of course, he felt he had an important contribution to make—*he* mattered! No reason for jealousy then.)

Directly or indirectly children try to tell us when they feel unlucky. Responding to their code directly is rarely helpful. Our major task is to be empathic. Each child must feel understood, included, and important. When a youngster is *sure* of this, he doesn't use devious devices to wipe out his disadvantage. He feels lucky and confident that he is *not* shortchanged.

PART V · DISCIPLINE AND SELF-ESTEEM

Discipline's meaning

Lectures on discipline bring parents out in droves. Small wonder. We live with its issues daily. Yet, in few other areas of child-rearing is there so much controversy and divergent advice. Reason, ignore, spank, deprive? When even experts disagree, what are we poor parents to do?

Much of the confusion comes from three major shifts in only three generations as to how parental authority is handled.

Before looking at the three basic approaches to discipline, we must get at this word's meaning. Here's an experiment. Let go of any thoughts you may have. Go blank. Ready? Now, catch hold of the first word that pops into your mind when you see this word:

DISCIPLINE.

Most people, confronted by the word, think of negative, repressive associations, such at "strict," "spank," "firm," "punish," "force," or "harsh." Did you? Is discipline only concerned with playing the heavy?

Webster's Third International Dictionary lists several definitions, including:

> "training or experience that corrects, molds, strengthens, or perfects . . .
> "PUNISHMENT: as a: chastisement self-inflicted as mortification or imposed as a penance or as a penalty . . .
> "control gained by enforcing obedience of order (as in a school or army) . . .
> "a rule or system of rules affecting conduct or action."[1]

Interestingly enough, "education" is listed as a synonym. Yet how many people think of "education" or "teach" when discipline is mentioned?

You probably hope that your particular discipline fits Webster's first meaning: "training that strengthens." Yet so many of us try to reach that goal by methods that fit his second or third meaning: punishment or control by force.

The word discipline stems from "disciple," a follower of a teacher. We do not think of a disciple following his teacher out of fear of punishment, but rather from inner conviction. As parents we prefer that our children follow rules because they believe in them, rather than because they fear reprisals. Anytime a child believes in a rule, it is easier for him to discipline himself. And,

the goal of discipline is self-discipline.

Rules that are embraced emotionally work toward self-regulation and high self-esteem. Herein lies the secret to constructive discipline. To see *how* you can work in this direction, let's look at each of the issues involved.

[1] By permission. From Webster's Third New International Dictionary © 1966 by G. & C. Merriam Co., Publishers of the Merriam-Webster Dictionaries.

Much fuzzy thinking about this topic is avoided when a sharp distinction is made between

1. discipline as a set of *limits* (rules); and
2. discipline as a *method* by which rules are made and enforced.

Confusion results when the word is used interchangeably for both limits and methods.

Four basic questions are tied to discipline and need to be considered separately:

1. Are limits necessary?
2. What kind and how many should be set?
3. Who should establish rules?
4. How can rules be enforced constructively?

Are limits necessary?

The very fact that human beings live in social groups means that *some* rules are needed. If every person—child and adult—paid attention only to his own personal needs and whims of the moment without regard for the interests or safety of others, society would not run smoothly.

The family is a social group. And it is vital that it have rules enabling each person to meet his needs without constantly running roughshod over those of others. Besides, the family's task is to introduce children to a society that does have regulations. It's our responsibility to help children become contributing members of society.

So, the question of whether there should be limits on behavior, particularly in our complex society, is an academic one. The fact remains that families, classrooms, and groups in general are more likely to meet the needs of all when guidelines for behavior exist.

The real issues of discipline center around the kinds and

number of rules, and how they are made and enforced. These factors leave a dramatic imprint on self-esteem.

Kinds and number of rules

No two families can have the same number and kinds of limits. And no hard and fast rule of thumb can be laid down. We can't say, "When a child is six, there should be X number of rules in Y areas." Some basic principles, however, can guide you in deciding whether the kinds of limits in your family work for or against high self-esteem.

That children have differing needs from those of adults is a major source of conflict between parents and children. Both sets of needs may be legitimate, but too often we think in terms of either-or. *Either* adult needs have priority *or* those of children do. Some of us, of course, play the game of seesaw, "This time I'll meet yours; next time, it's my turn." We may be unaware that both sets of needs can often be met. (For specifics, see Chapter Twenty-three.)

The kinds of rules that consider the needs of all are more likely to be constructive.

Regulations must make it legitimate to be a child while protecting adult rights. The constructive solution lies in redirecting childish urges rather than nailing the lid on them. This means knowing that children need to explore, climb, dig, tear, pound, paint, run, splash, holler, and to be with other children who do the same.

Engineer an environment that allows your child to meet his needs without damaging valuable property. The younger the child, the fewer times he should be asked to mind because his surroundings fit his requirements.

Some family limits are reasonable when considered individually but there are too many of them. Children should not run into fence posts every time they turn around; otherwise, they learn to think something is wrong with them.

How many and what kinds of rules you press for will be closely tied to your expectations, images, and personal needs. As mentioned in Chapter Six, tight clinging to rigid blueprints may pad your insecurities but only transfers them to children.

Fewer rules are needed when family members feel friendly toward each other; safe encounters actively encourage cooperation.

In thinking about the kinds of rules to establish, remember that children first have to come to terms with family limits, then with those of the school, and eventually with the expectations of society. If rules at home are too much at odds with school and society regulations, children have more severe adjustments to make.

Betty's family protected her from tasks she did not enjoy. Someone always took over her dirty work. At school, however, there was no one to do this. And certainly as an adult, she'll find that any job has unpleasant aspects that she will need to handle whether she likes to or not. Home training that allows a youngster to take the sweet without the sweat is poor preparation for later life.

Here in America we have a particular problem insofar as the kinds of limits we establish. In some cultures the majority of parents hold similar values and establish identical rules. In pre-war Japan, for example, parents and teachers had similar regulations for children. But America is a fast-moving society representing many cultures. Many of our values are in a state of flux. Children see one set of values upheld at home, different sets followed in friends' homes, and still different ones espoused in classrooms and in society at large. In short, we do not, as in the past, have uniform values to support home regulations. It is therefore especially important that your family rules be clear cut, fair to all concerned, and emotionally embraceable. (See Chapter Twenty-three.) And, of course, when children see adults stick to the rules, they are more apt to follow in imitation.

Limits, then, are needed to ensure peaceful family living.

The number and kind established must consider individual needs and stages of growth. The strongest determinant as to whether rules work for or against self-esteem lies in *how* they are made. There are three basic methods by which rules are established and *each approach directly affects the kinds of self-statements children make.* Understanding these methods (discussed in the next two chapters) gives you a guide for evaluating whether or not yours is a discipline that strengthens.

TWENTY-TWO · OLD WAYS OF DISCIPLINE

Parents have power

The very nature of parenthood gives us power over children. We are bigger, stronger, more experienced, older, and ordinarily more verbal. Legally we are responsible for their behavior, so society reinforces our position of authority. But the child's dependence on us for his physical and emotional needs gives us our greatest wedge over him. *The more dependent he is, the greater our power.*

How we use power determines our approach to discipline.

There are only three basic approaches to limit-setting: *power kept, power given away, and power shared.*[1] And the method you use influences who makes the rules in your family and how they are enforced.

[1] I am indebted to Thomas Gordon for this concept.

Most parents believe they have only two alternatives; either they establish the limits or they abdicate their authority and let children dominate. They are unaware that a third alternative exists. In this chapter we will examine the first two approaches and their effects on self-esteem. In Chapter Twenty-three, we'll consider the third method.

Your view of your role

How you see children and your role as a parent has considerable bearing on your approach to discipline. If you see youngsters as lumps of clay to be molded, if you have little faith in their capacity for cooperative self-direction, you are more likely to see your job as the boss who issues directives. You *keep your power* and use the authoritarian approach.

If you believe children are damaged any time their needs are frustrated, if you believe they can handle absolute freedom at any age, you're likely to *abdicate your power* and be an over-permissive parent. Seeing children's needs as important as yours and trusting their capacity for reasonable cooperation make you more inclined to *share power*. Then, you can afford to be democratic in your discipline.

An important factor that affects how you discipline is your personal response to having power. Mrs. M. was strongly dominated as a child and imitated her own parents without questioning this approach when her turn came. To her, strong-arm tactics were part of being a "good" mother. Mr. L. was also ruled with an iron hand, but his intense distaste for authority made him prefer to give power away. He wanted no part in even sharing it.

Many of us cannot share power because we need to make up for our own lack of self-worth. Controlling others gives us a sense of importance. And our youngsters seem legitimate prey. There is little doubt that sharing power comes easier for those who like themselves.

To properly evaluate your approach to discipline, give serious consideration to your view of children, your specific attitudes toward the role of parenthood, and your personal response to possessing power.

Now, let's look at the details of the first two methods of discipline and their effects on the growing child.

Authoritarian approach

The authoritarian approach to discipline has existed a long time. In the "good old days," a parent's word was law. Children were expected to carry out rules laid down by adults. It was an era of "spare the rod and spoil the child," and "children are to be seen and not heard." Gradually, this approach softened to consider feelings, individual differences, and developmental tasks. But, in the final analysis *authoritarian parents make the decisions*.

On the surface this approach looks great. We pull the strings and children jump. Of course, when they don't jump, we run into the problem of enforcement. At that point we have four alternatives:

1. *Give up*	(But this puts us in the over-permissive camp where we abdicate power.)
2. *Nag*	(This may or may not work. In either event, nagging destroys friendly feelings between children and us and does absolutely nothing for our dispositions. Few of us enjoy prodding.)
3. *Enforce by punishment*	(We manipulate behavior by fear of consequences.)
4. *Enforce by rewards*	(We manipulate behavior by everything from praise to out-

and-out bribery. But sometimes we run out of rewards
or can't find appropriate ones.
And children soon discover
they have us over a barrel.)

Most parents dislike resorting to these measures, so when
children balk, they up their volume to pound home the rule.
But when this fails, the authoritarian parent is forced to use
rewards or one of the many variations of the rod.

Devices for control

What are some of our methods for control? And what effect
do they have? When children are young, spanking is a familiar
device to show who's boss. It seems effective because it usually
produces immediate results. Yet, we all know parents who say,
"I could spank Henry till he was black and blue and he
still wouldn't mind."

As was mentioned in Chapter Nineteen, every spanking
fills a child with negative feelings that may be translated into
further misbehavior. Whether the resulting anger is turned
outward or inward, the fact remains that children have feelings
about being spanked, and these feelings work against the best
interests of parent and child.

Spanking does not teach inner conviction. It teaches fear,
deviousness, lying, and aggression. No matter how we slice
it, spanking is a physical assault of a bigger person on a smaller
one. And yet we tell children they shouldn't hit someone
smaller or weaker.

We can all smile at the apparent contradiction of the mother
who slaps her child, saying, "I'll teach you not to hit!" Yet,
studies show that youngsters subjected to overt parental aggression are far more likely to be physically aggressive and
hostile in their relations with others.

Scolding is another device for control. It ladles out rejection, shame, and humiliation. Verbal assaults blast self-esteem. A sharp distinction must be made between scoldings—"you-judgments"—and honest sharing of your feelings toward behavior —"I-reactions." Reactions toward behavior are not classified as scolding; they are part of being open with children, as we saw in Chapter Nine.

As captive audiences to endless spiels, children may tune us out in self-defense. Lectures help us unload but they burden children or land on deaf ears.

When you feel the need to harangue, you're better off to express your feelings to another understanding adult first. Then send the child your "I-reactions" toward his behavior and get to the point *briefly*.

Some parents use withdrawal of love for control. This always hits at the core of self. "Mommy won't love you if you do that," or "Daddy doesn't like little boys who cry," tells the youngster that his personal value is strictly conditional. It is highly effective as a behavior manipulator because children *need* love, but its use carries a price tag that may have life-long consequences.

Some parents use denial of food to enforce rules. "All right, go to bed without any dinner!" Because the child associates food with love and approval, this method of control symbolizes the withdrawal of love.

Withholding privileges is another popular device for control. Every time Billy misbehaves, his parents take away his motor scooter. They use the one thing he loves to keep him in line. Even if it makes him mind, this builds resentment and emphasizes helplessness. It makes a child long to escape the clutches of those who pull their rank. And it can make him hunger for power.

Isolation is yet another way to enforce rules. It may be desirable to remove a child from a situation, but it is always preferable for an adult to stay with him while he works through his feelings. If behavior is deteriorating, the chances are the child needs a booster shot of confirmation, understanding, or recognition. Isolation asks a child to repress feelings or to work them out alone—a job he may not be up to.

In discussing children's reaction to punishment, Sears[2] has said, "Our evaluation of punishment is that it is ineffectual in the long term as a technique for eliminating the kind of behavior toward which it is directed." If parents and teachers fully considered this finding, they would look at authoritarianism with a far more critical eye. And as nurturing adults we must concern ourselves with the *long-range effects* of our methods of child management.

In an effort to avoid punishing, many authoritarian parents turn to rewards and praise. The purpose is the same: to get a child to follow adult-made rules. You just use honey instead of castor oil.

Almost any day in a grocery store you can hear a parent say, "Now, if you sit still in the cart, I'll get you a gum ball when I'm through shopping." Some say, "You'll get a dollar for every 'A.'" Another parent goes in for gold stars; still others use praise, "There's a good boy. Run and get my sewing basket."

Rewards, of course, have to be sufficient to motivate the child in the desired direction; they have to be given immediately following the act if learning is to occur, and they have to be doled out consistently. *Bribery and praise*, however, simply *dangle power in a child's face.* You're far better off to avoid them altogether. (See Chapter Nine for the difference between praise—"you-judgments"—and positive "I-reactions.")

There is no question that the authoritarian approach works —at least for the moment. As long as your child is sufficiently dependent, you can manipulate much of the time by dishing out rewards or threatening dire consequences. Over the years,

[2] R. Sears, E. Maccoby, and H. Levin. *Patterns of Child Rearing.* New York: Harper & Row, 1957, p. 484.

however, authoritarianism defeats us. In evaluating any approach to discipline you must consider

1. its long-range effects;
2. whether it works toward responsible self-discipline based on inner conviction; and
3. its effect on self-esteem.

Let's look at authoritarianism with respect to these issues.

Effects of authoritarianism

Behavior controlled by outside authority usually lasts as long as the authority figure is present. We've all seen children from authoritarian homes run wild as soon as they escape the watchful eye. Some children are convinced that they need to follow the autocrat's rules when his back is turned, but not all of them reach this conclusion. The authoritarian is never fully free to take a leave of absence.

Rules imposed from on high are not likely to be embraced emotionally—from sincere inner conviction.

A profound disadvantage is that *authoritarianism encourages dependency*. It says, "Listen to me; I'll tell you what to do." A child's confidence is then not in himself but in outside authority figures. It clearly teaches children to put their center of gravity in others. In addition, dependency creates hostility and surely none of us wants such a harvest.

If you are sufficiently highhanded, you can break a child's spirit. Authoritarianism is great training for children who will live under dictatorships, but far from adequate for children who will be expected to think independently.

The most damaging aspect of authoritarianism is its effect on self-esteem. It literally instructs youngsters not to trust their own capacity to reason or judge. It is daily proof of our lack of faith in their capacity to work with us on the limits that make for cooperative living.

The child convinced that father knows best is hardly full of *self*-confidence. Being treated as a second-class citizen unworthy of a voice in his own affairs eats at self-respect. The youngster living with authoritarian discipline can conclude, "My ideas aren't worth much; I need regulating by others far wiser than me." Such convictions work against emotional maturity, intellectual growth, and self-respect. (And as we'll see in Chapter Twenty-four, it discourages creativity.)

Because the autocrat focuses on overt behavior, he can produce children who conform outwardly but seethe within. Hostility, resentment, and guilt are a few of the feelings authoritarianism fosters. We've all read accounts of model children who suddenly cut loose in rebellion. Some youngsters don't seethe inwardly; the rebel openly right from the start. In the long run authoritarianism is risky business.

Does this mean that you must *never* make a decision without consulting your children? Aren't there some situations where you have to put your foot down?

Yes, indeed. There are times when you have to say no, and flatly. Some of a child's ideas and behavior will be unacceptable to you. If your preschooler wants to play with a friend who has the measles, you have to say no unless you want him exposed. You may suggest a phone call or a visit through the window. But if he insists on playing directly with him, you are justified in retaining your power.

Whenever health, safety, or the law are concerned, you have to stand firm. Far more often than we realize, however, we can find acceptable solutions for his urges while remaining true to our convictions and responsibilities.

No matter how justified you may be, your child will probably have feelings about your retaining your power. Your best recourse then is to listen empathically to his disappointment, frustration, or irritation toward your limits. (Keep in mind that he has the right to these reactions even when they differ from yours.)

Resorting to authoritarian control *once in a while* doesn't damage irreparably. It is when power is *predominately* retained that an unhealthy climate exists.

Over-permissive approach

As evidence accumulated about the damaging effects of authoritarianism on mental health and emotional adjustment, experts in child guidance began advocating an entirely different method of discipline. The pendulum swung to the opposite extreme and parents were advised to set no limits on children's behavior. They were told that frustrating children was liable to make them candidates for the psychiatric couch. "Enlightened" parents switched gears and abdicated power. Fear of repression ushered in the day of child rule. There was no problem of enforcement because the child did whatever he wanted. (Of course, this left many parents feeling that they needed the psychiatrist's couch themselves!)

Over-permissiveness was not the cure-all it was supposed to be. In fact, the results were disastrous. These children were *more disturbed* than those reared under authoritarianism. Children from such homes were self-centered and demanding. They failed to consider the rights of others. Their social relationships ran afoul, and they had trouble adjusting to the limits of classrooms and society in general. They expected others to cater to their whims just as their parents had, and they were invariably disappointed. Abdication of power does not encourage responsibility and self-discipline.

Probably the single greatest disadvantage to over-permissiveness is that it eventually leads to *rejection*. Few parents can genuinely accept all the behavior of a child; even if they can, others cannot.

When George's behavior got on the nerves of his over-permissive parents, they told themselves that eventually he'd shape up and meantime their needs weren't as important as his. They took pride in their forward-thinking selflessness, suffered in silence, and chanted, "George needs to express himself." And

George proceeded to "act out" whenever he pleased. Their words said, "Just as you like, darling," but their body language moaned, "You're impossible and obnoxious!" George's self-respect went down the drain. He'd been told, "Anything goes," but he learned such wasn't the case.

The child from an over-permissive home invariably sees his parents as weak. Walking all over their needs can create anxiety and guilt. Unlicensed freedom is overwhelming and makes a child feel lost. Even more important, it smacks of disinterest and desertion.

Many a child from such a home says, "My parents should make me mind." On the surface, this sounds like a plea for authoritarian control. *But it is actually a cry for concerned involvement.* Morris Rosenberg's study[3] of 5000 high school students underscored the fact that the youngster who sees his parents as indifferent is less likely to have high self-esteem. As Carole put it, "My folks let me do whatever I wanted. It made me feel that I wasn't worth caring about."

As with the authoritarian approach to discipline, there will be times when you want to follow a hands-off policy and give children the full power to make their own decisions.

Lena comes to her mother undecided as to whether to ask Joel or Hank to the Leap Year Dance. Her mother listens empathically but she feels that the final decision should rest with her daughter. Greg is undecided about whether to take chemistry or biology next semester. His dad listens carefully to his pro's and con's and tosses out a few personal reactions, but he leaves the decision to Greg.

As long as a child's decisions don't interfere with health, safety, or the needs of others, you can comfortably back off. But a *consistent hands-off policy* invites all the disadvantages of over-permissiveness.

[3] Rosenberg, Morris. *Society and the Adolescent Self-Image.* New Jersey: Princeton University Press, 1965, p. 145.

Causes of over-permissiveness

Many parents, reacting against their own authoritarian up-bringing, refuse to become involved in establishing limits for children. Others are over-permissive because they unthinkingly repeat the pattern of their own parents. Still others, because of low self-esteem, believe they have no rights. Some fear involvement and the open sharing of feelings. They prefer withdrawal to confrontation.

Discipline that is too lenient or too harsh, too permissive or too authoritarian, does not strengthen. These extremes disturb the building of a healthy conscience, a responsible commitment to others. Neither approach—power kept or power given away—used *exclusively*—builds confidence and healthy self-discipline. Heavy use of either of these two approaches is destructive to a child's best interest. Children need strong parents who care enough to become actively involved, not dictators nor pale lumps of putty who smile wanly from a distance.

Still another danger lies in wait for the child who is reared in a home where the mother is extremely passive and overindulgent, never asking the youngster to take hold or assume any responsibilities. If this child has a highly authoritarian father or one who masks his true feelings (he is present physically but not psychologically), the foundations for a basic predisposition toward alcoholism in adulthood are laid.

Since the mother is Mrs. All-giving and Mrs. Nothing-you-don't-want-to-do-dear, the child is much more drawn to her. If this child is a boy, he may then tend to identify more with her and fail to establish a firm sense of masculine identity. If his identification with her is strong enough, he may develop homosexual interests. If not, at least he will be unable as an adult to stay married over the long haul to a woman who wants a husband rather than a son.

As an adult, such a boy will hunger for freedom from *emotional* responsibility and commitment, in addition to needing alcohol to shore up his basic feelings of inadequacy. Naturally, this dynamic is bound to influence how he handles his job, his marriage—in fact, all his human relationships. If as a parent, you are playing the overindulgent game, you are playing with fire—in terms of your child's future and the future of all those he comes in contact with.

Now, let's look at a more constructive approach to discipline.

TWENTY-THREE · CONSTRUCTIVE DISCIPLINE[1]

Democracy in discipline

Democracy is anchored in the belief that people deserve a voice in determining what happens to them. We adults appreciate living in a democracy, but we may overlook that children are equally as eager for a voice in the issues that touch their lives. Democracy in government has little meaning to a child unless he feels the daily benefits of it at home.

Few of us would willingly live under a dictatorship or in a state of anarchy, yet we may be guilty of establishing such conditions in our homes. This may sound rather harsh, but we must face the facts: too often we insist on democracy for ourselves but deny its benefits to our children.

We don't do this because we're mean, nasty, and self-centered. It happens because many of us were never accorded this privilege as we grew up. Or we have never had this discrepancy called to our attention. If we do think about it,

[1] I am indebted to Thomas Gordon for a number of the details in this chapter.

our first response is likely to be, "But children are too young and inexperienced to participate in decisions governing behavior."

Sometimes this is the case and we *do* have to make decisions for children, as was noted in the last chapter. But, too frequently, we make this assumption falsely. As more and more parents gain understanding about *how* to put democracy to work in the home, they are finding that children *can* handle its mechanics in many, many situations. The benefits to family living and the impact of this method of discipline on a child's development are worth examining because democracy strengthens self-esteem, self-reliance, intellectual growth, creativity, and responsibility.

"We use democracy in our home," said Mrs. A. "We hold weekly family councils and each person airs his grievances. My husband and I listen carefully and try to make rules that consider those gripes that are reasonable."

Does the existence of a family council ensure democracy in the home? *Definitely not.* Yet, countless parents mistakenly believe it does. The A.'s children live with *benign autocracy.* Their needs are aired and considered, but in the final analysis, *their parents draw up the rules.* This is not democracy.

Discipline is democratic when parents *share* power, when adults *and* children work together to establish rules that protect the rights of all. In democratic homes children have an equal part in working out limits. The family works as a unit to establish broad general policies while permitting flexibility within those limits. When conflicts arise, those individuals involved work them through together to everyone's mutual satisfaction. The democratic approach is founded on mutual respect, trust, and faith.

Many of us are democratic with infants. And, tiny as they are, even they sense when they're allowed a voice in their affairs. When a baby rebels at the taste of mashed meat, the mother may mix it with fruit to make it more palatable. Then, both her need that he have a balanced diet and his need for a pleasant flavor are satisfied. She finds a mutually satisfying solution. (Had she ignored his reaction and forced the meat down, she would have been authoritarian. Had she given up and subtracted meat from his diet, she would have been over-permissive.)

Frequently adults confuse democratic discipline with over-permissiveness. Sharing power, is a far cry from giving it away.

Democracy doesn't mean withdrawal; over-permissiveness does.

Democracy means mutual involvement.

Such an approach has nothing to do with a hands-off policy.

Prerequisites for establishing democracy

A combination of attitudes and skills is necessary to foster true democracy in the home. Unless certain basic attitudes exist on your part, its mechanics run aground. As you read, check your own outlook. (These attitudes are discussed earlier in relation to empathic listening, but it is important to see their relationship to democratic discipline as well.)

Democratic attitudes

Democracy works better when you see your child as neither an extension nor carbon copy of you. This means that you don't see yourself as owning your children—you see them as owning themselves and their feelings. You don't see them as objects to manipulate but rather as *persons distinct in their own right*.

Democracy is in fertile soil if you like people. Whenever we like others we *want* to treat them with respect. (Remember: how much you like others is related to how much you like your-self.) When a child feels valued and loved, he wants to coop-erate; he is more interested in negotiating conflicts. Warm, positive relationships already established make it easier to put the mechanics of democracy into practice.

This does not mean, however, that families whose "friendliness quotient" is low cannot move toward democratic discipline. It does mean that initial sessions may be stormy as pent-up resentments are released. It may be comforting to realize, however, that the democratic method is a potent remover of antagonisms.

Those of you who come to parenthood with a strong need for power will find that sharing authority cuts across this inner hunger as has been pointed out earlier. Most of us have grown up under the shadow of edicts handed down by parents, teachers, and employers. Once we get into a position of power it is only natural to want to call the shots.

You must, however, constantly keep the long-range view in mind. The underdog rarely admires, respects, or cherishes the dictator.

Seeing children as unique persons with the right to their own feelings, respecting your needs as well as theirs, liking youngsters, and wanting to share authority are the attitudes that help you get home democracy started.

Democratic skills

Democratic rule-making has a far greater chance of success if the rules established do not cut across developmental tasks. Much rule-breaking is eliminated when expectations and limits are grounded in the needs of selfhood. (See Part III.) The knowing parent pushes for limits that make it legitimate to be a child.

An additional aid in making democratic discipline work is skill in handling feelings. Parents who know that negative emotions lie behind negative acts are more apt to help children express feelings so that misbehavior and rule-breaking occur less frequently. Unless you remember that negative feelings can sabotage your best efforts to establish rules democratically, you may steer directly toward setting up rules, *forgetting* or *ignoring* feelings. Then, the method bogs down. Finally, sharing

"I-reactions" rather than "you-judgments" is essential to keep lines of communication and negotiation open.

Democratic attitudes, realistic expectations based on selfhood tasks, and skill in releasing and sharing feelings are major prerequisites for establishing democratic discipline.

The mechanics of democratic discipline[2]

The process for working out family rules jointly is similar to that being used increasingly in business and industry today. You first have to know what the problem is, what needs are involved, and work together for a solution to those needs that everyone can live with. Let's look at these steps more closely.

Stating the problem

Before working on a problem, you have to be clear about what it is and who owns it.

A messy kitchen, for example, may not bother the child. Most often it is one or both parents who own this problem; it is their need for order that is being crushed. On the other hand, one youngster may want order while another may not. Assuming the parents don't mind disorder, then the child who is bothered owns the problem. Any conflict may belong to only one person in the family or several. The ownership of the problem—whose needs are going unmet—should be clearly stated at the outset.

Even when you think a problem is clearly defined, you may discover that the problem presented is not the real one.

The G.'s had been democratic in handling family conflicts for some time. One day eight-year-old Gina asked for a conference. Here's how it went:

Mr. G: "Gina, we're all together now. What's on your mind?"

---

[2] In some communities Parent Effectiveness Training classes give specifics necessary for home democracy.

Gina: "It's Pat. Every night after we're in bed, she pounds her feet on the wall. It keeps me awake and I don't like it."

Pat: "Well, if it bothers you, I won't do it."

Gina: "You say that now, but you'll wait a few nights and then you'll start banging your feet again."

Pat: "No, I won't."

Gina: "Yes, you will. I know you."

Pat: "Well, if I do, you can—a-a-h, you can pick one of my toys, any one, and keep it forever."

Mrs. G: (Reflecting Pat's message) "You're willing to back up your promise with a guarantee, is that right, Pat?"

Pat: "Sure, because I already said I wouldn't bang on the wall any more."

Gina: "I don't trust you." (Angrily) "You say one thing but you do another!"

Mr. G.'s ears pricked up at Gina's tone. He heard anger and knew that agreements might be sabotaged unless it was released. "Gina, you're really mad at Pat," he said.

Gina: (Bursting into tears) "I sure am. Yesterday, I told Pat a big, important secret and she promised she wouldn't tell. And then she turned right around and told four different kids!"

Mrs. G.: "Boy, you sure don't like not being able to trust Pat!"

Gina: "No, I don't!"

Here is a classic illustration that the originally presented problem (wall-banging) was only superficial. The real issue was Gina's reaction toward betrayal. Had Mr. G. been insensitive to Gina's feelings or brushed over them in his hurry to reach a solution, the family might have spent fruitless time on a problem that camouflaged a more fundamental one.

Now the discussion shifts away from wall-banging to the subject of trust, and here is an appropriate time for some parental teaching. Such teaching, however, will always be more efficient after feelings are drained and if the teaching is *directly related to the child's own experiences*. Mr. G. says gently, "Pat, how would you feel if I promised you I wouldn't eat your piece of cake and then when you weren't around I went ahead and ate it?" (Notice, he uses an example that will have personal meaning for her.)

Pat: "I wouldn't like it."

Mr. G.: "Why?"

Pat: "'Cuz I want to eat it myself. And you told me you wouldn't touch it."

Mr. G.: "Yes, and how would you feel the next time I promised not to eat something of yours?"

Pat: "I might not believe you 'cuz you did it once before even when you said you wouldn't."

Mr. G.: "Yes, indeed. When people promise us something and then they don't keep that promise, we soon stop believing their words. We stop trusting them. And it's not very comfortable to live with people day after day that you can't trust. That's exactly how Gina feels. She was counting on your word and now she feels let down. This is important to remember because all the people you know will want to be able to count on your word when you give a promise."

Even though her father has done some teaching here, he knows that learning abstract concepts like trust, honesty, cooperation, and so on are as complicated as learning to read. He knows that future teaching may be in order on other occasions, but he also understands that such learning takes time. Most important, as he teaches he sticks to facts and studiously avoids making her feel guilty.

This example illustrates the importance of getting feelings expressed even in the initial stages of handling conflicts. Empathic listening brings real issues to light and makes a child more willing to listen to others.

It cannot be emphasized too strongly that

empathic listening throughout each of the steps of the democratic process is needed for productive results.

Expressing needs

As we saw in the example above, stating the problem and getting needs expressed may occur at the same time rather than involving two separate steps. If not, once the issue is presented to the family, get everyone's reactions.

If the parent is upset by a situation, his job is to look within carefully to see what personal need is frustrated. (Unless you're aware of your real feelings and willing to share them, you cannot accurately express your needs.) It may take some soul searching to discover why you're bothered, but it is time well spent in terms of reaching a constructive solution. Ask yourself, "What need of mine is being stepped on?" And let your family know.

In expressing your needs, remember to send "I-reactions." Assume the responsibility for your own frustration instead of foisting the responsibility off on a child by judgmental accusations. If you forget "I-reactions," a youngster feels attacked; then, instead of listening to your needs, he may immediately dig in his heels. "You-judgments" rarely get past defensive walls; then, communication bogs down.

Putting democracy into action requires open lines of communication. To ensure this, focus on "I-reactions" and empathic listening. *Failure to follow these two procedures can defeat all your efforts.*

Considering solutions

Once the problem is defined and all needs expressed, the issue at hand is "What solution will meet these various needs?"

Avoid the temptation to use democracy as a gimmick to railroad through your preconceived solutions. Do *not use the democratic approach if there is only one acceptable arrangement.* If a child truly has no choice (he may not drive the car until he has a permit or license, or he may not refuse to take his medication), he should not be led to think that he does.

If a situation exists that must be corrected and one particular alternative is unacceptable to you, clearly state this at the outset. The R.'s, for example, lived on a busy street; traffic was heavy at all times of the day. The parents could not accept their children playing in the street, so the group searched for an acceptable alternative that everyone could live with.

You may decide not to give youngsters a choice on one aspect of a problem but be interested in negotiating on other aspects of it. The B.'s gave their youngsters no choice as to whether they would help around the house. They felt the need for assistance. But they wanted to allow each child to choose his particular chores and establish his own time for doing them.

As solutions are offered, guard against insistence on conformity. As much as possible, protect individual preferences. A common pitfall is to protect your own needs but fail to protect children's. Mrs. J., for example, didn't want to be tied to a definite commitment as to which day she would vacuum her daughter's room so that Vicky knew when to pick it up. But she insisted that her daughter do her chores before school. In short, she wanted flexibility in her schedule but didn't accord Vicky the same privilege.

The freedom with which family members express their needs and offer alternative ideas for solutions depends heavily on the psychological climate. An atmosphere of pressure for conformity, disregard for personal integrity, judgment, evaluation, fear, and animosity shuts the doors to communication. Jerry's parents thought they were democratic, but they jumped on his ideas so regularly that he gave up being an active participant during family meetings. It was clear that his parents only wanted a rubber stamp. *Democracy in name only has no value.*

To foster independent thinking and self-reliance, give children the first opportunity to suggest ideas.

The H. family was working out a policy regarding television. They'd run into heated conflicts about who decided on the program to be seen. Various suggestions for solving the conflict were made.

"Why can't we get another television set?" suggested Quincy.

"There isn't enough money for one right now, son," replied his father. "The only way to buy a new set this year would be to cancel our vacation plans and spend our two weeks at home."

"Oh, no," said Mrs. H. "I'm not comfortable about that idea at all. I really need to get completely away from the house, especially this year. We've had so much illness that I'm ready for a vacation right now. The thought of canceling it would bother me no end."

"How about if Quincy wants to watch a program and I don't, he can go over to a friend's house and watch their TV set?" said Mickey. (Typically, children think of solutions that meet *their* needs solely until they get used to the idea that only solutions that meet *everyone's* needs are acceptable.)

"Both you boys sure hate to give up any of your favorite programs, don't you?" reflected their mother empathically.

"Sure," they chimed in.

"I don't feel we should impose on neighbors," said Mr. H. "If either of you gets a special invitation, that's one thing, but we can't shift our TV problem onto another family."

"How about if we draw lots every morning and whoever wins gets to choose the program that day?" suggested Quincy. (Now he thinks in terms of compromise.)

"Ug," replied Mickey. "That'd waste too much time. Besides, what if one person got to choose several times in a row? That wouldn't be fair!"

"Well," said Mrs. H. "I really don't have any programs I especially like before nine o'clock when you boys are in bed. And Dad only likes to watch the news for a half hour, so it seems as if we mainly have to find a fair arrangement for you two boys—working around Dad's news time."

"Yeah, but on Wednesdays my favorite program—in fact, one

we both like to watch—starts just when Dad's news begins," said Mickey.

"If we can work out something that stops this endless bickering, I'll catch the late news," said Mr. H. "Guess I can hold off one night a week."

"How about on the even days of the month Mickey chooses the programs? And on the odd days of the month I get to," suggested Quincy.

"Hey, good deal," said Mickey.

Many suggestions were made and personal reactions were shared, but the family continued working until they found an arrangement acceptable to all.

It makes no difference whether adults or children contribute the eventual answer to the problem so long as the solution is one everyone can buy. The criterion is that *no one is forced to accept a particular policy.*

With very young children, offering different solutions rests largely with parents. Try first one idea and then another; the child will let you know by his behavior when he accepts.

If your children continue to offer ideas that meet only their needs, don't despair. It takes a certain degree of maturity to think in terms of others. At such times, remind them that a workable solution has to meet everyone's needs. Then, continue to search for that solution.

Finding a solution

How long it takes to find a satisfactory answer to any one problem depends on the problem and particular family needs.

Family democracy does not involve voting. If three youngsters are happy about one idea but the fourth is not, keep working. Voting results in problems of enforcement. An outvoted child is invariably the one who drags his feet in carrying out the rule.

If no agreement can be reached, use the approach of the professional negotiator. State the areas of agreement and those of disagreement. The log jam needs to be clearly defined. Then, make an appointment for another session within a few days. When children understand that a basic policy must be worked out and that they will have to search together until a satisfactory solution is found, they are more apt to try creative thinking.

When you hit a stalemate, you may be tempted to toss out the democratic process and revert to authoritarianism or to throw in the towel and become over-permissive. If you do, family democracy disappears. Instead, work, talk, *listen for feelings,* and try to think creatively. Sometimes, it is helpful to bring in an outside person whom the group can accept. Several meetings may be required to break an impasse. A temporary policy may be needed to handle a situation while you seek to break the deadlock.

Once solutions are reached, check with each member involved regarding his acceptance and then write them down in case of later uncertainty about the solution. Agreed-upon rules need to be clearly stated.

Reactions toward solution

A solution that looks good while you are negotiating may not work in practice. Some facet of the problem may not have been considered or new circumstances may arise that make it impractical. So, the last step is to check with the group to see how they feel about the rule after they've had a chance to work with it.

Family policies will need revision from time to time to allow for changing needs. Leave the door open for later evaluation by saying, "Let's try this idea and see how we all feel about it. If we run into any snags, we'll work out a new arrangement."

Specific issues

Using democracy in setting limits does not necessarily mean a formal conference over every issue. Julia wanted to wear her new velvet party dress to school. Her mother said, "Honey, I'm afraid your dress will get torn or dirty at school. I can't wash it in the machine and dry cleaning is expensive. But you really do want to wear it, don't you? How about putting it on after dinner while you watch TV?" Julia bought the idea, and both sets of needs were met. The problem was handled on the spot.

In establishing rules or working out conflicts, involve only those concerned with the issue. If a member of the family is uninvolved with the problem but wants to join the conference, there's no reason why he shouldn't, provided those who own it agree. Who knows, he may be the one to come up with the creative solution!

Include children in setting up basic family policies whenever possible. Allowances and how they are to be handled, television hours and programs, home chores, care of pets, bedtime routines, homework, the use of the car and telephone are well suited to this process. These issues affect their daily lives and children need to be involved in working out the rules.

Some parents object that the democratic process takes too much time. Granted, it is quicker for adults to lay down the law. But consider the hours needed to get children to follow authoritarian edicts, to say nothing of the problems of enforcement and the total effect on self-esteem. Rules nagged about are most often those imposed without giving children a voice. They are the ones likely to be broken when your back is turned. The time needed for the democratic process is short, indeed, when you know the benefits it brings.

If you aren't already using democratic discipline, let your children know a change is being made in how most rules will be worked out. Indicate that you are starting a new policy involving everyone in setting up rules and resolving conflicts. Point out the steps of the process, stress that joint agreement means no ramrodding of solutions, and get started.

Even if you are sold on this approach, you may find yourself slipping back into former methods. When you do, head for make-up work. Get the group together, tell them you're dissatisfied with your handling of the issue, and that you want to replay the scene. Children are remarkedly cooperative when given a voice, even if belatedly.

If any family member falls down on his end of the agreed-upon solution, get those concerned together to find out what went amiss. You may find that the rule failed to take everyone's needs into consideration, that the agreement was forgotten, that feelings got in the way of its being carried out, that it was bought even when it wasn't genuinely acceptable to everyone, or that it was a limit that a child could not realistically carry out because it was developmentally beyond him. Pinpoint the reason for the breakdown and work from there.

When Debbie failed to carry out her part of the family rule, her parents called the group together to see what went wrong. "Oh," said Debbie, "I was tired of working on the problem that day and I agreed to Dick's idea even though I didn't like it."

"Well, Debbie, we need your ideas and reactions if we're to make these rules stick. Let's get your objections out in the open and find an acceptable answer," said her father.

Mr. and Mrs. K. discovered that their family rule about picking up toys wasn't working because it was unrealistic for their four-year-old. He needed help in straightening his room, so they altered their policy to take his stage of growth into account.

Frank continually forgot to do the home chores he chose. His parents felt his choices were compatible with his stage of growth; they found no underlying negative feelings that might interfere. The forgetting seemed to be a case of his simply being busy. However, they did not want to remind. At their conference his father said, "All of us forget once in a while, but still when we do our whole policy breaks down. How can we handle forgetting chores? Whatever we work out has to apply to all of us, grown-ups as well."

Now the burden of enforcement becomes the problem to be solved. This approach removes parents from the role of the policeman and involves children in establishing their own consequences. It is amazing to see how much more acceptant they are of "reminders" they've helped to design. Frequently, children get so carried away that they go in for overly severe consequences. When this happens, hold out for less dire ones.

Involving the family in working on the problem of strict adherence to democratically made rules is a far cry from strict enforcement of the autocratically made rules. *Strict or not strict is not the issue.* The focal point is how power is handled. And in democratic homes it is shared. The whole process of home democracy means

cooperation through unanimous consent.

It is how family rules and conflicts are worked out that affects whether discipline strengthens or weakens.

Benefit of democratic discipline

The particular solution to a conflict is *not* of central importance, but the

process by which conflicts are resolved is crucial.

Democracy builds high self-esteem by leaps and bounds.

When a child is consulted, when his contributions matter, when he experiences his needs as having equal validity with others in the family, then he knows he is a person of worth. He doesn't have to wonder.

The very willingness to share power proves respect. The mere fact that *no one person wields all the power* prevents children's being victims of an autocratic steam roller or a disinterested parent. Allowed to be joint architects in matters affecting them reinforces feelings of control and autonomy. Yet, it does not give *unlicensed* freedom to do as they please.

The democratic process says "Yes" to children. It says, "We believe in your rights and in your capacity to contribute just as we believe in similar rights for ourselves." It says, "We need you! And we need to work together." Children's attitudes toward life and themselves are affected accordingly. When you establish true democracy at home, you *involve* children in life. Life has more purpose and meaning when a child is given an active part in decisions affecting him. Remember:

The push toward independence is the push toward self-direction.

Part of mastery involves the ability to plan and help make decisions. Each child needs experience to develop self-reliance; democratic discipline gives him the necessary practice.

Democratic discipline fosters *responsibility* and *self-discipline*. Children rarely sabotage rules they've helped design. They can follow them with inner conviction. And, unlike rules imposed from on high, they are more apt to follow them whether or not adults are present. In addition, *shared power shifts the responsibility for enforcement* (should this be necessary) *to all members of the family.*

Democratic discipline fosters a wholesome respect for authority. If you have any doubt, ask yourself whom you would truly respect more:

a boss who wielded his power over you and used force or rewards to manipulate your behavior;

a boss who simply let you do whatever you wanted and refused to become involved; or

a boss who shared his power through respectful involvement and asked you to take part in the decisions affecting your life?

Too often we think of respect for authority in terms of outward obedience—based on fear of consequences. But *genuine respect is born of admiration and inner conviction.*

Increasing evidence indicates that youngsters who are raised in democratic family atmospheres as young children come into adolescence with less need to rebel. They are less troubled and resentful, as well as being less rejecting of parents. When youngsters are consulted as they are growing, they have not spent twelve to eighteen years as underlings to power, nor have they lived with total disregard for the rights of others. Who among us wants to rebel and reject when we've been treated with friendly respect and given a genuine part in self-regulation?

In addition, youngsters from democratic families show increased intellectual growth, as we'll see in Chapter Twenty-four.

We cannot afford to ignore the data. *Democracy in the home has far-reaching, positive benefits for children.* It directly nurtures the qualities most of us want in our youngsters: self-respect, emotional stability, self-confidence, social responsibility, nonaggressive leadership, meaningful involvement with life, and the unfolding and development of potential.

Real democracy grows real people.

You cannot be casual about establishing a democratic climate if you intend to nurture. Democracy proves love to children.

Democratic homes strengthen our country. Should a large percentage of our future citizens feel low self-worth, our country will be weakened. Studies show that the child with low self-esteem is less interested in public affairs (internal problems capture their attention). They are less likely to take part in public issues (they feel threatened by expressing opinions, doubt the value of their ideas, and are self-conscious about expressing themselves). They do not have the courage of their convictions. When you help children to high self-esteem, you take active steps to ensure that our democracy remains strong.

Misbehavior and discipline

Sharing power with youngsters in every area possible is constructive discipline that strengthens. But it does not completely eliminate misbehavior.

"Kenny is acting up again!" Such a comment needs careful scrutiny. What is misbehavior?

No pat answer can be given. Is Kenny's behavior out of line because he's coming down with a cold, because he's tired, because he has been cooped up too long, or because adult expectations or family tensions are too high? Perhaps his environment is unsuited to his needs, or he is in a particular stage of growth, or his emotional needs are unmet.

Are family rules too strict or too lenient? Is Kenny locked in a power struggle with his parents? Is he laboring under too much competition? Perhaps rules are unclear or there are too many of them. Maybe he is full of negative feelings or his self-esteem is low. Some children labeled behavior problems actually have mild neurological handicaps.

Behavior is caused. Whenever misbehavior is continuous, you must deal with its source to eliminate it. *Chronic* misbehavior is a child's way of telling us that something is awry in his life. Take a serious inventory and eliminate the deficits you find.

There will be times when you keep your power and make decisions regarding your child's behavior. There will be other times when you give your power to the child to make his own decisions. But to build high self-esteem and responsible self-discipline, there will be *more* times when you share power and work out your rules together. Remember: *how* you discipline affects *how* your child lives his life.

PART VI · MENTAL GROWTH AND
SELF-ESTEEM

TWENTY-FOUR · MOTIVATION,
INTELLIGENCE, AND CREATIVITY

The push from within

A stranger to our planet, every normal child is born curious. He interacts freely with what he discovers around him, unencumbered by set ideas. He manipulates, experiments, and explores. The child whose curiosity is accepted as valid is given the green light to learn.

By three or four, the average child is virtually a walking question box. "Why is grass green?" "What holds clouds up?" "How come fire's hot?" "Do you see when you're dead?" "Who ate that hole in the moon?" "Where does the wind go when it stops blowing?" "Is God married?" "Why?" By five, most have formed basic attitudes toward learning—attitudes shaped by their parents' reactions toward their early explorations.

Children learn whether it is safe to learn.

Unfortunately, some children learn very early *not* to learn. How does this happen?

Tommy upends his new wagon and twirls its wheels. He

hears, "No, Tommy, wagons go this way." He is fascinated by the bright, gay packages at the grocery store. "Stop that, Tommy, keep your hands off!" He reaches for a strange garden creature. "Oh, Tommy, icky! That's a germy snail; don't touch it." Repeatedly, Tommy is discouraged from investigating and using fresh approaches to the things he finds. Wonder gets him into trouble; he learns it's unsafe to explore.

For safety's sake, sometimes Tommy's investigations must be restricted, but far too often he is *needlessly* limited. His urge to discover is not supported and he turns off his curiosity to avoid disapproval.

Is there any harm in Tommy's experimenting with a wagon upside down? He can't run wild in the grocery store, but can his parents hand him objects to feel and touch and smell? Can they let him hold the snail to discover personally what it's like and wash his hands later?

Tommy's many questions too often meet an annoyed, "Go outside and play; don't bother me." He is literally encouraged not to be inquisitive. Approval comes when he is passive, conforming, and quiet. He learns to set his wondering self aside.

In the morning, Tommy is told, "Here let me tie your shoes; I can do it faster." (Do we have to race *every* morning?) If too many things are done *for* him, Tommy may lose his drive for self-reliance. Whenever he is forced to choose between self-reliance and approval, the child may prefer to give up resourcefulness. Love has priority for little folks.

When youngsters start school they have five or six years of teaching behind them—teaching that has an important bearing on their entire attitude toward learning. When curiosity is taboo, enthusiasm for learning dies.

Questioning and experimentation with the unknown form the basis of advance in every field. Stamp out these qualities that are present in every normal newborn child to some degree, and you literally hold back progress for the human race. Every parent and teacher is responsible for keeping the lights of curiosity burning in children. Every child must know that it *pays to wonder*. He must think no less of himself because of his push to know.

What stimulates learning

Children not only need an atmosphere that encourages curiosity and exploration, they need rich exposures to a wide variety of experiences. Increasing evidence indicates that rich stimulation early in life affects intellectual development. Each child needs as much direct experience as possible. Only in this way can he come to know about his surroundings personally.

We women like to read or hear about a new fabric on the market, but nothing substitutes for our actually seeing, feeling, and working with it. Direct experience tells us far more than learning secondhand. The more *firsthand* experiences a child has, the more knowledgeable he is about his world; this adds to his security and confidence.

Academic progress is related to direct exposures. When city-bred Bobby saw the word "cow" in his primer, he had no previous associations to bring to the black symbols on the page. He was told it was an animal that had certain ways and he was shown a picture of it. His brain received its impression about cows through other people's experience and by looking at an abstraction on a page.

When farm-raised Nelson saw the symbols spelling cow, he brought a wealth of previous associations. He had touched and smelled and heard cows. He knew how they chewed their cuds and swished their tails; he had watched them give milk and feed their young. His brain had received impressions about cows *directly* through his own eyes, ears, nose, and fingers. Many neural connections had been established that gave personal meaning to the printed symbol.

Impoverished early childhood environments actually result in varying degrees of mental retardation. Early stimulation gives more extensive networks of associations to bring to the abstract symbols on which schools rely so heavily.

Along with extensive, direct contact a child needs practice putting his experiences into words. A youngster may have much stimulation but be unable to verbalize his responses. Schools, of course, place heavy emphasis on the spoken and written word. Plenty of practice at home develops a skill highly valued at school.

Impoverished language environments handicap academic progress.

You encourage a child to talk by your examples and by your respect for his ideas and feelings. Communication that is truly open only flourishes in a climate of safety.

In addition, children need early practice in problem-solving. Experiments with animals have shown that those subjected to successful problem-solving situations early in life are more adept at problem-solving later in life than those that are not. What does all this mean in terms of you and your child? It means you encourage intellectual growth by providing rich, firsthand experiences early in life and encouraging him to *talk* about what he saw and did and how he felt. Help him find answers to the questions he raises. Let him run up against problems, stand by with needed support, and encourage him to find his own solutions.

Buddy's mother was preparing a salad for dinner while her son watched.

"Whazat?" asked her three-year-old.

"It's an avocado," said his mother slowly. "Can you say a-vo-ca-do?"

Buddy tried, "A-da-va-do."

"Watch my mouth, Buddy. A-vo-ca-do." And together they said the word till Buddy had it.

"Wha zit fo'?" asked Buddy.

(His mother could have thought, "Dopey, I wouldn't put anything in a salad if it weren't to eat!" But his question is not unintelligent. He has seen straws in milkshakes and they weren't for eating. He has seen parsley that's used only for decoration.) His mother supports his curiosity by saying, "It's to eat. We don't eat this part," holding up the skin, "or this part," picking up the seed. "Why do you s'pose we don't eat the skin or the seed?"

Buddy picked up a piece of peeled skin and bit into it; he felt the seed. "Too hahd," he said.

"Yes, now try this part," she said, giving Buddy a slice of avocado meat.

"Ooh, gushy!" said Buddy disdainfully.

"How does it taste to you? Would you like to smell it? Try squishing it in your fingers."

"Like the soft, but no like it taste," said Buddy. "I no smell nuffin'."

"No, it doesn't have a smell like pineapple or lemon. I didn't like the taste at first either, but now I do. Sometimes we put avocados in salads when we like the taste. Next time we're at Aunt Mary's I'll show you her avocado tree. Avocados grow on trees the way the oranges do in our back yard. Here, let's put this seed over some water in a jar and see what happens!"

Buddy's mother directly enhanced his attitude toward learning. Her response accepted his curiosity; she helped him experience a strange object directly through all his senses. She encouraged his talking about it and respected his personal reactions. Together the two of them shared a learning experience.

One day Warren yelped in frustration when his wagon caught on a rock. He couldn't dislodge it by pulling it forward. His mother could have lifted the wagon off the rock for him but she would have missed a splendid opportunity to let her son test his problem-solving ability. Still she didn't desert him.

Instead, she said, "Looks like the wagon is stuck and it won't come off by pulling it forward. I wonder how else you could get it free?"

Her five-year-old surveyed the situation, got down on all fours, then ran for his shovel. He dug around the rock and pushed it out from under the wheel. The wagon was free.

"It was interesting," said his mother later. "I would have lifted the wagon or pushed it backward, but his approach was to dig out the stone. I thought my way was easier but I felt it was important to let him use his own imagination to solve his problem."

Both these mothers encouraged their sons' learning. If continued, their support will be reflected in their boys' later intellectual development.

Within the limits of safety children need to interact with the things in their environment without interference.

The guiding principles are: respect childish curiosity and exploration; find acceptable outlets for the push to know. Self-esteem is enhanced when your attitude and behavior say, "Your curiosity is important. I will help you experience and understand."

What is intelligence?

"My, but Bill is intelligent!" Such words are music to the ears of proud parents. Ordinarily, when we say this, we mean that a child is quick to learn. And we usually think in terms of the abstract learning ability needed in school. There are, however, many kinds of intelligence.

Bill may be sharp at manipulating mathematical symbols yet have only average ability to read. Martha may have little capacity to learn from books, but her sensitivity to others makes her socially adept. Ted may do poorly in school but be highly gifted musically. Even an IQ (intelligence quotient) score has different meanings for different children.

Libby, Jean, Harry, and Mack all have tested IQ scores of 126, yet their abilities are unequal. Libby's keen memory pulls her score up; she does well in subjects where memory is an advantage. But she has only average reasoning ability. She has to work hard in subjects requiring this skill. Unlike Libby, Jean's score is influenced by her marked talent for reasoning and comprehension. She has little ability, however, for rote work. Harry, on the other hand, is an exceptionally gifted child whose potential far outshines the two girls'. His score is depressed by emotional blocks. Mack, unlike the other three, comes from a culturally deprived background. His score, therefore, carries a different meaning than theirs.

A single IQ score should not be relied on, for mental growth is more rapid at certain periods than at others. Many factors, such as physical health, the degree of rapport between child and examiner, and cultural exposures, influence test performance.

Richards[1] studied the development of a young boy over a period of seven years to see if there was a relationship between his IQ scores and his life experiences. Sure enough, when the boy's home and school environment were most confirming (sending positive reflections), his IQ score increased to 140; when they were least nurturing it dropped to 117. The psychological climate surrounding any child has a strong influence on his mental functioning.

An IQ is no more than a *score* roughly estimating the over-all ability available for use at that time to handle mental abstractions (words, numbers, concepts). Because schools focus on the manipulation of abstractions, the IQ is necessarily useful for their purposes. Taken by itself, however, it tells little about even the ability to handle abstractions. You have to look at each subtest that makes up the total test to know where particular strengths and weaknesses lie. You have to examine performance as a whole to determine whether the score reflects true capacity or whether potentials are being depressed.

Parents, particularly in upper middle-class neighborhoods,

[1] Richards, T. W., "Mental Test Performance as a Reflection of the Child's Current Life Situation, A Methodological Study," *Child Development*, XXII (1951), pp. 221–33.

are often heard tossing around children's IQ scores as if they had innate meaning in themselves. Unfortunately, in some communities, such scores are status symbols for parents.

(In terms of their children's adjustment and happiness, how much more realistic if these parents were concerned with their youngsters' self-esteem quotients! Brilliance at manipulating abstractions is not to be derided, but it does not guarantee that a child will function fully as a whole human being.)

A high IQ doesn't necessarily mean high performance or motivation. Grades in school are more often a reflection of motivation than innate capacity. As one counselor put it, "It's not so much a matter of how intelligent a child is as what he does with what he has." With an IQ of 120, Olga outstrips Perry, whose IQ is 165. Her burning curiosity and desire to learn push her to use her ability while Perry daydreams and worries about what others think of him. Self-confidence permits a child to perform; whereas, brilliance may be trapped in low self-esteem.

IQ tests do not measure creative ability, leadership, imagination, motivation, artistic or musical talent. This doesn't mean that IQ scores are worthless; it simply means that they should be seen for what they are.

Is intelligence fixed?

It used to be thought that intelligence was fixed and could not be changed. Today, we know this is untrue.

The IQ's of adopted children are closer to those of their adoptive parents than to those of their natural parents. In culturally advantaged neighborhoods about twenty-five to thirty percent of the children score 125 or above on IQ tests. In neighborhoods where children are culturally disadvantaged only about six percent of the children score this high. (This finding results partly because IQ tests reflect exposures to books, conversations, and material gadgets.) When disadvantaged children are provided enriching experiences, many of their IQ scores rise dramatically.

A long-term study of 300 children by the Fels Research Institute of Antioch College revealed that IQ's fluctuate considerably. It revealed that many IQ scores decreased steadily during the first six years when the children were dependent on parents. But more than half of the youngsters began to score higher when they reached school and were challenged to self-reliance.

A great deal of evidence exists that intelligence as measured by IQ tests is not fixed. Parents can do much to increase their children's mental ability and they markedly affect their desire to learn.

Roadblocks to learning

Even when curiosity is encouraged and the environment is richly stimulating, some children do not use the ability they have. The causes may come from any one or a combination of sources.

Physical handicaps can block learning: poor hearing or eyesight, neurological handicaps, hormonal imbalances, or slow physical maturation affect how well or rapidly any child learns.

Whenever a learning problem exists, the possibility of physical defects should *always* be checked *first*. Too often a child labeled slow-learning is later found to have a physical abnormality.

Many learning problems stem from emotional problems.

Intellectual growth does not occur apart from emotional growth; the two are intertwined.

The child whose emotional needs are unmet is less likely to do well academically. The starved man has little motivation to learn from books. First, he must satisfy his hunger, then he can concentrate on learning. As we've pointed out earlier, the child convinced that he is a failure has little motivation to try. And the child with a backlog of repression has little energy for school challenges.

Parents frequently say, "I wish I knew how to motivate my child." Remember: *high self-esteem is the mainspring for motivation.* The child's belief, "I have capacity! I can do! I have something to offer!" turns on his "go-power." Challenges are fun when you think you can handle them. When you feel you can't cope, interest quickly sags. As Emerson said, "Self-trust is the first secret of success."

Constantly watch your expectations for children. The *commonest cause of learning blocks,* particularly in children from middle-class families, *comes from undue pressure to achieve goals beyond their reach.* Such children learn how to fail.

"You got a B in social studies, why not an A?" is a charge many a middle-class child faces. One of the strongly entrenched values in suburbia is pressure for rapid achievement. Ever since Sputnik, academic pressures in America have increased, moving steadily down into the lower grades. The tune is excel, excel, *excel!* Unthinkingly and unintentionally, many well-meaning parents communicate to their children that they are more lovable and worthwhile if they top their class.

Remember: overambition comes through to children as nonacceptance. Unrealistically high expectations mean strong disappointments. And disappointments slam against self-esteem. They turn off "go-power" and then the child doesn't even turn on his engine.

Another roadblock to intellectual growth is discipline that is too lenient, too protective, or too strict. As we saw in Chapter Twenty-two, dominating parents breed hostility, dependency, and inadequacy—feelings that block intellectual functioning. Overprotective parents or ones who refuse to involve themselves in establishing limits make children feel inadequate and unloved. These approaches work against high self-esteem, which in turn affects motivation to learn.

Democratic discipline fosters intellectual growth by stimulating involvement, reasoning, creative thinking, and responsibility. Sharing power in rule-making plays a genuine part in fostering mental competence. The Coleman study revealed that the biggest factor motivating the child to learn is his feeling, "I have some control over my destiny." Democratic discipline allows youngsters to make this statement.

The Fels research study found that those children whose IQ's continued to rise over the years reached out for more and more self-reliance. They were confident, sure they were loved, at ease with others, less excitable, and more original in their thinking. In short, they bore the trademarks of high self-esteem.

IQ's dropped for those children who were dependent, less sure they were loved, less able to become involved in projects of their own, and who needed a great deal of direction. They were children who shied away from responsibility. Their characteristics describe children with low self-esteem.

High self-esteem strongly affects whether a child uses the abilities he has.

Another stumbling block to learning occurs when communication lines are clogged or closed. Research indicates that children who do well on mental tests and in schoolwork are more likely to come from homes where there is a great deal of open communication. When parents and children are warmly interested in each other and their activities, when children feel *safe* to share ideas and feelings, intellectual growth is stimulated.

Families in which there is guarded, tense, and coded communication fail to stimulate each other's thinking. Mental capacities shrink, become twisted, or fail to develop in such atmospheres.

In considering the roadblocks to learning we should not overlook the importance of good schools, inspired teachers, and flexible curricula geared to children's interests. Self-confident, motivated children can lose their zest for learning when they are jammed into overcrowded classrooms and taught by poor instructors using inferior techniques. In addition, when children are given an active part in planning the curriculum around their interests, they respond quite differently than when they are treated as empty pitchers into which stale textbook knowledge is poured.

Mr. S.'s social studies class was especially concerned about a particular issue in the community. They personally planned the approach to be used in gathering data for their survey study and they interviewed those involved with it in their town. Brainstorming sessions based on the accumulated data resulted in a series of recommendations presented to the city council. And many of their ideas were put into use. "The absentee rate in my class dropped to zero when we tried this approach," said Mr. S. "And students who dragged their feet about studying were reading as never before. The whole class came to life." Actually digging into personally relevant material makes it almost impossible to drag students from it. Direct experience and participative learning beat textbook cramming every time.

Far more important, however, this kind of educational experience says to a student, "Your concerns are important. Let's bring them into the classroom and work with them. We believe you are eager to learn and competent to confront genuine problems. We want you to actively participate in their solution." What a boost to feelings of self-worth!

Cluster grouping, team teaching, open classrooms, programmed learning, and independent projects and research in a child's area of interest are making inroads on the lock-step teaching that has held sway in classrooms for generations. But in spite of these advances, we have a long way to go in education to overcome the "Now, hear this" approach in which teachers decide what, when, and how children shall learn. Perhaps the time is not far off when teachers will be truly free to become resource people who encourage the natural curiosity of children.

Additional ways to stimulate learning

Each of us is our child's first reading, art, and music instructor. When first introduced to a new medium, a youngster's primary interest is to get acquainted with it. Whether book, clay, or autoharp, let the youngster enjoy the encounter without having to meet some goal.

Two-year-old Vicky holds her cloth book upside down, pokes at the pictures, and then puts it in her mouth. She is gathering firsthand information about something new; later she can hear the story.

Mike brings a brown smear on his paper for his teacher to admire. "Would you like to tell me about it, Mike?" asks his teacher. (She purposely avoids asking, "What is it?" Such a question focuses on the product and makes a child feel he should produce something.)

"Sure," says Mike, "that's a turtle under the mud." Initially, Mike made a primitive turtle and then discovered, as he swished the colors with his brush, that everything turned brown. Undaunted, he used his discovery that red, blue, and yellow make brown to give his turtle a home. He was in control.

Each product needs to be accepted and respected as this child's particular interaction with the medium or as his way of seeing. Accuracy is not important; enjoyment of expression is.

Reading aloud to children long before they can read themselves increases interest in books. Gear the story to the child's interest level and attention span. Story hours work against interest when interruptions, questions, and sharing are ruled out. Getting to the end of the story is not the goal; stimulating discussions have more value. Accept each child's personal reactions to nurture positive attitudes.

Take children to the library while they are still young, include them in the story hours there, and let them have their own check-out cards as soon as they are old enough to sign their names. Youngsters need to see you reading, discussing, and enjoying books. Books used as baby-sitters or as devices for withdrawal from life defeat your purpose.

Hobbies, crafts, tools, and gardens of their own help children learn more about their world. Always leave room for experimentation and discovery. Reference materials (a globe, dictionary, atlas, encyclopedia) within easy reach are important resources for growing minds.

Making maps of places familiar to children and playing map games make geography real. One family that moved frequently kept a log of the places they'd lived with accompanying maps of their travel routes. "We had endless hours of fun doing this together," said the father, "and out of it came all kinds of questions that led our boys to independent reading and projects they initiated."

When Paul asked a question, his father usually said, "Let's look it up," rather than "Go look it up." Sharing the search for answers until the consulting habit is well established makes learning more attractive.

Family bulletin boards for displaying art work, collections, or stories increase interest in learning, as well as stimulating creativity. They give children recognition and a feeling of importance. (Kitchen cabinets and refrigerator doors make excellent bulletin boards if you're cramped for space.)

Records and music of all kinds enrich children's lives. Making their own instruments, songs, and dancing free-form invites creativity.

Television is a source of heated contention in many families. Used indiscriminately or as a baby-sitter, it encourages passivity and works against creative involvement. By being selective, however, you can find worthwhile programs. Even when programs turn out to be poor, you can capitalize on the fact by involving children in thinking about changes for improvement.

As we've mentioned earlier, the democratic process is well suited to selecting programs, but you needn't feel you are stepping on self-esteem to veto some programs for viewing. None of us would invite murderers and thugs into our homes each day to entertain our children. And even though the bad guys come out on the losing end, a steady diet of muggings and knifings is hardly constructive fare. Some degree of latitude in choosing his own programs is desirable, but if your youngster seems to crave a continual stream of programs that specialize in violence, it may be a clue that he has hostile feelings that need release in other ways (active listening, clay, active sports, punching bags, even counseling help). If he pushes for constant television watching, his preference may indicate that his social relationships are providing little satisfaction. Many a child is willing to leave the tube when a family game or reading hour is suggested.

Puppets bring the theater into your home, along with helping youngsters work out feelings in socially acceptable ways. Homemade ones—as simple as paper bags or old socks with faces drawn on them or as elaborate as those made of papier-mâché—are almost always preferable to those commercially made.

Creative writing and creative telling provide hours of warm family enjoyment. Write out a small child's story for him, read it aloud, and see if any of your youngsters would like to draw pictures illustrating it. This supports the need for achievement and recognition. "Instant tall-tales" (making up a two-minute story about three totally unrelated things—a kangaroo, a banana peel, and an icicle) give outlets for creative imagination.

Trips of all kinds provide fertile opportunities for discovery and discussion. They must be planned with the child's attention span and interest level clearly in mind. Excursions that result in disciplinary tirades defeat their very purpose. Exploration and learning aren't fun under such circumstances. Trips should never press children beyond their limits of endurance or your limits of patience.

These ideas are but a few of the many ways to stimulate children intellectually. But remember: *how you relate to children during these shared experiences is the key to whether their appetites are whetted for more.* Make them periods for criticism and pressure and they'll come to be dreaded. Make them opportunities for warm and respectful closeness and they'll come to be treasured. *Nurturing love turns on mental growth. The climate's the thing.*

Important as rich exposures are, every child needs time alone —unscheduled, free time. Outside stimulation can be so constant that he never develops inner resources. Many parents recognizing the importance of rich exposures bombard their children with lessons and trips. They operate on the principle that if some is good, more is better.

One study of highly gifted people found that by circumstance many of them spent large portions of time alone, apart from others and continuous stimulation. A balance between stimulation and unscheduled time is best—too much of either can be detrimental.

Creativity

Most of us think we want our children to be creative. But what does creativity mean? What is the creative child like? How can you foster creativity in children?

The creative person is one who brings the new into being. He sees things in fresh ways. The highly intelligent child is *not* necessarily the highly creative child. A youngster may be a keen imitator or an avid manipulator of symbols and yet not be creative. On the other hand, the person of only average book-learning ability may be a highly creative cook, seamstress, woodworker, musician, painter, or interior decorator.

Original ways of seeing and responding to life are gifts every normal child brings with him, in varying degrees, into the world. Many of us think of creativity in terms of great works of art, music, literature, or science. But we frequently overlook that creativity blossoming in small ways is just as authentic as creativity expressed in a grand manner.

Each of us can probably think of someone who won't go down in history as a creative genius but who uses his own individuality to bring novelty into his daily life.

What characteristics distinguish creative youngsters from noncreative ones?

Creative children tend to be independent, rather unconcerned with group pressures or conformity, and disinterested in what other people think of them. They retain their capacity to wonder and question and see things afresh. They are flexible, imaginative, spontaneous, and playful in their approach to problems. They are highly receptive to their senses; they tend to see more, feel more, and drink in more of what is around them. Creative youngsters are equally open to themselves and what is going on within. In short, they are highly responsive to both their inner and outer worlds.

Such children are willing to risk paying attention to intuition and trying the new. It requires a certain degree of confidence and security to work with the disorganized, the complex, the inconsistent, the unknown, and the paradoxical. Creative youngsters are not particularly concerned with neatness or promptness and are easily bored with routine.

Frank Barron, who has done extensive research on creativity, distinguishes between two kinds: that which comes from the repressed unconscious and that which flows freely from an unfettered unconscious.

The person creating from repression grinds out monotonously similar productions. They are outlets for personal repressions and hungers. The person who creates freely expresses his uniqueness in wide variety, each product novel and new.

John's poetry snaps with vivid imagery and arresting rhythms, but over and over it rehashes the same blood and gore. Arnold's verse wells up from his unique responses to a wide range of experiences: a touching tribute to filtered forest lights, a teasing testimonial to a tadpole dance, the seething wrench for a cause that's lost, the sparkling foam-song from a frosted wave. Open to all that's around and within, he responds accordingly. His creativity is unencumbered by psychological axes to grind.

How can you foster creativity in children?

When children know uniqueness is respected, they are more likely to put theirs to use. The reactions each child receives in his early attempts at originality determine whether such impulses flourish or wither.

Creativity needs a climate of safety from judgment and freedom of expression.

If you value conformity, stereotyped thinking, constant order, and compliance, you are not likely to nurture creativity. Your attitudes and values are felt and reacted to. Can you tolerate imperfection and failure? Your child is more likely to try out new ideas if he knows *in advance* that approval is not tied to the outcome of his project.

Creativity and self-esteem

The relationship between high self-esteem and unfettered creativity is extremely strong. By its very nature, creativity is a deviant act. It says, "I see things *my* way and I am willing to let you into my private, perceptual world." It takes self-confidence to make a personal reaction public.

Studies show that the freely creative youngster is high in self-confidence, emotional maturity, calmness, and independence. He has the capacity for sustained concentration and involved absorption in his projects.

These findings are not surprising because the child whose experiences have taught him that he is unconditionally loved and worthwhile is free to listen to his inner promptings; he trusts his personal reactions and intuition. His *belief in himself* supports the urge to carry out his unique ideas. His energies —not wasted in self-defense—are free to tackle the new. He does not believe that personal worth is at stake in each production.

Being more socially independent and inwardly peaceful, he is less restricted by the thinking of others. Group pressures are less likely to limit his expressions. High self-esteem frees a youngster to play with a whole repertoire of possibilities, confident that he can choose those of greater merit. He can afford to stand up for his ideas and opinions. For creativity, a child must trust his own perceptions and have confidence in his ability to express them. The youngster with high self-esteem has this kind of confidence.

The child with low self-esteem may have unique ideas but being socially dependent, he is more likely to set them aside for the safety of approval. He is more sensitive to criticism because he has already judged himself negatively. He, therefore, prefers working under others. He shies away from creative, independent decisions, responsibility, and leadership. He shrinks from the limelight; it only exposes him to further criticism. Competition threatens; he prefers to submerge his talents. Conformity is less risky than creativity. Working on his psychological needs has priority over adventure into the unknown. In fact, the unknown threatens the child with low self-esteem. He doesn't expect to be successful handling it; he has had enough of failure.

Although it is important to the youngster with low self-esteem to surge ahead to earn positive reflections, his lack of self-confidence gets in his way. He has high goals, but little hope of success. Projecting an image of inadequacy, he convinces others of his lack of worth by his very behavior.

Building self-esteem in children actively nurtures intellectual development, motivation, and creative expression. (Interestingly enough, the psychological climate that produces the freely creative, productive child is made up of precisely the same ingredients that compose the climate of love. See Part II.) The youngster with self-confidence surges ahead to develop his particular potentials and talents.

Safe encounters, reasonable standards, rich exposures, and democratic discipline ensure learning and creativity. Each child's push to know needs support and he must be sure that mistakes are not catastrophic. When children live with parents who provide such an atmosphere, they unfold in all directions.

As a parent who cares, actively support educational movements that work toward the removal of restrictive school practices: grading by which one child is compared to another, uniform teaching, overcrowded classrooms, and heavy reliance on teacher-directed activities. Children carry their feelings and hungers and self-attitudes into the classroom. More parents and teachers need to be aware of the role that self-esteem plays in the lives of children. Education *must* concern itself with children's emotions and self-attitudes or it does not deal with the whole child. And all education begins in the cradle.

Parents and teachers must work together to help youngsters embrace all parts of themselves so that they are free to learn and create. It is only as a child's total uniqueness is respected that he can permit his individuality to unfold.

PART VII · SEX AND SELF-ESTEEM

TWENTY-FIVE · THE WEDDING OF SEX AND LOVE

The meaning of sex education

If sex education only involved teaching the facts of reproduction, our responsibilities could be dispatched with a father-son talk, a mother-daughter conference, or a good book. This, however, is not the case, for facts rarely prevent trouble. It is, instead,

> **attitudes toward sex and self that determine how youngsters handle sex.**

And for many of us, the sticky part of sex education lies right here. Why is sex such a problem and how do we teach healthy attitudes?

Why sex is a problem

Although we live in the twentieth century, the belief from former centuries that sex is evil and dirty still lurks in many of our minds. We may not consciously admit to this outmoded view, but we act as if we do.

In the fifteenth and sixteenth centuries, earthly pleasure was regarded as sinful. Sex was seen as necessary for the continuation of the race, but wholehearted enjoyment of it was publicly viewed as the work of the devil; sex symbolized man's fall. Even between married couples, it was not respected as a positive force; it only pointed out the beast in man. And for a woman to enjoy sex meant she was immoral, if not downright depraved! Sex went underground; repression and the double standard ruled.

Gradually, the subject has been brought into the open; in fact, today sex receives exaggerated attention, no doubt a reaction from being kept under wraps. Now, sex-as-recreation is continually thrust at us from all directions: advertisements, television, movies, novels, art, and clothing styles.

Some parents reacting against their own puritanical upbringing believe they are enlightened by providing their daughters with the pill and retreating into the background. Yet, many young people who have tried the sex-for-gratification route find it wanting. A new morality is emerging and with it has come the struggle to put sex in fresh perspective.

Sex deserves its rightful place as a creative, nurturing life urge to be dealt with openly. But it is a force that must also be respected. It can be a weapon for control and exploitation. Or it can be related to love, responsibility, and commitment. Misused, sex destroys human relationships; used responsibly, it can nourish and enrich.

Healthy sex attitudes

Every normal human being has sexual feelings. A positive attitude toward sex means accepting these urges as vital and proper. It means that sensual feelings are not seen as shameful. A healthy outlook is based on a youngster's comfort about his particular sex and sexual role.

How any one youngster handles his sexual urges is tied to all of his experiences with life and love. And his attitudes are formed from birth on. To teach positive attitudes toward sex, it helps to be aware of the various sources that affect each child's outlook.

Sex and love

The urge to mate and to nurture has long been considered instinctual. Harry Harlow's work with monkeys, however, suggests that these so-called instincts may, in fact, be learned. Those monkeys raised in isolation from their mothers showed little or no interest in mating as adults and rejected the offspring they bore as a result of artificial insemination.

Evidence indicates that the strength of the adult sex drive and the urge to nurture (to "mother") are colored by the kinds of warm, cuddling, touching experiences each individual has during infancy. It seems that for the human being to *give* love one day, he must first *receive* it.

Each time you cuddle, rock, pat, bathe, and feed your baby, you give experience in taking in love. How he is touched and treated affects whether he finds physical contact pleasurable or not; it influences his future capacity to enjoy intimacy. Warm tenderness and respect for an infant's body and his needs are a child's first exposure to love, and, therefore, to sex education.

When you provide safe encounters (trust, cherishing, non-judgment, empathy, separateness, focused attention), you teach that psychological intimacy and personal involvement are not to be feared. You teach that opening oneself up psychologically to important life persons is nurturing rather than dangerous. You give silent lessons in love—lessons that are part and parcel of constructive sex education. The child who is clobbered when he dares to get close finds intimate contact too risky. He may prefer alienation and physical sex to the vulnerability of genuine psychological intimacy. If so, he is slated for counterfeit relationships, for one overriding fact is clear: *physical intimacy is no short cut to psychological intimacy.* In and of itself, intercourse does not remove loneliness and estrangement. Yet, countless people (young and old) believe it will. And they are invariably disappointed.

Sexual contact is always more fulfilling when it comes in the context of tender caring, openness, and sensitivity to the best interests of the other. As Edmund Bergler has put it, "*Sex 'tastes' better when combined with tender love.* This is an experience that has nothing to do with moral attitudes."[1]

Love that has any depth means involvement. When sexual release comes in the context of trust, commitment, and safety, its pleasures take on heightened meaning. The youngster who has lived in a climate of love is more apt to bring his sexual feelings into this framework. He is less interested in sex-as-recreation.

Sex and negative feelings

Helping a youngster express negative feelings affects his future sexual relationships. As we've seen, repressing negative emotions holds down positive, loving ones as well. The guarded individual doesn't set aside his controls when he hops into bed. His sex life lacks the quality of open spontaneity and remains primarily physical.

The person who represses feelings may use sex as an outlet for release. Jack's typical device for retaliating against his wife when pressures built up between them was to arrive at a sexual climax before she did, leaving her frustrated and angry. His was a powerful, if unconscious, device to get even. When couples fear working through their inevitable conflicts by openly expressing their reactions, the breakdown in communication is invariably reflected in their sexual adjustment. Impotence and frigidity can result from unhealthy attitudes toward sex, but they can also be symptoms of repressed negative feelings and damaged lines of communication.

When a youngster's parents resolve their frictions by open

[1] Bergler, Edmund, M.D., *Divorce Won't Help*, New York, Harper & Row, 1948, p. 226.

discussion and when they help him release his negative emotions, he receives positive sex education. He learns that confrontation doesn't wipe out commitment and love. And he doesn't have to release his repressions from other areas of his life through the disguise of sexual maladjustments.

Obviously, parental arguments that are intense, prolonged, and destructive can overwhelm and frighten a child. They may teach him that marriage is frightening and should be avoided.

Children sense the kind of relationship their parents have and form impressions about love relationships from what they see lived out in front of them day after day. As a result of such experiences, they can conclude, "Marriage is rewarding," or "Marriage is destructive."

Sex and the body

Every child forms attitudes toward his body and its various parts. And these attitudes color his view of sex. How you feel about your body is communicated to your children. If you believe the organs for elimination and reproduction are nasty or shameful, your youngsters are likely to develop similar reactions.

Pammie was only three but she habitually said, "Gotta cover up my nasty," as she pulled up her panties after going to the bathroom. In a very short time she discovered that certain parts of her body were dirty and had best not be looked at.

Where did Pammie get this idea? No one ever said anything about bodies being nasty. It all happened rather indirectly: her mother's facial expressions when she changed her diaper; her distaste when Pammie brought the potty with her first proud production in it; her slapped hand when she leaned over to examine her vulva; older children snickering when a two-year-old took off his bathing trunks at the beach; a "Stop that!" when she stooped to watch her dog urinate. These and other reactions told Pammie that bodies had unacceptable parts, that elimination was dirty, and that certain talk was strictly hush-hush.

Each time you bathe, dress, or toilet train your child, your attitudes toward his body are as influential as when you answer specific questions about bodies, babies, and sex. You teach sex education both nonverbally and verbally.

Your handling of your child's early body explorations has a marked effect on his attitudes toward his body. The day Mrs. G.'s infant discovered his hands and spent the morning examining them, she smiled at the wonder of his delightful discovery. That evening she warmly shared the incident with her husband. But the morning he discovered his penis and tried to examine it, she grew tense and confided to her husband that their son had gotten to *"that"* stage.

Every child wants to explore each part of his body from all angles. Such investigations give evidence of alert curiosity and are part of self-discovery. When you treat explorations in one area as acceptable but get upset about others, you teach that particular parts of the body are taboo.

Sooner or later all youngsters discover their genitals and that they evoke pleasurable sensations. All of them engage in self-exploration and in some mutual exploration or sex play.

What do you do when this happens? Your reactions speak to youngsters. Do you frown, shame, or threaten? Or do you give them a name for the body parts and discuss the differences between boys and girls? Do you say, "Yes, those parts give good feelings, but you aren't to play with other children to get them?" Do you see the young child's genital play as normal or as dangerously precocious?

The word "masturbation" is emotionally charged for many parents. Some adults today still believe, *falsely,* that masturbation causes mental illness, mental retardation, and delinquency. *There is no truth in this belief;* masturbation does not cause any of these things. It is true that many mentally ill, retarded, and delinquent people engage in masturbation, but their self-manipulation is not the cause of their problems. Problems exist first: self-manipulation comes afterward.

Masturbation is an almost universal occurrence during three

stages of normal development. During infancy, the healthy, alert child feels and investigates the genital area with the same curiosity that he pokes at his ears or fondles his teddy or pulls at his cat's tail. Since the nerve endings there are quite sensitive, he naturally experiences a generalized pleasant sensation. But this feeling is not the intensely exciting feeling of the mature adult. You cannot prevent this initial discovery, but if you handle it unwisely the youngster concludes that the genitals and the feelings coming from them are bad and wrong.

The second period of genital play comes between three and five when children are emotionally attached to the opposite-sexed parent. Children handle some of their sexual feelings at this stage by self-manipulation. Because boys have a noticeable organ for elimination that is pleasurable to touch, they are more apt to play with themselves than girls.

"What do you do when your four-year-old boy holds his penis in public? If I make him feel comfortable about doing this whenever he wants to, he's going to run into rejection from others," said Mrs. W.

Certainly, this is true. You help a youngster learn the ways of society by telling him that if he wants to hold his penis, he needs to do so in the privacy of home. Say, "You know there are some things we do in front of others and there are some things we do only in the privacy of our families. We don't run around outside without clothes on, but if we want to do this at home, we can. If you want to hold your penis, wait till you're home."

By three or four, a child is aware that there are two sexes and that he is a boy or girl. His curiosity about the differences between bodies and ways of urinating carries no more significance than his interest in noticing that chickens and cats eat in a different fashion.

Many forward-looking nursery schools provide for youngsters to see members of the opposite sex urinating by having a common bathroom for boys and girls with the doors from the toilet cubicles removed. This practice has *not* resulted in youngsters becoming sexually precocious nor has it accentuated sex play. It has, instead, fostered an acceptance of sex differences and eliminated snickering exposures to satisfy curiosity. After a few weeks, there is no more interest in watching another child urinate than there is in watching him get a drink of water.

The third period for self-manipulation occurs in adolescence when the specific activity of the sex glands makes itself felt. Because direct outlets for sexual expression are restricted until they are older, adolescents turn to masturbation to handle the new intensity of their feelings.

Some genital play, then, is part of normal development. Avoid any implication that masturbation is dirty, makes the child sick, causes insanity, impotence, or that it is a sign of moral weakness.

You *should* be concerned when masturbation is prolonged and excessive. When this happens, it suggests that the *child's relationships with others may give him so little satisfaction that he is forced to turn to himself.*

Masturbation can be a tension-reliever. When excessive, it signals that a youngster is unhappy or is laboring under too many pressures. It can indicate that he has too few meaningful involvements in life. His tensions may come from holding in negative feelings, unrealistic expectations, excessive competition, feeling inadequate, bored, or lonely, or from discipline that is too strict or too lenient. It is almost always accompanied by other indications of unhappiness.

The job is to deal with the cause and not the symptom, which is all excessive masturbation is. The more you provide a relaxed, accepting, nurturing climate, the fewer inner tensions your youngster builds. Happy, involved children are much less apt to cling to masturbation to get satisfaction in life. The pleasures of self-manipulation rarely outweigh the joy of feeling loved and worthwhile. Masturbation gives only a temporary, lonely relief that cannot compete with the deep satisfactions of meaningful involvements with others.

A little masturbation at certain stages, then, is common; a lot means that you need to attend to the climate surrounding the child and see that he has experiences that build self-esteem.

Self-respect is nurtured by wholehearted acceptance of the body and its sexual feelings, even though such feelings may not be expressed indiscriminately. Even though your attitudes and teachings are positive, children are bound to run into negative attitudes from other sources. All you can do is to make sure that your training is positive and point out that other attitudes exist. Remember: the child with high self-esteem is less likely to absorb such negative attitudes.

Sex and role identification

Nothing is more devastating than a child's belief that he is the wrong sex. Feeling that his particular sex is second best tears at self-respect because he is helpless to alter it. And it can interfere with identifying positively with his sex.

Mr. G. assumed that, of course, his first child would be a boy; he planned all sorts of activities the two of them would do together. When the much-wished-for boy turned out to be a girl, he was crushed. Although her name was Elaine, he called her "Bud" and jokingly introduced her as "his son." Elaine never felt quite right about herself. Her recourse was to become a masculine girl. Her low self-esteem, lack of female identification, and her anger toward her father's masked rejection noticeably affected her total adjustment to marriage.

If you resent a child's sex, look inside yourself for the cause. You must take *active* steps to correct such rejection, otherwise your youngster feels unacceptable at a very basic level. Part of any child's high self-esteem is feeling, "I'm glad I'm a boy," or "I'm glad I'm a girl." Your child cannot be glad if you aren't.

Sex and relationship to parents

Every girl's attitude toward boys is colored by her relationship with her father. And every boy's way of seeing girls is affected by how he and his mother have gotten along.

Dominated by his mother, Henry avoided getting under the thumb of another female, for to him women necessarily meant domination. He never married; he saw sex as a vehicle for controlling women in his never-ending attempt to get even with his mother.

Gertrude's hatred for her father generalized to dislike for all men. Although she married, she was dedicated to making life miserable for her husband. The only reason her marriage lasted was that she picked a man with a deep need to be punished.

Friendly feelings between a child and the parent of the opposite sex contribute to his enjoyment of the other sex and his future sexual adjustment.

Sex and developmental tasks

Emotionally immature adults do not handle their feelings maturely. And sexual feelings are no exception. Each time your child completes a task of selfhood, he moves toward emotional maturity. Helping him with the normal steps of growth is positive sex education. A task left undone or surrounded by guilt adds to immaturity and less adequate sexual functioning. Every person brings his total person into the intimate communication of adult sexuality. And he behaves accordingly.

Sex and discipline

Because discipline is concerned with how family members meet each other's needs, the type children live with has its impact on their responses to the needs—including the sexual needs—of others and themselves. A dominated youngster may use sex to control; intercourse may be more rape-like in spirit than mutually enjoyable. Or, if a youngster is crushed by authoritarianism, he may become a sexual door mat.

Over-permissiveness made Larry think only of his own needs. He "loved 'em and left 'em." It was no skin off his teeth if girls read love into his need for self-gratification. Eventually, when he married, his wife tolerated his selfishness but got back at him by devious devices. Their marriage bed was an arena for ploys, counterploys, selfish victories and hurtful defeats.

Democratic discipline gives youngsters a pattern of mutual respect to carry into their sex life. It nurtures commitment and involvement that become a total way of life. It, therefore, becomes a powerful force for positive sex education.

Sex and the self-image

As we've seen, a youngster's image of himself influences his behavior, including how he behaves sexually.

Les felt deeply inadequate as a male. His Don Juan antics were his attempt to prove his virility to himself and others. His major interest in dating was to get the girl into bed to verify his sexual prowess. As a married man, he could not remain faithful because he continually had to gather fresh evidence indicating he was thoroughly masculine.

Tom's inadequacy splashed over into his sex life. To maintain internal consistency, he had to behave as a sexual incompetent.

Nancy was exceptionally attractive and had a fine mind, but she believed she had little to offer. By sixteen she had had a series of affairs. In a group counseling session she spoke about her promiscuity. "All I have to offer a boy is my body. Sex is date insurance; it means I won't be left out." Not believing her person was worthy of respect, she didn't believe her body was either.

Nancy's frankness encouraged another girl in the group to open up. Margaret said, "I don't belong. All my life I've wished I could be 'in.' Sex is my admission ticket. Who cares about a reputation? It doesn't keep you company on the sidelines!"

"I know I run around with a no-good gang, but at least they're like me," admitted June. "We're all a bunch of rejects; we've got that in common. Sure, I'd like to get in with the other kind of kids, but when I'm around them, I don't even know how to talk. They're all so sure of themselves. Makes me feel lower than ever. I could never make it in their circles, so why try?" June's lack of self-respect was reflected in the company she kept and in her consequent behavior.

"I think my reason for sleeping with every guy I go out with has nothing to do with sex or dates or wanting to be 'in,'" said Bonnie. "I think I do it to get even with my mother. She ruled me with an iron thumb from the time I can remember. I don't really like sex all that much. But, this is *one* place where she can't rule me. Besides, frankly, it's fun to get a guy going. Gives me a feeling of power and I like that."

Instant and indiscriminate sex makes for shallow relationships; it sanctions noninvolvement and feeds alienation.

Indiscriminate sex is the urge for pleasure without pressure from commitment or conflict. The person who wants only self-satisfaction but not responsibility will gravitate toward others with similar interests. The emotionally mature do not seek superficial involvements. In fact, reaching out for responsible relations is a mute statement: "I have something to offer another and I can handle a long-term commitment."

Indiscriminate sex is the cry to avoid maturity. It is the obvious way to duck out from under the stresses which *all* commitments involve. Responsibility to another is what separates man from the animal in mature sex. Self-seeking never results in self-fulfillment.

Sexually promiscuous youngsters use sex to work out more fundamental problems—ones unrelated to sex. Their sex life rarely leads to the warm satisfactions they seek. Pathetically, their symptom leads them down blind alleys that invariably create new, more complicated problems.

Promiscuity, then, can stem from a number of sources: emotional hungers, negative reactions toward parental values, over-control, or over-permissiveness. Of course, it can also result from parental example.

Promiscuity in boys is more apt to be sanctioned by society. "Boys will be boys!" we say.

Our culture is steeped in the belief that young men need to sow their wild oats. Many a father is secretly proud of his son's sexual escapades, believing that they underscore his son's virility. But male promiscuity has *nothing* to do with masculinity; in fact, it may signify precisely the reverse. The Don Juans have to concentrate on conquests to shore up their doubts about their sexual capacities.

Barring psychological factors (unmet emotional needs), adolescent male promiscuity is probably a function of the intensity of the male sex drive, coupled with cultural pressures that delay the age of marriage. In girls it is more a factor of psychological (*not sexual*) hungers.

The reality of the strong sex drive in boys has contributed heavily to our society's general acceptance of a double standard for sexual behavior. Contraceptive pills, antibiotics, and the revolution in moral ethics are causing some parents to accept a similar standard for their daughters. Other parents are at a loss as to how much sexual activity to sanction outside marriage.

Early marriage may seem like a solution to the problem; yet, statistics show a high incidence of divorce for those who marry in their teens. No doubt some divorces occur because the marriage only provided legal status for a forthcoming child. But many other youthful marriages falter even so.

Probably one major cause for these divorces is that the

adolescent is still evolving his potentials and working out his sense of identity. The mate who looks compatible to a youngster at seventeen may be completely unsatisfactory when he has fully matured. So, early marriages are not the simple solution they appear on the surface.

The idea that sexual urges cannot be controlled or released through active, vigorous participation in sports and other activities just isn't true. Indiscriminate sexual activity is *not* the only way out for young people.

> **The evidence suggests that the best insulation against indiscriminate sexual behavior when the herd instinct runs high in adolescence—when sexual urges are intense—is a high degree of personal worth.**

A sense of personal value insulates a youngster from selling himself short and lessens interest in irresponsible sexual behavior. The youngster who likes himself seeks wholesome relationships that nourish self-esteem rather than meaningless ones that tear it apart. Belief in himself makes a youngster less wary of commitment—he knows he can handle it. And he is freer to take a firm stand on moral issues. And as we've seen, his self-respect makes him seek others who handle their lives similarly.

The youngster with low self-esteem has had negative experiences with love and, once burned, prefers fly-by-night arrangements that permit him to remain uncommitted, irresponsible, and uninvolved. Such a youngster may marry, but he usually chooses a person who also shys from psychological intimacy. He cannnot grow and flourish, of course, without genuine intimacy, but he prefers this hunger to the proven danger of closeness.

Building self-esteem is fundamental to a positive sex-education program, for self-respect underlies the healthy, nurturing marriage.

What they should know

Along with an acceptance of himself and his feelings, every youngster needs specific information about the reproductive process. Almost every library has books written for appropriate age levels that present the facts of reproduction. Looking through some of them will give you a general idea about how and what to tell a child. Specific facts, however, should be given *when* specific questions are asked.

Guard against giving more information than a child asks for. Too much detail too early only confuses and may be absorbed incorrectly.

Prior to adolescence, each youngster should be familiar with reproductive facts and the contributions that both male and female make. He should know how babies are started (conception), how they grow during pregnancy (gestation), and how they are born (childbirth). He should understand the basic facts about heredity, menstruation, and nocturnal emissions.

Children should be taught that the process of childbirth is perfectly normal. Too many youngsters, girls particularly, are scared to death of this normal human function because they have heard exaggerated tales or read dramatic accounts of difficult and painful births.

"My mother told me that having a baby was the worst experience in her life," said Beth. Such statements can make the Beths (and there are many of them) feel guilty or bad for the pain they caused their mothers, as well as fearful of ever becoming mothers themselves.

Mothers who have had unpleasant experiences in childbirth should let their daughters know that difficult deliveries are the exception rather than the rule. Boys need this information as well so that they won't carry exaggerated fears into their relationships with their wives or worry about the pain they may cause them.

When discussing sex with youngsters, point out that sexual feelings will probably be strong and powerful. They need advance preparation. They must be taught that mature sexual expression means personal responsibility to the integrity of the other person involved. They need to know that only in this framework can sex truly nurture. Casual sex always hurts someone because almost invariably one or the other becomes emotionally involved. Meaningless encounters are rarely constructive.

Listening to a youngster's ideas and attitudes before giving facts helps clear up misconceptions picked up from others or from his own imaginings.

Point out the difference between male and female sexual urges. Both sexes must understand that a boy is much more quickly aroused than a girl and that his feelings are not necessarily related to love. Because a girl's sexual urges are more frequently associated with romantic love, she's apt to interpret advances as a sign of love. What may be a one-night stand for Harry may be a deep commitment for Marge. Many a young girl's heart has been broken because she was not fully aware of this *fundamental* difference between the sexes.

Girls should know that boys are stimulated visually; they should be aware that provocative clothes, postures, and "come-on's" are completely unfair to boys who are trying to handle their feelings responsibly. On the other hand, girls should understand that it is not an insult if a boy makes a pass, and by the same token, it is not an insult to the boy when she says no.

"Well," said Ginny, "I did say no and Greg never asked me out again." Ginny might consider that if Greg asked her out only for sexual release, he probably wouldn't remain in the relationship once he got what he wanted anyway.

Girls should know that most boys are not interested in lasting relationships with promiscuous girls. Serious, committed involvements are built on trust, and promiscuity destroys trust.

The boy who is seriously in love doesn't reject a girl simply because she refuses sexual intimacy. If he's serious, he'll stay around until they are both ready to assume the responsibility of marriage. Her standards increase his respect for her as a person with the courage of her convictions. Few boys remain permanently interested in an easy mark.

Our society abounds with the philosophy, "You-can-have-anything-for-nothing." "Have-it-now; pay-later" has become an American byword. As a parent, you have to actively counteract this attitude by teaching and example. Youngsters must realize that deferred payment costs—and often dearly.

Every youngster has to take a stand at some time or another in the management of his sexual feelings. Emphasize that *he* holds the power of choice as to where he wants to go and how he eventually lives his life. The ultimate decisions lie in his hands.

Youngsters need to think *ahead* about the consequences of their actions both to themselves and others. Thinking through in advance about handling difficult situations prepares youngsters so that they are not caught unaware or in the heat of emotion.

How you manage your life—whether you behave responsibly and live by a moral code—has its impact on your children. When you know clearly what you stand for and *act* on your beliefs, you give youngsters convincing models. Teen-agers, as we've seen, are particularly involved in working out a meaningful value system and they need strong, dedicated adults. They are quick to detect hypocrisy. Every adolescent needs a positive philosophy to handle sex wisely. Strong affectional bonds with your children give them the necessary cushion to be true to their ideals.

How to present the facts

Ideally, youngsters should get the facts of reproduction from parents who feel comfortable about sex themselves. But from a practical point of view, many of us feel squeamish discussing this topic. The important issue is not whether you are comfortable but whether you can be *open* about how you *do* feel.

Children quickly detect attitudes. "Mother gave me the whole spiel about the facts of life," said twelve-year-old Cindy. "She got through the details without batting an eye, but, man, could you tell it was loaded for her! Her face flushed at certain words, and she acted like she was swallowing a bad pill."

Remember: trust is vital; therefore, put your cards on the table frankly. Say, "I'd like to answer your questions about sex without getting all flustered, but frankly I can't. As I grew up, this subject wasn't discussed and I feel uncomfortable with it. I'll answer the questions I can, even if I flounder, and I'll get you books for fuller details. I only hope you'll be more relaxed talking about this subject when you're a parent."

Honesty about discomfort in discussing sex—if it exists—makes it clear that the *subject* is legitimate but that your past training is responsible for your lack of ease. This is an important point in positive sex education.

You may be able to reduce personal discomfort by developing an adequate working vocabulary. Familiarity with the terms of reproduction makes discussion easier. If certain words are emotionally charged, say them to yourself a hundred or two times. You'd be surprised how this helps.

Reading four or five books on sex education written for your aged child can familiarize you with ways to present facts. Better yet, read them aloud to yourself. Your ears *can* get used to those "loaded" words and ideas.

Present facts *accurately*. You can't get away with fairy tales or the brush-off when your child is four and give him the straight scoop when he's thirteen. You destroy trust, and curiosity doesn't wait for your convenience. You have to decide whom you want your child's teacher to be: you or another child?

Some of you may feel that no amount of reading or practice will result in comfort about sex talk. Then, say, "I would like to discuss this subject with you but because of my past training I can't. But you can talk to . . ." And make an appointment for your youngster with a doctor, nurse, school counselor, minister, or friend.

One word of warning: do not assume that a person is comfortable talking about sex because of his profession. No vocation guarantees relaxed, positive attitudes toward sex. Talk to the individual yourself and get a personal feel for his "comfort quotient."

By the time they are three or four, most children ask where babies come from. If they haven't, open the subject no later than age five at an appropriate time by commenting on a birth in the neighborhood, in a story, on television, or with pets. Ask, "Do you know how babies are born?" Or bring home a library book about sex written for preschoolers just as you bring home books on other subjects for reading aloud. Allow plenty of time for questions and discussion. Make a practice of getting sex-education books into your youngsters' hands at appropriate ages all during childhood even though you may prefer to give the initial introductions yourself.

Support they will need

The early or late bloomer profits from support and open discussion about his growth. The sting from other children's remarks is lessened when he is aware of the tremendous variations in rates of development. Slow growers are especially helped by developing specific skills. Competence offsets the "failure" of a small or late-developing body.

Regardless of awareness and skills, the child will have feelings about his development if it is noticeably out of step with his peers. Plenty of *active, empathic listening* helps him accept a situation he cannot change. Avoid logic and lectures like the plague. Usually discrepancies in development occur at the very time a youngster needs to feel just like everyone else. Knowing you *understand* his predicament is the greatest support in the world.

Adolescents need opportunities to discuss their various feelings—including their attitudes and fears about sex—with other teen-agers. Such discussions, however, won't be open (and therefore will be less productive) unless the seven ingredients of safe encounter are present. Teen-agers still need group support; facing their sexual feelings through mutual sharing is healthier than worrying about them alone. They are ordinarily freer to express true feelings if the adult leader is not one of their parents and if he is skilled in facilitating frank and honest communication.

At this point, you can appreciate the tremendous variety of factors that affects how a youngster handles his sexuality. Each one plays a big part in the sex education he receives. All aspects of a child's life influence whether he develops a responsible and committed wedding of sex and love in his attitudes and behavior.

TWENTY-SIX · IN CONCLUSION

At this point, hopefully, you have a new appreciation for the nature of the human fabric and the importance of self-esteem in every child's life. But this awareness may fill you with guilt. If so, read on.

Remember: human beings adapt and work around even the most unfavorable psychological environments. The push toward health flourishes even in those who have had little psychological nourishment and who are well advanced in years.

Everything you have done to date has probably come off of heartfelt intentions for your children's well-being. Any lacks in your parenting are the result of little or no training and not having received confirmation yourself. Blaming yourself, your mate, your parents, or your life circumstances only impedes your progress. You can decide to see your parental shortcomings as opportunities for growth or for beating yourself with the hammer of guilt and remorse. My hope is that you will embrace yourself as a human being still in the process of developing your own untapped potentials. You can start today and rectify deficiencies that exist; if the job seems too big, seek professional help.

The place to start in extending your nurturing is with *yourself*. Each move toward meeting your own needs and accepting yourself is an investment in the welfare of your family. A checklist of the basic ideas in this book is provided after this conclusion. Refer to it *frequently* for those booster shots we all need to remind us of the essentials.

Remember: *you don't have to be perfect*. As Lincoln said, "Look for what is wrong and you will surely find it." You probably have made mistakes in rearing your children, but can you honestly find a single parent who hasn't? If you think you know one, you don't have all the facts. All any of us can do is our best each day, but that "best" will never be perfect. And children do quite nicely with fully human parents who fall short here and there.

Look to the *climate surrounding your child now*. Regardless of the past, deal with the present, with where you and your child are at this moment. If you are uncertain about whether your look, talk, or expectation withers self-respect, put yourself in your child's shoes. Then, you'll have a clue as to the quality of the mirroring you do. Remember: no child needs positive mirrors at every moment in life.

Each of your children is most likely to fulfill his promise in a climate that confirms and allows him to grow in his own time, in his own way. Your child needs your active understanding as he travels the uneven path from dependence to independence. Given the necessary elements he has no choice but to like himself.

Remember: the healthy child is true to himself; this gives him personal integrity. He does what he can with what he has and is at peace within. The unhealthy one lives by borrowed standards. At odds with himself, he masks his unacceptable parts and judges himself and others accordingly. Each of us gives daily answers to the question, "Can I let my child be true to himself?" A line in the song, "I Gotta Be Me," goes, "I can't be right for somebody else if I can't be right for me." This is a modern version of Shakespeare's, "This above all:

to thine own self be true, and it must follow, as the night the day, thou canst not then be false to any man."

Aristotle knew the truth that psychology verifies today. Over two thousand years ago, he said,

**"Happiness
is
Self-contentedness."**

Living with your child so that he is deeply and quietly glad that he is who he is gives him a priceless legacy: strength to meet stress, and courage to become committed, responsible, productive, and creative—a fully *human* person. Then your personal investments of nurturing love, time, energy, and money will bear fruit endlessly into the far reaches of time. Helping your child like himself is the greatest gift you can give. It spells L-O-V-E in a most profound way.

For a practical step-by-step program to increase your own self-esteem, refer to CELEBRATE YOUR SELF by Dorothy Corkille Briggs, Doubleday, 1977.

CHECKLIST OF BASIC IDEAS

Here are the kernel ideas we've talked about. Such a checklist has proven popular with parents in my classes for a quick review of the nurturing they provide. It can be a roadmap for increasing your effectiveness.

The Basis of Emotional Health

1. How your child feels about himself affects how he lives his life.
2. High self-esteem is based on your child's belief that he is *lovable* and *worthwhile*.
3. Your child must know that he matters just because he exists.
4. He needs to feel competent to handle himself and his environment. He needs to feel he has something to offer others.
5. High self-esteem is *not conceit*; it is your child's quiet comfort about being who he is.

Mirrors Create Self-Images

1. Every child has the potential for liking himself.
2. Your child *learns* to see himself as the important people around him do.
3. He builds his self-picture from the words, body language, attitudes, and judgments of others.
4. He judges himself according to his own observation of himself in comparison with others and others' responses to him.
5. High self-esteem comes from positive experiences with life and love.

Mirrors Influence Behavior

1. Your child's behavior *matches* his self-image.
2. He may feel confident in one area but not in another; how he acts gives you clues as to whether he feels he operates from a position of strength (positive self-statements) or weakness (negative self-statements).
3. If your child sees himself as inadequate, he *expects to fail* and acts accordingly. Personal sureness, however, gives him the courage and energy to tackle tasks. It allows him to *expect to win,* and he acts accordingly.
4. Belief in himself ensures that your child will relate more successfully to others. Then, personal happiness is more likely to be his.

The Price of Warped Mirrors

1. Your child is seeking self-respect.
2. If he feels inadequate, he may submit to a self-effacing life, withdraw, or erect various defenses to keep his self-esteem.
3. Neurotic defenses are put up around the belief, "I am unlovable and unworthy."

4. When defenses push others away, the youngster defeats his need for positive reflections.
5. Your positive reflections allow your child to avoid paths that cut into the fullness of living.

The Trap of Negative Reflections

1. Ordinarily, your child's view of himself is continually changing.
2. If he becomes convinced that he is no good, he must, to remain internally consistent, refuse to let in positive messages about his competence.
3. Low self-esteem that is rigid results from many negative factors operating over a long period.
4. Negative self-attitudes *can be changed* to high self-esteem by providing your child with a nurturing climate of acceptance and experiences with success.

Polishing Parental Mirrors

1. We all see our children through filters of inexperience, borrowed standards, unfinished business, unmet hungers, and cultural values.
2. Filters become expectations by which you measure your child; they influence how you treat him.
3. If your expectations do not fit your particular child at his particular stage of growth, you will probably be disappointed in him.
4. If your child feels he consistently falls below your standards, he loses his respect for himself.
5. Your expectations are more likely to be fair if they are based on the facts of child development, alert observations, and sensitivity to his past and present pressures.
6. Check your expectations *frequently*; it is so easy for them to get out of line.
7. The more fulfilled you are as a person, the fewer unrealistic pressures you'll put on your child.

8. What you do to yourself, you will do to your child. Therefore, increasing your *own* self-acceptance allows you to be more accepting of your child.

Genuine Encounter

1. Every child needs focused attention—genuine encounter—to feel loved.
2. Love is not necessarily communicated by physical affection, constantly setting aside your own needs, overprotection, high expectations, time, and gifts.
3. Your child is likely to view continual distancing—concern with the past, future, schedules, and tasks—as lack of love. He can only *feel* lovable if you take time to be fully *with his person.*
4. Make a habit of being open to the wonder of your child in the here-and-now. Check yourself *frequently* on your focused attention rating.

The Safety of Trust

1. Trust is the most important ingredient of a psychologically safe climate.
2. Your child must be able to count on you for friendly help with his needs.
3. Your words must match your body language if he is to trust you.
4. He needs you to be *appropriately* open with him about your feelings, your reservations, and your ambivalences.
5. Your child needs your humanness; be real with him. This helps him accept his own humanness, giving him a model that allows him to embrace all parts of himself. Then, he is not alienated from himself or others.

The Safety of Nonjudgment

1. The second ingredient of safety comes when judgment goes.

2. Direct your "I-reactions" toward behavior; give up "you-judgments" of your child's person.
3. When your child sees his person as separate from his acts, he's better able to build *solid* self-respect.

The Safety of Being Cherished

1. Cherishing your child's specialness, even though his behavior may not be acceptable, is the third ingredient of psychological safety.
2. Refuse to take your child's uniqueness for granted, treat him with the same respect you want, focus on his positive qualities, avoid seeing him as the same as his acts, and work toward valuing yourself. Then, your cherishing will come through.
3. When your child feels cherished, he will seek more realistic goals, accept others as they are, learn more efficiently, use his creativity, and like himself.

The Safety of "Owning" Feelings

1. The fourth ingredient of psychological safety comes with letting a child "own" his feelings without withdrawing your approval.
2. You respect separateness when you avoid asking your child to match his feelings and reactions to yours.
3. Offer your child many experiences, but treat his reactions to them with respect. Avoid forcing lessons on him when *he* doesn't enjoy them.
4. Plan actively for differences among your children, both in expectations and family activities.
5. Respect for differences and uniqueness nurtures your child's self-esteem.

The Safety of Empathy

1. Empathy is understanding your child's viewpoint without judgment, agreement, or disagreement. Be atten-

tive to body language as it is more accurate than words.

2. Empathy must come from your heart to be genuine.

3. When your child is upset, his secret wish is for empathic understanding; he needs it before explanations, reasons, or reassurance.

4. If you see your parental role as that of a nurturer, if you respect your child's integrity, if you are in touch with and comfortable about your own feelings, empathy comes easier.

5. Empathy erases alienation; it is powerful proof of love. And it actively builds your child's love for you.

The Safety of Unique Growing

1. The sixth ingredient of psychological safety is the freedom to grow uniquely.

2. Growth proceeds in spurts interlaced with regressions and plateaus.

3. The push toward growth is built into your child.

4. When your child feels safe to retreat, he is free to grow.

5. The seven ingredients of safe encounter intertwine to form the climate of love. They ensure that your child will *feel* your caring; then he develops wholehearted self-respect and can unfold in all directions.

Journey of Self: Over-all Plan

1. Human growth follows a logical plan; completing each step successfully allows your child to feel competent and worthwhile.

2. Familiarity with the plan helps keep your expectations realistic, spares you needless worry, helps you be more accepting, and can enable you to work *with* your child's psychological homework so that he is free for the next task ahead.

Journey of Self: First Six Years

1. Autonomy, mastery, initiative, attachment to the opposite-sexed parent, self-centeredness, and preference for the same sex are the tasks of the first six years.
2. Selfhood tasks are worked on at the same time that your preschooler learns what his body will do, what the world around him is like, and what it is to be a member of a family.
3. Your preschooler has a huge assignment; go easy; he needs slow, nonpressurized teaching.
4. The conscience only begins to emerge around six; it needs strong outside support.

Journey of Self: Middle Years

1. Your middle-aged child needs to refine autonomy and increase mastery while defining himself with reflections from agemates.
2. He is making the move from self-centeredness to other-centeredness but it is *gradual.*
3. Your eight to ten works on getting hold of the feel of what males and females do by imitating the same-sexed parent. He needs sustained exposures to a strong, warm adult of the same sex. Seek a substitute model for him if there isn't one in your home.
4. From eleven to thirteen, your youngsters will seek same-sexed models outside the family.
5. You smooth the way for your youngster's increasing competence and self-respect by encouraging him to join groups his age, offering opportunities to develop skills in activities he enjoys, accepting his movement away from the family, and especially by providing safe encounters.

Journey of Self: Adolescence

1. Your teen-ager needs to sever his dependence on the family and agemates, while reevaluating his picture of himself. He needs new answers as to his identity to fit the changes in himself and in his roles.
2. He needs to establish healthy relationships with the opposite sex, plan for a life work, and build a meaningful set of values by which to live.
3. Many roadblocks exist in our culture that directly stand in the adolescent's way as he tries to build a sense of identity.
4. The more you can give your teen-ager a sense of personal security (safe encounters and democratic discipline), the better he will withstand the outside pressures.
5. It is not until late adolescence that your teen-ager's conscience will be able to stand without outside support.
6. Many factors can make your teen-agers a personal threat to you. Looking honestly at those threats can make them less overwhelming.

Handling Children's Feelings

1. Most of us do not handle children's feelings as we want ours handled.
2. All children have all kinds of feelings that tradition has taught us to avoid dealing with directly.
3. Handling negative feelings by reason, judgment, denial, advice, reassurance, or diversion pushes a child away. It forces him to think less of himself and to repress or disguise his true emotions.
4. Repressed feelings do not disappear; they work against physical, emotional, and intellectual health.
5. The power of feelings evaporates when emotions are

accepted with understanding and channeled into acceptable outlets.

6. Your child needs you to be an *active* listener, not a *passive* one.

7. To get rid of negative acts, get rid of negative feelings first; they are the *cause*.

8. Acts may need to be limited, but expression of feelings should be limited only in terms of to whom, when, and where they are released.

Cracking the Code of Anger

1. The normal feeling of anger masks an earlier feeling.

2. When you accept anger by *active* listening, your child will usually lead you to the *underlying* emotion. Channel his feelings into safe outlets.

3. Times of anger can be reduced but never completely eliminated. If your child is frequently angry, check: Are his physical and emotional needs being met, is he up against too many frustrations, is he getting abundant exercise? Check your expectations, type of discipline, competition, comparisons, family tensions. Is he getting large doses of safe encounters?

4. Coming to terms with your own hostilities helps you work with his.

5. Send your *first* feelings as "I-reactions."

6. Most tantrums are a sign of lost control and extreme frustration, not bratty behavior.

7. Indirect signs of anger are constant teasing, tattling, sarcasm, acting-out aggression, hitting out at adult values, continual accidents, unrealistic fears, model behavior, depression, and psychosomatic symptoms.

8. Your acceptance of your child's anger prevents his using indirect outlets or repressing. It permits him to accept his total humanity.

Lifting the Mask of Jealousy

1. Jealousy is a normal feeling in families, particularly since each child wants to be the favorite.
2. Jealousy masks your child's real or imagined feeling that he is *disadvantaged*.
3. Internal or external pressures can decrease your child's feeling of adequacy; then, he is apt to feel jealous.
4. With high self-esteem, your child has an inner sureness that protects him from frequent and intense jealousy.
5. Jealousy grows when favoritism, comparisons, or lack of respect for individuality is present. Avoid using one child to meet your own unmet needs. A relaxed family atmosphere based on cooperation and democratic discipline reduces its frequency.
6. Indirect signs of jealousy are a sudden increase in dependency, regression, demands for material things, and increased misbehavior.
7. When jealousy comes, help your child express it by active listening. His feeling is real for him regardless of the facts.
8. Help your child to feel understood, included, and important; then, he doesn't feel shortchanged.

Disciples in Discipline

1. Discipline refers to *rules* for behavior and to the *methods* used to make and enforce them.
2. Discipline teaches children to get along with others. They can mind from fear of reprisal or from inner conviction.
3. The end goal of discipline is self-discipline.
4. Some limits are necessary to help people meet their needs as they live together.

5. Rules are more likely to be constructive when they consider both your children's *and* your needs.
6. Fewer rules are needed when you provide appropriate outlets for children's urges, suit the environment of childish needs, keep expectations realistic, and provide a climate of love and respect.
7. The kinds and number of rules in your home can support or undermine your child's confidence in himself.

Old Ways of Discipline

1. Authoritarian discipline means you *retain* your power, make the rules, and enforce them by reward or punishment.
2. Over-permissive discipline means you *give* your power to your child to do as he pleases regardless of your needs.
3. When relied on *exclusively*, either of these two approaches works against responsible self-discipline, inner conviction, a healthy conscience, and high self-esteem.

Constructive Discipline

1. Democratic discipline means working *with* children to establish mutually agreeable limits and solutions to conflicts. You *share* your power.
2. To establish democracy you need democratic attitudes of mutual respect, realistic expectations, skill in releasing negative feelings, and a willingness to share your feelings and power.
3. Democratic procedures involve a clear statement of the problem, the expression of each person's needs, searching for a solution that meets those needs, and reacting to the solution after the family has worked with it.
4. Unless you listen *actively* and send "I-reactions" continuously, the lines of communication will bog down and defeat your efforts at home democracy.

5. Democracy's benefits are widespread: it fosters friendly feelings between you and your children; it encourages responsibility, independence, motivation, creative thinking, intellectual growth, personal involvement, and respect for those in authority. It directly enhances high self-esteem, for it is powerful proof of love, faith, and trust.

Motivation, Intelligence, and Creativity

1. Your child is born curious and with a push toward self-reliance.
2. Support his explorations, curiosity, and moves toward self-reliance if you want him to be intellectually stimulated and to use his creativity. He must know he is safe to wonder and discover.
3. You stimulate his intelligence by providing rich first-hand experiences, broad language exposures, successful problem-solving experiences, and family examples and attitudes that value learning and independence.
4. Your child's intellectual growth is affected by: physical handicaps, emotional hungers, repressed feelings, undue pressure for unrealistic goals, nondemocratic discipline, closed lines of communication, overcrowded classrooms, inadequate teachers, and poor teaching techniques.
5. A climate of safe encounter motivates your child to learn and to capitalize on his inborn uniqueness. There is a direct relationship between unfettered creativity and high self-esteem.

The Wedding of Sex and Love

1. Sex education means more than teaching the facts of reproduction. It involves fostering healthy attitudes toward the body, feelings, sex roles, and the self.
2. Attitudes toward sex are colored by cuddling, feeding, dressing, bathing, and toilet training experiences; prog-

ress in developmental tasks; how negative feelings are handled; the kinds of models provided; the values youngsters see lived; the type of discipline used; as well as by influences from outside the home.

3. Your attitudes toward sex are contagious. Be open about any squeamishness you may have. Place the responsibility where it belongs: on your past training rather than on the subject.

4. Present the facts of reproduction *when* your child asks questions. If he doesn't ask, open up the subject yourself. Give introductory information no later than age five. Get appropriate sex education books into his hands at each stage of development.

5. Positive sexual adjustment is more likely if your child is emotionally mature.

6. Self-esteem directly affects sexual behavior. Strong self-respects enables your youngster to establish an enriching, responsible, committed marriage to a person with similar self-regard. Such a couple is most apt to breed self-confidence in their own youngsters.

How do you spell love to your children? If they live with realistic expectations, safe encounters, cooperation with tasks of selfhood, understanding acceptance of all feelings even when you limit acts, and democratic discipline, they will *feel* loved. *And that feeling is the basis of high self-esteem.* With this solid inner core, potentials will unfold, they will be motivated, creative, and see a purpose in life. They will relate successfully with others, have inner peace, be stress resistant, and have a greater chance for a happy marriage. They themselves will become a nurturing parent.

Hopefully, at this point, you are convinced of the importance of knowing all you can about the most important job in the world—parenthood. The following reading guide can help you continue growing.

READING GUIDE

Books give only guidelines; they are not yardsticks by which to measure children. Here are some that can be springboards to your further learning about the nature and needs of children:

1. Do you want more information about what to expect developmentally?

   a. Gesell, Arnold & Ilg, Frances. *Infant and Child in the Culture of Today*. New York: Harper, 1943; *The Child from Five to Ten*. New York: Harper, 1946; *Youth* (10–16) New York: Harper, 1956.

   Organized by ages. Describes typical behavior and suggests specific techniques for handling.

   b. Hymes, James L., Jr. *The Child Under Six*. Englewood Cliffs, New Jersey: Prentice-Hall, 1963.

   A must for understanding all ages because if child hasn't completed tasks of first six years he carries them as unfinished business into later years.

c. Ilg, Frances & Ames, Louise. *Child Behavior*. New York: Dell, 1955 (pocketbook).

Organized by topics (eating, tensional outlets, etc.). Suggests causes and methods for handling. Index (pp. 349–53) gives references for each age level up to age ten. Chapter Two is a must.

d. Public Affairs Pamphlets, 22 E. 38th Street, New York 16, New York.

Enjoy Your Child, 1, 2, 3. (Excellent for all ages.)
Understanding Your Child from 6 to 12.
Keeping Up with Teen-agers.

e. Spock, Benjamin. *Baby and Child Care* (Revised pocket edition). New York: Pocket Books, Inc., 1957.

Specific, practical suggestions on child management on pp. 304–436.

f. Stone, Joseph L. & Church, Joseph. *Childhood and Adolescence*. New York: Random House, 1957.

Basic and chockful of essential material.

g. Superintendent of Documents, Department of Health, Education & Welfare, U.S. Government Printing Office, Washington 25, D.C.

A Healthy Personality for Your Child
Your Child from One to Six
Your Child from Six to Twelve
Adolescent in Your Family

Excellent, inexpensive pamphlets. Others available for children with special handicaps.

2. Would you like additional tips on living with preschoolers?

  a. Harlan, Mary. *First Steps in a Grown-up World*. New York: Abelard Press, 1952.

   Short and specific suggestions that work by a nursery school teacher.

3. Do you want more information on helping your child build a healthy conscience?

  a. Fraiberg, Selma. *The Magie Years*. New York: Scribner's Sons, 1959.

   Excellent suggestions by a practicing child therapist although I disagree with her belief in earned love. (p. 282).

4. Do you need more specifics on handling negative emotions and active listening?

  a. Axeline, Virginia. *Play Therapy*. Boston: Houghton Mifflin, 1947.

  b. Baruch, Dorothy. *New Ways in Discipline*. New York: McGraw-Hill, 1949.

  c. Baruch, Dorothy. *How To Live With Your Teen-ager*. New York: McGraw-Hill, 1953.

  d. Ginott, Haim. *Between Parent and Child*. New York: Macmillan Co., 1965.

  e. Ginott, Haim. *Between Parent and Teen-ager*. New York: Macmillan Co., 1969.

   All are excellent for understanding human nature and give specific suggestions. Easy reading; musts.

5. Would you like more material about jealousy and rivalry?

    a. Neisser, Edith. *Brothers and Sisters.* New York: Harper, 1951; *The Eldest Child.* New York: Harper, 1957.

    Both are excellent for gaining insight into the pressures on the child in relation to siblings. Easy reading; musts.

    b. Science Research Associates, 57 West Grand Avenue, Chicago, Illinois.

    "Helping Brothers and Sisters Get Along."

    An excellent, inexpensive pamphlet.

6. Are you interested in more material about discipline?

    a. Hymes, James L., Jr. "Discipline." Bureau of Publications, Teachers College, Columbia University, New York.

    An excellent, inexpensive pamphlet.

    b. Hymes, James L., Jr. *Behavior and Misbehavior.* Englewood Cliffs, New Jersey: Prentice-Hall, 1955; *Child Development Point of View.* Englewood Cliffs, New Jersey: Prentice-Hall, 1955.

    Both are short, easy reading, and give essential information.

    c. See listings under 4 (b. through e.).

7. Would you like some suggestions for stimulating your preschooler's intellectual potential?

    a. Frankel, Lillian. *What to Do with Your Preschooler.* New York: Sterling Publishing Co., 1953.

b. Hymes, James L., Jr. *Before the Child Reads*. Evanston, Illinois: Row, Peterson & Co., 1958.

c. Ward, Muriel. *Young Minds Need Something to Grow On*. Evanston, Illinois: Row, Peterson & Co., 1957.

All are short, easy reading, and give specific suggestions.

8. Do you want some guidelines on art and reading for the young child?

a. Bland, Jane Cooper. *Art of the Young Child* (3-5 years). New York: The Museum of Modern Art, 1957.

Discusses fundamentals for fostering artistic ability (pp. 33-47). Gives principles and examples of the meanings of art exposures at each age level. Short, easy reading, full of ideas.

b. Mitchell, Lucy Sprague. *Here and Now Story Book*. New York: E. P. Dutton & Co., 1921.

The fifty-page introduction ("What Language Means to Young Children") gives basic principles by which to choose children's literature. The rest of the book gives stories well loved and written by children (grouped by age levels: two-seven).

9. Would you like more information about creativity?

a. Anderson, Harold, (Ed.). *Creativity and Its Cultivation*. New York: Harper, 1959.

A collection of leading authorities share their ideas about the nature of creativity and how it can be encouraged.

b. Barron, Frank. *Creativity and Personal Freedom*. Princeton, New Jersey: D. Van Nostrand Co., Inc., 1968; *Creativity and Psychological Health*. Princeton, New Jersey: D. Van Nostrand Co., Inc., 1963.

Excellent material for showing how attitudes toward self affect creative expression.

10. Would you like to read more about the self-concept?

a. Axeline, Virginia. *Dibs: In Search of Self*. Boston: Houghton Mifflin, 1964.

A beautiful and moving account of one child's movement in therapy. It illustrates dramatically the ingredients necessary for a child to become fully himself. Highly recommended.

b. Coopersmith, Stanley. *Antecedents of Self-Esteem*. San Francisco: W. H. Freeman & Co., 1967.

This is a doctoral dissertation on the self-esteem of a group of junior high boys. It is academic reading but the conclusions listed at the end of each chapter are worth being familiar with.

c. Hayakawa, S. I. *Symbol, Status, and Personality*. New York: Harcourt, Brace & World, Inc., 1963.

Read Chapter 4. Easy reading and witty.

d. Horney, Karen. *Neurosis and Human Growth: The Struggle for Self-Realization*. New York: W. W. Norton, 1950.

Excellent source to learn more about how the neuroses develop around low self-esteem. Not simple reading but well worth the effort.

e. James, Muriel, and Jongeward, Dorothy. *Born to Win.*
Reading, Mass.: Addison-Wesley Pub. Co., 1971.

A gold mine for improving your own self-worth; easy
reading; filled with exercises for self-help. A must.
Paperback.

f. Moustakas, Clark (Ed.). *The Self.* New York: Harper
& Row, 1956.

Each of the nineteen chapters is written by a different
author. Some chapters are highly academic; some are
not. If you have time for only one chapter, read the
last one.

g. Newman, Mildred, and Berkowitz, Bernard, with Jean
Owen. *How to Be Your Own Best Friend.* New York:
Random House, 1971.

Outstanding. Simple yet profound. Only 53 pages
long but chock-full of nuggets for self-growth.

h. Putney, Shell and Putney, Gail. *Normal Neurosis—
The Adjusted American.* New York: Harper, 1964.

Read Chapter Three.

i. Rosenberg, Morris. *Society and the Adolescent Self-
Image.* New Jersey: Princeton University Press, 1965.

This is a report on over 5,000 high school seniors and
their self-images. Quite academic but the discussion at
the end of each chapter presents the findings briefly
and clearly.

j. Satir, Virginia. *Conjoint Family Therapy.* Palo Alto,
California: Science & Behavior Books, Inc., 1964.

Read Chapters Two through Six. Although written for professionals, the style is non-technical, short, and to the point.

k. Satir, Virginia. *Peoplemaking*. Palo Alto, California: Science & Behavior Books, Inc., 1972.

Excellent and easy reading. Really helpful to check what's going on in your family relative to self-worth.

11. Do you want more information about the fully functioning person and what he needs to flourish?

a. Association for Supervision and Curriculum Development. *Perceiving, Behaving, Becoming: A New Focus*. National Education Association, 1201 Sixteenth Street, N.W., Washington 6, D.C. 1962 yearbook.

The first four chapters are written by four leaders of the Third New Force in psychology. They discuss the fully functioning personality; the remainder of the book gives specific suggestions for providing a nurturing classroom climate. However, the ideas are equally applicable in the home. *Definitely a must.*

b. Hayakawa, S. I. *Symbol, Status, and Personality*. New York: Harcourt, Brace & World, Inc., 1963.

Read Chapter Five. Easy reading.

c. Maslow, Abraham. *Toward a Psychology of Being*. New York: D. Van Nostrand, 1962.

Read Chapter Four. It points out what stops growth.

d. Rogers, Carl. *On Becoming a Person*. Boston: Houghton Mifflin Co., 1961.

Outstanding, from one of the leaders in the Third New Force in psychology. Chapters Three, Six, Eight, Nine, and Sixteen are musts.

12. Do you want further ideas about being a nurturing parent?

a. Hymes, James L., Jr. "Being a Good Parent." (See 6, a, for address to obtain this pamphlet.)

b. Hymes, James L., Jr. *Understanding Your Child*. Englewood Cliffs, New Jersey: Prentice-Hall, 1952.

Simple, witty, and direct. Definitely a must.

c. Overstreet, Harry. *The Mature Mind*. New York: Norton, 1959.

Read Chapter Ten, "The Home as a Place for Growing."

d. Public Affairs Pamphlet (see 1, d, for address). "Making the Grade as Dad."

e. See listings under 4 (b through e).

13. Would you like to learn more about yourself?

a. Briggs, Dorothy Corkille. CELEBRATE YOUR SELF. New York: Doubleday, 1977.

b. Harris, Sidney J. *Winners & Losers*. Illinois: Argus Communications, 1973.

c. Missildine, Hugh. *Your Inner Child of the Past*. New York: Simon & Schuster, 1963.

d. Powell, John. *Why Am I Afraid to Love?*. Illinois: Argus Communications, 1972.

Why Am I Afraid to Tell You Who I Am? Illinois: Argus Communications, 1969.

e. Pietsch, William. *Human BE-ing*. New York: Lawrence Hill & Co., 1974.

Each is outstanding, easy reading, and develops self-insight.

14. Do you want a closer look at the need for perfection?

a. Clarke, John R. *The Importance of Being Imperfect*. New York: David McKay, Inc., 1961.

Humorous, easy to read, and an eye-opener.

15. Are you interested in some short but excellent pamphlets on specific topics?

a. Child Study Association of America, Inc., 9 E. 89th Street, New York. Here are a few titles:

"Aggressiveness in Children."
"Adolescent Years."
"What Makes a Good Home."

b. Science Research Associates (see 5, b, for address). Here are a few titles:

"Why Children Misbehave."
"Building Self-Confidence in Children."
"How to Live with Children."
"Developing Responsibility in Children."
"Understanding Hostility in Children."

c. Public Affairs Pamphlets (see 1, d, for address). Here are a few titles:

"The Shy Child."
"Coming of Age: Problems of Teen-agers."

"Saving Your Marriage."

"How to Tell Your Child about Sex."

16. Do you want more reading about sex education?

   a. Baruch, Dorothy. *New Ways in Sex Education.* New York: McGraw-Hill, 1959.

   Presents basic understandings and concrete suggestions for developing healthy attitudes and giving specific facts. Excellent and easy to read.

17. Would you like some books on sex education for appropriate age levels?

   For the child under five:

   a. Faegere, Marion. *Your Own Story.* Minneapolis: University Press, 1943.

   b. Langstaff, Nancy. *A Tiny Baby for You.* New York: Harcourt, Brace & World, 1955.

   c. Selsam, Millicent. *All About Eggs.* New York: W. R. Scott, 1952.

   For the child from six to nine:

   a. DeSchweinitz, Karl. *Growing Up.* New York: Macmillan Co., 1967.

   b. Gruenberg, Sidonie. *The Wonderful Story of How You Were Born.* New York: Doubleday & Co., Inc., 1952, 1970.

   c. Gruenberg, Sidonie. *Let's Hear a Story.* New York: Doubleday & Co., Inc., 1961.

   For the child from ten to twelve:

a. DuVall, Evelyn. *About Sex and Growing Up*. New York: Association Press, 1968.

b. Gruenberg, Benjamin & Sidonie. *Wonderful Story of You*. New York: Doubleday & Co., Inc., 1960.

For the child from thirteen to fifteen:

a. DuVall, Evelyn. *Facts of Life and Love for Teen-agers*. New York: Association Press, 1956.

b. Landis, Paul. *Your Dating Days*. New York: McGraw-Hill, 1954.

c. Levine, Milton. *Wonder of Life*. New York: Golden Press, 1968.

d. Shedd, Charlie W. *The Stork Is Dead*. Waco, Texas: Word Books, 1972.

For inexpensive material on sex education, write:

a. American Institute of Family Relations, 5287 Sunset Boulevard, Los Angeles, California.

b. American Medical Association, 535 Dearborn Street, Chicago, Illinois.

c. American Social Hygiene Association, 1970 Broadway, New York, New York.

In any book you will probably find some ideas that appeal and some that don't. Think of reading material as a kind of mental smörgåsbord. Sample the ideas, test them, and use those that make sense to you.

INDEX